MEMORY, PATRIARCHY AND ECONOMY IN TURKEY

MEMORY, PATRIARCHY AND ECONOMY IN TURKEY

Narratives of Political Power

Meral Uğur-Çınar

EDINBURGH
University Press

For Kürşat and Bahar...

Edinburgh University Press is one of the leading university presses in the UK. We publish academic books and journals in our selected subject areas across the humanities and social sciences, combining cutting-edge scholarship with high editorial and production values to produce academic works of lasting importance. For more information visit our website: edinburghuniversitypress.com

© Meral Uğur-Çınar, 2024

Edinburgh University Press Ltd
13 Infirmary Street
Edinburgh EH1 1LT

Typeset in 11/15 EB Garamond by
IDSUK (DataConnection) Ltd

A CIP record for this book is available from the British Library

ISBN 978 1 3995 1448 4 (hardback)
ISBN 978 1 3995 1449 1 (paperback)
ISBN 978 1 3995 1450 7 (webready PDF)
ISBN 978 1 3995 1451 4 (epub)

CONTENTS

FIGURES

ACKNOWLEDGEMENTS

This book is a product of years of thinking, research and writing. But equally, it is a product of the conversations I had with so many great minds over the years. Acknowledgements are one of my favorite parts to read in the books of others, and it is a pleasure to write one for this book. Yet at the same time, I know that I will not be able to do justice to all those who contributed to what has now become this book.

Over the years, I have presented parts of this research and have gotten feedback for it at various talks, workshops and conferences. I presented different parts of my work that culminated in the chapters of this book at several Annual Meetings on the following panels: 'Gezi Park Protests: Debating the Terms of Politics, Democracy and Participation' (2014 Middle East Studies Association), 'Patriarchy, State and Legitimacy in Turkey' (2015 Middle East Studies Association), 'Revolutions and Counterrevolutions' (2016 American Political Science Association Annual Conference), 'Historical Memory and Remembering in Democratic and Authoritarian Politics' (2021 American Political Science Association), 'Populism and Populist Discourse: National Cases and Comparative Perspective' (2021 International Political Science Association) and 'Populist Practices in Comparative Perspectives' (2021 Canadian Political Science Association). I deeply appreciate the contributions of the participants of these events. I would particularly like to thank the discussants of my papers, John Vanderlippe, Özlem Altıok, Isaac Kamola, Dovile Budryte, Mark Farha and Isabelle Cote for their insightful comments and their engagement with my works in progress.

I would also like to thank the participants of the Turkish–German Frontiers of Social Science Symposium (TUGFOSS), which was held in Potsdam in 2018, for their feedback. I am especially grateful to Erdem Aytaç and Selin Akyüz, who invited me to present my early ideas on populism and political narratives at the symposium and provided me with invaluable feedback. At the Middle Technical University, I received very insightful feedback from the participants of the Political Science and Public Administration Departmental Seminar in 2021, especially from Ayşe Ayata, Aslı Çırakman and Başak Alpan with regard to populism and collective memory in Turkey.

Also, I would like to extend my gratitude to the participants of the 2022 European Consortium of Political Research Joint Sessions Workshop 'Gender and the Rise of Authoritarianism', Cristina Chiva, Petra Guasti, Pär Zetterberg, İrem Tuncer-Ebetürk, Berfin Çakın, Lynda Gilby, Natalia Kovyliaeva and Alexandros Tokhi, especially Cristina and Petra, who not only organised the panel, but also provided impeccable feedback on my work as discussants. I would also like to thank Luca Manucci, who, as the editor of *Populism Interviews: A Dialogue with Leading Experts* (Routledge, 2022), not only made me part of that project, but also gave me reasons to think deeply about the relationship between populism and collective memory with his thoughtful questions.

More recently, I was fortunate enough to be part of a panel at the University of Pennsylvania titled 'The Construction of National Citizenships: Competing Paradigms' organised in honour of Rogers Smith's retirement. I am thankful for the participants of this panel, particularly Ian Lustick, Jeff Green, Nancy Hirschmann, Elspeth Wilson, Sarah Song and Harris Mylonas for inspiring me to reflect on some of the most pressing domestic and global issues regarding narratives and politics. Ian Lustick, my dissertation supervisor more than a decade ago, still continues to have a lasting effect on what and how I write thanks to his sharp intellect and conscientious approach to politics. Likewise, my conversations with Rogers Smith, and his work on stories of peoplehood, have been a constant source of inspiration and intellectual development for me over the years.

I would also like to thank the editors at the Edinburgh University Press, Gillian Leslie, Ersev Ersoy, Emma House and Louise Hutton for all their efforts along the way. They were the best editors one could hope for. I am truly grateful. The series editors, Alpaslan Özerdem and Ahmet Erdi Öztürk, also provided invaluable, constructive insights that improved the book tremendously. Of course, I am also extremely grateful to the anonymous reviewers for providing the most helpful, intellectually stimulating, and knowledgeable feedback possible. Parts of Chapter 3 have appeared in *The Political Quarterly* (2015, 86 (3): 359–63) and *METU Studies in Development* (2017, 44 (April): 47–67). I would like to thank the journals, their editors and the anonymous reviewers for their feedback. I am also grateful to Koç University-VEKAM for letting me use images from their archive.

I would like to thank my friends and colleagues Tekin Köse, Senem Yıldırım Özdem, Alev Çınar, İlker Aytürk, Bülent Batuman and Daniel Just for their insights, support, encouragement and wisdom. Our graduate students, and my co-authors on other projects of collective memory, historical narratives, and narratives of the Left, Ali Açıkgöz, Berat Uygar Altınok and Gökhan Şensönmez: it has been a source of joy and pride to see how you have become the wonderful thinkers and scholars you are.

I am thankful to my mother Sıdıka Uğur, my father Behzat Uğur, my sister Emel and my niece Nehir for being my family and making life more meaningful for me. My husband, Kürşat Çınar, who has witnessed all the stages of this work and contributed to it with his insights and endless support, deserves a special 'thank you'. I would also like to thank my daughter Bahar so much, for the hope in her eyes, for her kindness and warmth, and for motivating me along the way, by saying, '*yaz, anne, yaz*'.

1

INTRODUCTION: NARRATIVES
AND POLITICS

This book is written in an effort to understand the multifaceted and dynamic role narratives play in politics in general, and in Turkish politics in particular. Narratives play crucial roles in politics and open fruitful areas of research. Narratives help us comprehend separate phenomena by weaving them into a comprehensible web of relationships. They turn 'temporally distributed events into interpretable wholes' (Wertsch 2000, 515). Narratives also reduce the number of possible interpretations of events by emplotting them in a certain way (Ewick and Silbey 1995, 213; Wertsch 2000, 515), and they give stories a sense of reality due to the common-sense properties of their truth claims (Bridger and Maines 1998). Narratives do not only help us comprehend the world but also our place within it. As Somers (1994, 625) maintains, identity formation takes shape within 'relational settings of contested but patterned relations among narratives, people, and institutions'. In addition to making sense of our lives and ourselves in narrative form (Taylor 1989; Brockmeier 2002), we also express and transmit our ideas through narratives. Political narratives are key to our understanding of the role of ideas in politics as they are the vessels through which ideas are carried.

As Polletta (1998) points out, narratives can serve us better in understanding political communication than other discursive communication units such as frames or discourses for a number of reasons. Narratives have a temporarily configurative capacity, they rely on emplotment rather than explanation and they tend to be more vague, leaving room for personal interpretation and actually requiring our interpretative participation to 'fill the gaps and resolve the ambiguities'. Relatedly, while the success of frames depends on how credible, logical and explanatory they are, narratives rely on 'emotional identification and familiar plots rather than on testing or adjudication of truth claims' (Polletta 1998). The temporal dimension and sense of movement also distinguishes narrative from discourse and frame (Miskimmon, O'Loughlin and Roselle 2013, 7). As Ewick and Silbey (1995, 200) argue, the temporal and structural ordering inherent in narratives 'ensure both "narrative closure" and "narrative causality": in other words, a statement about how and why the recounted events occurred'. In this sense, narratives are not only descriptive but also evaluative (Brockmeier 2000, 60) and prescriptive.

While narratives are studied extensively in fields such as literary criticism, health sciences, social work and psychology, there are only a few studies that are concerned with the influence of narratives on political outcomes.[1] In addition to attempting to start filling this gap, with this study, I also hope to respond to the call in the political science literature to enhance our understanding of ideational and discursive political phenomena (Béland and Cox 2010; Berman 2010; Blyth 1997; Rueschemeyer 2006) and to study the interaction between ideas and institutions through discursive constructs (Schmidt 2010). In Chapter 2, I analyse the role historical narratives play in hegemonic power struggles among political parties. In Chapter 3, I trace how economic development narratives affect prospects of democratic practices and institutions. In Chapter 4, I delve into the narrative resources upon which populist regimes draw. In Chapter 5, I analyse how protesters subvert dominant notions of citizenship through their engagement with dominant narratives, including patriarchal narratives. In Chapter 6, I look at the relationship between political narratives and political regimes, particularly visions of citizenship regimes and nationhood in a global perspective, focusing on the political implications of exclusionary narratives such as the Replacement Theory and on the prospects to counter far-right politics with narratives.

As will be discussed further in Chapter 5, this book also responds to the call to bring together state theories and theories of gender and feminism (Adams 2005; Ugur-Cinar 2017). While state theories have so far not made sufficient use of the findings of the feminist literature, feminist theory has not sufficiently incorporated theories of state formation (Adams 2005, 32–3). What is more, as the chapter will try to demonstrate, with the study of gendered narratives, we can go beyond the conceptualisation of patriarchy as solely 'male domination' and we can provide a novel approach to patriarchy that exposes its use as a political legitimisation tool.

The empirical focus of the book is primarily Turkey but I also discuss the broader theoretical and empirical implications of the findings. In Chapter 4, I discuss the Turkish case in conjunction with the Austrian and Hungarian cases in the context of populism and, in Chapter 6, I combine my theoretical discussion with illustrative examples particularly focusing on the US, German speaking countries, and France. The Turkish case is useful in tracing continuity and change in the views of collective memory, development and patriarchy of those who hold power and those who challenge the incumbents. Turkey is a case of deep divisions and harsh hegemonic struggles and also a place in which there are actors who are motivated to transcend such cleavages and form a more inclusive, pluralist society against all odds. Narratives provide a useful lens through which to analyse these competing notions and their interaction with the institutional setting in which they operate.

Conceptual and Methodological Framework

Based on the existing definitions of a narrative (e.g. Brockmeier and Harre 1997, 266; Miskimmon, O'Loughlin and Roselle 2013, 5; Somers 1994, 616), we can count actors, events, a plot, temporal dimension, a setting and space as key elements of narratives. Sometimes one or more of these elements are fully fleshed out and sometimes only hinted at. Following Andrews (2004), Patterson and Monroe (1998), Polletta (1998), Polletta and Callahan (2017) and Polletta and Chen (2012), among others, I use the terms narrative and story interchangeably.

Narrative analysis is concerned with the ways in which perceptions of the world are mediated and transmitted through narratives and aspires to understand how different actors 'make use of stories to interpret and bolster their arguments, and how they integrate narrative as strategy' (Groth 2019, 5, 11). As Lueg, Bager and Lundholt (2021, 4) argue, narrative inquiry is both a theoretical and a methodological approach. In this line, the methodology of this book is closely linked to the theoretical approach followed.

The data for this research is derived from texts such as public speeches of political leaders, official statements found in museums, as well as visual texts such as graffiti and posters from protests. To analyse the selected material, I mainly follow a thematic narrative analysis in order to identify and analyse patterns in the data (Riessman 2008). In order to provide a coherent and compelling interpretation, which is grounded in the data (Braun *et al.* 2019), I follow an iterative process. I first develop initial themes in light of 'prior and emergent theory' and then go back and forth between primary data and existing scholarship in an attempt to analyse data and provide novel theoretical insights from the data (Riessman 2008, 54, 66, 74). The data analysis method of this book is thus abductive, as it moves 'back and forth between theory and empirical data' (Wodak 2004, 200).

As is typical in narrative analysis, the sampling in this study is purposeful and the selection of the texts analysed also depends on how exemplary they are, and on the richness of the data (Ewick and Silbey 2003, 1138; Riessman 2008, 60). In the process of familiarising myself with the data, I initially went over some exemplary speeches of the leaders, whom I have been following for a decent amount of time now, given my research interests. I read these texts in light of the theoretical background in fields such as feminist theory and collective memory studies. Initial texts included, for example, Erdoğan's speeches on the Gezi movement, on the 17–25 December 2013 corruption investigations, the presidentialism debate, constitutional referenda, and commemorative events. In addition, ethnographic material from museums and landmark places, old and new, such as brochures and exhibits were also selected for narrative analysis. In the case of Gezi, available graffiti and banners were also included. Once the themes started to emerge and I began to identity certain narrative patterns in the speeches, I utilised quotes from the texts in order to provide illustrative examples that substantiate my argument (Riessman 2008, 55).

In addition to thematic analysis that is focused on content, the book also draws on structural analysis to the extent that it looks at how the stories are told, what the specific starting points of stories are, where they end, what is selected and what is left out in the narratives that are told. As the book will demonstrate, such choices are not trivial but instead have important implications in terms of moral judgments and issues of identity. The narrative configuration, such as the selection of the beginning of a story, also makes claims to power and authority and the transformation of actors into characters within a plot imply moral judgment (Freistein and Gadinger 2020, 222; Opperman and Spencer 2018, 275). Accordingly, I pay close attention to the beginning, the ending and sequencing of the stories as well as the implications, hints, inferences, assumptions of the storylines. My analysis is also attentive to the temporality of the storyline. While studies in developmental psychology, for example, have shown us the role temporality plays in individuals' reconstruction of developmental processes (Demuth and Mey 2015), this book analyses the ways in which temporality is instrumentalised for political ends in the narratives told.

In addition to the content and structure of the narrative, the context of the narrative is also significant (Esin 2011, 97). The interactional-performative model (Riessman 1993; Mishler 1995) is attuned to the role of the storyteller as one who tells the story in co-construction with the listener. This approach necessitates attention to the 'contexts, including the influence of researcher, audience, setting and social circumstances on the constitution and performance of the narrative' (Esin 2011, 109). While the work in the interactional-performative model is mostly focused on the immediate audience, like in an interview setting (Mishler 1995), in this book, I focus more on the dialogical character between the narratives and the addressee of these narratives at the collective level. A case in point will be the Gezi protest slogans that engage with the patriarchal narrative of the government and the citizenship model such narratives envision.

Narratives, Power and Culture

As the title suggests, power is a central concept for the book. This is the case because first, in addition to forming the basis of solidarity, consent and coherence of identity (Taylor 1989), narratives play key roles in power struggles (Özyürek 2006; Shohat 1999; Zerubavel 1995) and second, when multiple narratives compete for public meaning (Bridger and Maines 1998), those who are in power, especially for a long time, have the advantage of institutionalising certain stories through resources such as textbooks, commemorations and museums (Wertsch 2004, 50; Hayward 2010). These resources, along with public utterances, TV series, media, landscape design, architecture and archaeology make dominant stories asymmetrically more powerful compared to counterhegemonic ones.[2] Political entrepreneurs are also more likely to get their stories heard because of their financial resources and political connections as well as because they are seen as better suited to tell stories than, for example, marginalised groups (Polletta *et al.* 2011). As such, the book is attentive to understanding how power interacts with narratives in the process of reinforcing political projects and in the struggles for hegemony.

Against all odds, narratives can also serve counter movements in creative ways. The discussion of the changing force of certain historical, developmental and patriarchal narratives in Turkey in the last century gives us a chance to delve deeply into how dominant narratives are counteracted and to what effect. As I demonstrate in Chapter 5, even if counter movements do not always get the chance to tell a full-blown alternative story, they can nevertheless destabilise the main tenets of dominant power structures. The dialogical nature of narratives (Bakhtin 2013; Wertsch 2000), discussed further in the respective chapter, is a focal point of the analysis as I try to show how new stories engage with the old ones rather than being told from scratch.

In light of the criticism against internally homogenising essentialist uses of the concept of culture (Abu-Lughod 1991; Abu-Lughod 1997; Appadurai 1988; Clifford 1988; among others) and in line with the call for a more dynamic, semiotic and non-essentialist approach to culture (Wedeen 2002), such a dialogical approach helps us steer away from cultural accounts that risk turning the cultural field into a closed one and treating it as a timeless reality. Following the journey of narratives in the Turkish political context maps the cultural terrain while being attentive to power, resistance and dynamism. This helps us avoid an essentialised depiction of the culture–politics nexus. Though narrative analysis, I am thus able to take a set of pictures over Turkey's recent history and contemporary politics without ossifying the findings in a timeless cultural domain. Beyond the Turkish case, such an analysis also advances our understanding of how tension and coherence, continuity and change play out within the cultural and societal realm through the distinct role narratives play. I want to show that it is through narratives that we bring the cultural into the political repertoire and it is again through narratives that we engage with culture in order to fight political battles.

Narratives of Collective Memory, Economy and Patriarchy

The book focuses particularly on how narratives of economic development, collective memory and gender influence politics while at the same time being influenced by it. These three types of narratives are deeply embedded in the cultural terrain that contains global as well as local elements as I will discuss briefly below and elaborate on in the respective chapters. Gendered narratives are deeply embedded in patriarchy. Economic development narratives are bound by capitalism, particularly neoliberalism, as well as the drive for modernisation. Historical narratives are closely tied to the predominance of nation states and nationalism.

We can best understand these three types of narratives in relation to the discussion of broadly conceived master narratives[3] or deeply running schematic narratives.[4] Somers' discussion of meta-narratives is particularly useful in this regard. Meta-narratives, or master narratives, refer to narratives in which we are embedded historically and socially (Somers 1994, 619) so deeply that they are difficult to recognise and are often uncritically adopted (Patterson and Monroe 1998, 325). Master narratives 'permeate the petit narratives of our everyday talk' (Bamberg 2004, 361) and these are also the narratives that politicians rely on when they speak in narrative form, as will be demonstrated in this book.

In addition to, and in conjunction with, global narratives regarding capitalism, progress and the like mentioned by Somers (1994), or security narratives which are discussed by Wibben (2010, 43) as grand narratives, local contexts also provide centres for gravity for deeply embedded unique meta stories. Somers (1994, 630) herself notes that 'the extent and nature of any given repertoire of narratives available for appropriation is always historically and culturally specific; the particular plots that give meanings to those narratives cannot be determined in advance'. Localising such deeply running narratives, Wertsch (2004, 56) talks about 'a generalized narrative form' that 'underlies a range of specific narratives in a cultural tradition'. Hence, globally and locally embedded narratives play an important role in shaping the parameters of politics as this book will try to demonstrate.

Relatedly, when we talk about narratives, we do not simply mean the narration of singular events but we refer to 'narrative networks' that provide meaning to particular narratives within this network (Andrews, Kinnvall and Monroe 2015, 142; Somers 1995). Similarly, Polletta and Chen (2012, 495, 501) argue that hegemony operates not by the identical repetition of a single story over and over again but rather by the 'promotion of stories that thematize familiar oppositions'. As such, in the Turkish case, narratives related to gender, economic development and collective memory are anchored in narrative networks in which they resonate. This is not to say that they evoke the same sentiment across all listeners but they resonate in the sense that they provide intelligibility and common understanding across the community. In Wedeen's (2002) words, they became the hub of a 'system of signification'. It is around this understanding that consent and contention are built as will be explicated in the book.

Patriarchal stories, which rely on assumed gender and familial roles, normalise hierarchies among the ruler and the ruled. Given the highly hegemonic standing of patriarchal narratives in Turkey and beyond, they can be conceptualised as meta-narratives (Somers 1994) or grand narratives (Wibben 2010). While patriarchal narratives provide the basis of political allegiance, compliance and legitimacy across the political spectrum, they can also sometimes serve to unsettle the political system and question its legitimacy when mobilised in narrative form, which is a point so far left unexplored in the literature. In other words, patriarchal narratives can also be engaged with in multiple ways and some of these engagements can challenge the entire order these narratives represent as will be discussed in detail in Chapter 5. Existing studies on grand narratives of patriarchy mostly focus on individual level stories. For instance, Squire *et al.* (2014) focuses on sexual narratives of educated young women and their mothers in relation to Turkish modernisation. This book, on the other hand, tries to move the analysis further into the realm of collective political action. To do so, it will trace gendered narratives and the interaction between them in relation to hegemonic struggles, state-citizenship debates and prospects for democratisation.

Patterson and Monroe (1998, 325) point at narratives of mastery and progress, including economic development narratives as part of meta-narratives, or grand narratives. Narratives of development play a central role, particularly in countries such as Turkey, which are eager to catch up with more economically developed countries. In fact, the literature on Turkey has pointed at the central role of development and state-led developmentalism (Adaman and Arsel 2012; Keyman and Gümüşçü 2014). Modernity and development have come to mean different things to different groups in the history of the Turkish Republic

(Özyürek 2006, 19) ranging from cultural modernity and Westernisation, particularly before the 1980s (Buğra and Savaşkan 2014, 30; Kasaba 2008, 2), to visions of modernity based on economic development and industrialisation (Göle 1993, 201) and even full-blown neoliberalism (Cinar and Ugur Cinar 2018, 20) Thus, one needs to account for multiple stories of development that accumulate over time in a dialogical fashion. To that end, Chapter 3 traces the history of changing notions of development in Turkey, observing the implications of such narratives for the political field, particularly for the prospect of and threats against democracy and democratic institutions. It does so by tracing the political speeches of high-ranking Turkish government officials and journalists close to them to show how these people use narratives of economic development as a tool to politically legitimise interventions to liberal democracy.

Finally, collective memory, with its strong ties to the nation-building effort is another deeply running narrative field in which we can observe varying narratives competing for hegemony. As Wertsch (2008) argues, collective memory is deep because narrative tools that organise it are largely inaccessible to conscious reflection. To this end, this book takes stock of such varying narratives, always trying to pay attention to how power, through institutions and organisations, interacts with political actors in the context of competition for domination over the memory of the nation. Chapter 2 traces the historical narrative–political identity nexus by focusing on struggles over (re)defining a nation through historical narratives. It concentrates on the Ulus district of Ankara to compare how the secularist and Islamist versions of Turkish nationalism turned this place into an epicentre of hegemonic struggle by writing different historical narratives thorough different museums, 'pilgrimage' sites, monuments and ceremonies.

Chapter 4 brings together all three types of narratives, namely economic, historical and patriarchal, to show how these stories co-constitute populism and provide legitimacy for it. Using contemporary Turkey, Hungary and Austria as cases studies, it will show how stories of history, development and patriarchy are deployed by populist leaders, Erdoğan (Adalet ve Kalkınma Partisi: AKP), Orban (Fidesz), and Strache (Freedom Party) to (re)define the people and justify inclusion and exclusion based on historical, economic or patriarchal grounds. A narrative approach to populism allows us to better make sense of how populism is politically constructed and how its appeal is widened and deepened. By approaching populism from this angle, the book also hopes to address another gap in the literature, namely the lack of attention to the relationship between political narratives, particularly historical ones, and populism.[5] Chapter 6 demonstrates how the relationship between political narratives and populism plays itself out at the global level and reflects on the potential to use stories in the struggle against authoritarian, exclusionary and monist political movements and political leaders.

With this point, we are back to the motivation of this book, mainly providing a well-rounded look at political narratives embedded in their cultural and institutional context. The main purpose of this book is to utilise narrative analysis in order to understand the political. I believe that such a multifaceted and dynamic approach to the topic at hand provides a welcome addition to the literature, hopefully paving the way for more studies to come.

Notes

1. On the influence of historical narratives on citizenship policies, see Ugur Cinar 2015a. On the role of conflict-supportive narratives on peace processes, see Oren, Nets-Zehngut and Bar-Tal 2015. On the role of narratives in shaping understandings of security, see Mehta and Wibben 2018.
2. See for example, El-Haj 2002. Oren, Nets-Zehngut and Bar-Tal (2015) argue, for instance, that in addition to being disseminated by institutions, conflict-supportive narratives in Israel are also shielded from counter-narratives via various mechanisms: control of information, discrediting of counterinformation, monitoring and punishment.
3. Zerubavel (1995, 6) defines a master commemorative narrative as 'a broader view of history, a basic "story line" that is culturally constructed and provides the group members with a general notion of the past'.
4. Wertsch (2004, 51) distinguishes between specific narratives and schematic narratives. While the former refers to the specific events in texts regarding collective memory, the latter 'involve a much more abstract level of representation and provide a narrative framework that is compatible with many instantiations in specific narratives'. Wertsch (2007, 31) also thinks that schematic narratives are much more resistant to change due to their resistance to counterargument and imperviousness to evidence.
5. On the lack of studies regarding populism and collective memory, see Cento Bull 2016 and Savage 2012. For a recent study addressing this relationship, see Ugur-Cinar and Altınok 2021.

2

TWO TALES OF A NATION: ULUS AS A SITE OF COMPETING HISTORICAL NARRATIVES

This chapter looks at two competing historical narratives in Turkey in their struggles over collective memory for the production and contestation of communal identities. As Art (2006, 18) notes, 'although many political scientists would agree that "memory matters", there have been few studies that trace the nexus between ideas about the past and political power'. In parallel, Kansteiner (2002, 184) similarly points out that 'despite this relatively obvious link, the connection between memory and identity has as yet been rarely discussed in memory studies'. As this chapter will illustrate, historical narratives open a fruitful strand of research into the study of society and politics that has so far been left relatively unexplored. In order to delve deeply into historical narratives at work in the Turkish case, this chapter focuses on struggles over (re)defining a nation through historical narratives by specifically focusing on the case of Ulus, Ankara. Ulus, which literally means 'the nation' in contemporary Turkish, became central first to the Kemalist modernisation efforts and later to the political Islamist goals of reshaping the nation once the political Islamists captured first municipal and then state level rule. The chapter compares how the secularist and Islamist versions of Turkish nationalism turned Ulus into an epicentre of hegemonic struggle by writing different historical narratives through different museums, 'pilgrimage' sites and monuments.

The past provides raw material for projects in the present and in the future. Like ideas, the past is not automatically transmitted either and it too needs to be mediated. History is narratological in character. It is always presented to us in narrative form, which attributes separate, objective facts, the continuity of a subject (Balibar 1992, 86). Narratives create a web of meaning around separate images and events of the past and facilitate the transmission of different perceptions of the past. Historical narratives create historical continuity between separate events. These connections are not necessarily predetermined and they involve political agency. It is always possible to narrate historical events in more than one way (White 1978; Zerubavel 2003) and different historical narratives have different political implications (Davis 2005; Ugur Cinar 2015a; Zerubavel 1995). Eviatar Zerubavel, for example, shows how different narratives constructing the past structure time sequence differently; for example, in linear, circular or zigzag fashion; separate historical periods differently from one another; and introduce different historical beginnings in order to justify the political claims they make in the present.

Events woven into a storyline can sometimes stretch even throughout centuries as Yael Zerubavel's (1995) discussion of the Zionist narrative shows. Zerubavel (1995) looks at the unifying and contentious aspects of collective memory through the case of the Zionist master narrative. To do this, she traces the evolution of three events central to the myths of the Jewish society in Palestine: the Fall of Masada (AD 73), the Bar Kokhba Revolt against the Romans (AD 132–5) and the defence of Tel Hai (no retreat) settlement (1920). According to Zerubavel, the Zionist commemorative narrative accentuates the perception of a 'great divide' between antiquity (as the golden age) and exile (with a negative and reductionist image). The positive aspects of exile are suppressed in order to promote the people–land bond, something Zerubavel sees as reinforced by Zionists' denial of centuries of Palestinian life in the land. Three historical events analysed in her book serve this master narrative: the defence of Tel Hai provided Israeli society with 'a myth of origin, a point in time that symbolized the rebirth of the nation and the beginning of a new era'. Zionism also emphasises a new national era and discontinuity with earlier past and symbolic rupture with the exile. The Bar Kokhba revolt symbolises the last struggle for freedom during antiquity in Zionist collective memory while also constructing a historical continuity between antiquity and the Zionist national Revival and Zionist pioneers. The Masada myth is also used to build historical continuity between antiquity and the Zionist national Revival. The activist interpretation of Masada both creates a connection to present heroism and provides a counter-metaphor to the Holocaust. In Zerubavel's view, these commemorations are not only powerful means to reinforce social solidarity but they also create an arena of struggle over power and control. She illustrates her point through the challenge posed to the secular nationalist interpretations of Jewish past by contending sides such as the nationalist–religious camp or by those who urge towards a more critical representation of the past in Israeli national tradition.

As discussed earlier, narratives help us comprehend separate phenomena by weaving them into a comprehensible web of relationships. This means that narratives demand that 'we discern the meaning of any single event only in temporal and spatial relationship to other events' (Somers 1994, 616) and turn 'temporally distributed events into interpretable wholes' (Wertsch 2000, 515). What is more, as discussed in the introduction, narratives also reduce the number of possible interpretations of events by emplotting them in a certain way (Ewick and Silbey 1995, 213; Wertsch 2000, 515), and they give stories a sense of reality due to the common-sense properties of their truth claims (Bridger and Maines 1998).

In addition to weaving separate events into a comprehensible plot and reducing alternative possibilities of making sense of the past, narratives are also crucial in constituting our identities. Individuals construct a sense of identity through narratives. Narratives are significant in memory practices and even more so when it comes to more complex constructions of meaning in our lives. A number of scholars have very aptly noted the close relationship between narratives and identity. As Kearney (2006, 3) argues, 'telling stories is as basic to human beings as eating. More so, in fact, for while food makes us live, stories are what make our lives worth living.' In Brockmeier's (2002, 26) words: 'If I do not only want to count the photographs from my past collected in that box and not only name the persons they show, but also want to point out why they mean anything to me at all, then narrative becomes the hub of my account.' Narrative plots, with their beginnings and ends, enable us to gain a certain sense of time that goes beyond chronology (Ricoeur 1980). As Taylor (1989, 47) argues, 'in order to have a sense of who we are, we have to have a notion of how we have become, and of where we are going', which, according to him, we reach with narratives. Yuval-Davis (2006, 202) actually argues, 'identities are narratives, stories people tell themselves and others about who they are (and who they are not)'. Jerome Bruner (1986; 1990; 1991; 1996) brings a cognitive psychology perspective to narratives. Bruner argues that human beings organise their experience and their memories of human happenings mainly in the form of narrative. Bruner (1987, 15) argues that the self-telling of life narratives, that is, our autobiographies, structure our perceptual experience, organise our memories and 'segment and purpose-build the very events of a life'. As a result, he states, 'we become the autobiographical narratives by which we "tell about" our lives' (see also Brockmeier 2000; Ezzy 1998). Brockmeier (2000, 59) argues that autobiographical narratives do not just describe or represent a self in time, but they also evaluate our lives in the light of moral assumptions and ethical convictions (see also Freeman and Brockmeier 2001).

Historical narratives are essential in constructing identity not only at the individual but also at the collective level. Narratives both tell us 'what is the sense of our political world in general and also of our place within it' (Bottici 2010, 920). Even stories about the individual, seemingly unrelated to group identities, mostly draw on collective identity narratives (Yuval-Davis 2006, 202). Thus, as Riessman (2008, 10) argues, 'connecting biography and society becomes possible through the close analysis of stories'.

Echoing our discussion of culture in the introduction, Somers (1994, 625) invites us to be aware of the culturally and socially embedded nature of identities and suggests following a narrative approach to understanding identities. She maintains that identity-formation takes shape within 'relational settings of contested but patterned relations among narratives, people, and institutions'. Somers (1994, 618–9) argues that ontological narratives, which are narratives social actors use to make sense of their lives, build on public narratives, which are 'narratives attached to cultural and institutional formations larger than the single individual, to intersubjective networks or institutions, however local or grand, micro or macro'. Agreeing with Somers on this matter, Patterson and Monroe (1998, 329) state that ontological narratives (or life stories) depend on public narratives, which are culturally available explanations of institutions, systems and relationships: 'Hence, what is told in the course of personal narrative draws, at least in part, on what is available in culturally shared understandings.'

Narratives provide an especially powerful point of departure in understanding political communication. This is due to a number of reasons. As

Polletta points out, narratives have a temporarily configurative capacity. They rely on emplotment rather than explanation and they tend to be more vague, leaving room for personal interpretation and actually requiring our interpretative participation to 'fill the gaps and resolve the ambiguities'. Relatedly, while the success of frames depends on how credible, logical and explanatory they are, narratives rely on 'emotional identification and familiar plots rather than on testing or adjudication of truth claims' (Polletta 1998).

Miskimmon, O'Loughlin and Roselle (2013, 7) argue that the temporal dimension and sense of movement distinguishes narrative from discourse and frame. Neither discourse nor frames 'feature a causal transformation that takes actors from one status quo to another' or demonstrate 'temporal and causal features narratives necessarily possess'. Similarly, Wibben (2010, 45) states that narratives' appeals lie in the relationship of the ending back to its beginning. As Ewick and Silbey (1995, 200) argue, the temporal and structural ordering inherent in narratives 'ensure both "narrative closure" and "narrative causality": in other words, a statement about how and why the recounted events occurred'.

With these characteristics, historical narratives are essential in the creation of national allegiance as well as in defining the indispensable elements of a 'nation'. With historical narratives, we are assured the existence of a people in the past and in the present and we are demanded a commitment to carry out a future plan (Moreno and Perez Garzon 2002, 276). Historical narratives have implications beyond national consciousness. With historical narratives, identities are built and fortified and political causes justified and contested. They are the basis on which social cleavages, friends and enemies, aggressors and victims, authenticity and artificialness, political problems and solutions are envisioned. As such, collective memory inevitably also provides a battlefield for different political camps (Cinar 2005; Özyürek 2006; Zerubavel 1995). Battles over collective memory lie at the heart of communal identity and politics, as reflected in the bitterness of disputes over the content of school curricula, since telling the past 'has as much to do with the here and now – who we are today and where we are going – as it does with events and people long past' (Patterson and Monroe 1998, 322).

As Polkinghorne (1995, 7) argues, the plots 'mark off a segment of time in which events are linked together as contributors to a particular outcome'.

These segments vary in terms of the time span they cover, ranging from the boundless to centuries, to lifetimes or to daily or hourly episodes. The configuration of the story and the knowledge selectively appropriated in it are directly related to power and authority as Freistein and Gadinger (2020, 222) maintain. As Freistein and Gadinger (2020, 222) argue, once the plot is established, actors are transformed into characters and this transformation also implies moral judgements, as will be illustrated in this chapter. Multiple narrative structures can operate simultaneously and compete for public meaning in an event (Bridger and Maines 1998). Even though some stories can be reproduced through generations, such reproduction is always selective and, in this process, 'identity narratives can shift and change, be contested and multiple' (Yuval-Davis 2006, 202).

Narratives are reinforced through reiterated performative practices (Bell 1999). As Yuval-Davis (2006, 203) puts it, 'specific repetitive practices, relating to specific social and cultural spaces, which link individual and collective behaviour, are crucial for the construction and reproduction of identity narratives and constructions of attachment'. In this regard, Ulus provides an indispensable site for the analysis of historical narratives that seek to mould political identities as will be seen in this chapter.

While most studies focusing on contested collective memory in Turkey focus on Istanbul, Ankara has so far been understudied in this realm. Once a small town during the late Ottoman era, Ankara became the heart of the struggle for a new beginning with the start of the War of Independence in 1919. With the promulgation of the Republic in 1923, it became the object of the new Republican project to create a capital city akin to its Western counterparts. In contrast to Istanbul, which is loaded with Ottoman, Islamic and monarchical symbols, Ankara offered a clean canvas. Ankara, the new capital, was envisioned as the modern, republican and secular alternative to Istanbul, the capital of the Ottoman Empire.

Mostly left to oblivion in the secularly dominated politics of the first decades of the Republic, the Ottoman past was taken to the forefront once the AKP and its forerunners came to power (Tokdoğan 2018; Kaya, Robert and Tecmen 2020). From 1994 until 2019, political Islamist parties ruled Ankara's metropolitan municipality and many local municipalities, starting with the Welfare Party, the AKP's predecessor. Ulus was shaped by AKP policies through the

Ankara metropolitan municipality and the local Altındağ municipality as well as through the steps taken and resources dedicated by the central government.

Ulus is an important place in constructing the Kemalist historical narrative of the formative years of the Republic. Ulus lies at the centre of Ankara and was once the model project of secularist Kemalist Turkey. What is now known as Ulus was known as Taşhan Square, named after the Taşhan building, which was built between the years 1895 and 1902. It first served as a caravanserai and then as a hotel. The building was demolished in 1936 and the Sümerbank building was erected in its place. In the 1920s, the square was renamed Hakimiyet-i Milliye (National Sovereignty) Square and then Ulus Square. Cobblestones were laid down to the otherwise dusty roads and the Atatürk statue was erected in 1927 (Vekam).

The first two parliament buildings of the Republic were built in Ulus, which now serve as museums of the Republic. The world-famous Anatolian Civilizations Museum and Ethnography Museum were built here during the early Republican era among other projects of modernisation such as ballrooms and statues. Once political Islam gained traction, however, Ulus became a centre of struggle. Especially with the AKP coming to power and controlling both the Altındağ and the metropolitan municipality, the district was subjected to large-scale transformation. In contrast to the museums that focused on the pre-Islamic history of the area or served as pedagogical instruments to orient citizens to Western-style arts, the AKP made interventions to the Ulus district that imposed a more religious, nativist and conservative counter-hegemonic national imaginary to the space.

The AKP era projects include, for example, the museumification of the Islamists poet Mehmet Akif Ersoy's house and the Ulucanlar prison, as well as the establishment of the Intangible Cultural Heritage Museum. Combined with the gentrification and 'renovation' project of the historical Hamamönü area – where especially during Ramadan, Ottoman style festivities are held – and the building of the Melike Hatun Mosque with 7000 prayer capacity as well as the expansion of the surroundings of the historical Hacı Bayram Mosque, Ulus is a hub of the AKP's rebranding of Turkey and its collective memory. This transformation is especially interesting as it happens in an era of neoliberalism in a state setting that has been historically known as a strong and centralised one. This chapter looks at this struggle through the alternative narratives told by both sides based on ethnographic fieldwork on the sites mentioned above as well as narrative analyses of texts provided by these sites and the relevant speeches concerning these sites.

Historical narratives can also help us make better sense of neo-Ottomanism as an appealing idea, among political Islamists, and particularly the AKP supporters. Tokdoğan (2018), for example, talks about the emotions triggered by neo-Ottomanism but does not analyse how these ideas are triggered and transmitted through the intertwined historical narratives that are told by the AKP politicians, and particularly by Erdoğan. The work mentions the fact that that Erdoğan's neo-Ottomanism is a reaction to the Kemalist outlook vis-à-vis the Ottoman Empire but it does not delve into the narratives' role in the transmission of these emotions or the dialogicality among competing visions of the Turkish past. A narrative approach to historical narratives will deepen our understanding of current discussions of the past in Turkey, including neo-Ottomanism and the juxtaposition between Kemalist and political Islamist historiography (Bozoğlu 2020a, 2020b). It will help us, among other things, to be attentive to the negotiations, silences and deliberate ambiguities in the AKP's effort to re-tell Turkish history.

The Kemalist Historical Narrative and the Kemalist Incarnation of Ulus

In order to contextualise the formation of Ulus in the early years of the Republic, in this section, we will first discuss the envisioned nationhood of the founders of the Turkish Republic and the historical narrative accompanying this vision. We will then focus on the most emblematic structures of the era to trace the Kemalist historical narrative within each individual structure as well as in a holistic manner to understand the overall landscape of Ulus of the era in relation to the narrative it aspires to tell about the past, present and future of the Republic. The Anatolian Civilizations Museum, the Ethnography Museum, and the First and Second Parliamentary Buildings will be analysed in this section.

The Turkish Republic was founded in 1923 as a result of a two-front war against the Allied occupation on the one hand, and the Ottoman Sultanate on the other. The Turkish National Assembly started to function as an alternative authority to the Ottoman Empire in 1920. The leader of the War of Independence, Mustafa Kemal Atatürk, became the first president of the newly formed state. When the new Republic was founded, one of the key aims was to build a Turkish nation that carried certain characteristics. Among these, being modern and secular as well as accepting Turkishness as the primary identity and erasing ethnic and religious particularities was key. Such an ideal Turkish nation, heir to a great history and capable of reaching the level of development of 'the contemporary civilisation' was articulated through historical narratives. One of the main aspects of this new historical storyline was to start the history of the Republic much earlier, going beyond the Ottoman Empire. Such a storyline could achieve multiple things: first, it could downplay the place of the Ottoman past and reduce any power claims based on the Ottoman past, and second, it could show the rest of the world, particularly the Western countries, that Turks possessed a great place in the history of civilisations. The following quote from Atatürk is illustrative in this respect:

> The history of the Turkish nation is not limited to Ottoman History. The history of Turks dates to much older times. Our ancestors who have established great states have also been the owners of big and far-reaching civilizations. It is our duty to search and study this history as well as to get to know the Turk and to introduce the Turk to the world. The Turkish child will find more energy in doing great deeds as it gets to know its ancestors.[1]

One of the tasks of the new regime therefore was to undertake an extensive history-writing project that could erase the Ottoman legacy. This process included the removal of the dominance of religion from the public realm and the multi-ethnic structure dominant under the Ottoman socio-political system. This history-writing effort was also a continuation of the struggle with the West as well as the desire to be admitted to the contemporary international order as an equal peer. While the new regime had turned its face to the West, it was also keen to continue an anti-imperialist struggle. Atatürk and historians close to him were bothered by the stereotypical and inferior representations of the Turks in Western historiography and social sciences (Inan 1939, 244). In fact, Afet Inan, Atatürk's adopted daughter and the prime historian of the regime, tells the following story regarding the motivation behind the new history-writing effort. Afet Inan recalls that she once came across comments on the Turks in a French geography book in 1928 that stated that Turks were from an inferior race. She explains that when she showed these remarks to Atatürk and asked his ideas on them, Atatürk's response was, 'No, that's impossible. Let's work on this matter.' In addition to acquiring the deserved respectable place in the international arena due to their glorious past, it was hoped that with this new historical narrative, a sense of pride could be reinstituted in the war-weary citizens. This sentiment is demonstrated well in the quote from Ataturk below:

> You Turkish nation . . . Even though political and social factors that targeted your existence have blocked your way and slowed down your march for a couple of centuries, your ten thousand years old ideational and cultural heritage still lives in your spirit as a pristine and infinite power. History, which maintains in itself the memory of thousands of years, also points at the place you deserve in the world civilization. Walk there and rise! This is both your right and your duty! (cited in Inan 1999 [1930])

In an attempt to institutionalise the new historical narrative, new state institutions, such as the Türk Tarihi Tetkik Heyeti (TTTH – Committee for the Study of Turkish History), which later became Türk Tarihi Tetkik Cemiyeti (TTTC – Society for the Study of Turkish History), and Türk Tarih Kurumu (TTK – Turkish Historical Society) were formed. The task of TTTC was to conduct research on Turkish history; publicise the findings via seminars, congresses, commemorations and expeditions; make excavations; publish books; and organise international congresses. The institution also prepared the first history textbooks (Inan 1999 [1930]) and convened The First History Congress on 2–11 July 1932 and The Second History Congress on 20–25 September 1937. Both congresses were under the ruling elite's close supervision. The leading cadre read all papers before they were presented and they attended the congresses. Atatürk himself attended both congresses and read the papers in advance. These two congresses, together with the history textbook *Türk Tarihinin Ana Hatları* (Guidelines of Turkish History; Inan 1999 [1930]) and the civics book *Vatandaş için Medeni Bilgiler* (Civic Instructions for Citizens; Inan 2000 [1931]), formed the general framework of the Turkish historical narrative.

According to what has come to be known as the Turkish History Thesis, Turks are depicted as the creators of great civilisations in their journey from Central Asia to the rest of the world. Contrary to the later, Islamist historical narratives that put emphasis on Turkish history in Anatolia after their mass conversion to Islam (the Manzikert War 1071 being central in this regard), the founding eras of the early Republican historiography deliberately dated back to pre-Islamic times. The civilisations that are claimed to belong to the Turkish heritage include, most notably, the Hittites and the Sumerians. The attribution of Turkishness to these civilisations 'allowed the Turks to claim to be the legitimate heirs (and, indeed practically the progenitors) of all civilizations that had existed previously on the soil of the new Turkish Republic' (Tanyeri-Erdemir 2006, 382). The focus on the Anatolian geography also needs to be understood as part of an attempt to put forward an antithesis of pan-Turkism that aspired to unite Turks, including those outside the borders, politically (Özdoğan 1998).

Elsewhere (Ugur Cinar 2015a), I have examined in detail how Turkish history textbooks depict Turks as a self-sufficient people with the historical mission of establishing the Turkish state on the Anatolian homeland. According to this storyline, Turks originated in Central Asia and founded high civilisations there but they had to migrate as a result of progressive desiccation of this area, carrying the arts of civilisation with them. In the places they arrived, Turks from Central Asia mixed with the locals. Yet instead of talking about a horizontal interaction between different civilisations, Turkish history textbooks tell the story as one in which other groups melt into the Turkish civilisation due to Turk's superior qualities in terms of administration and their just, fair and compassionate attitude toward the others.

In an effort to highlight Turkish contributions to world civilisation, the earlier textbooks tell us in an exaggerated manner that Turks established almost every important civilisation on earth. In earlier textbooks, Anatolian, such as Hittites, Phrygians and Lydians, Aegean and Mesopotamian civilisation as well as Etruscans, Egyptian, Chinese and Indian civilisations are claimed to be created by the Turks (for details see Ugur Cinar 2015a). These overt claims, mostly put together under the 'Sun language theory', which tries to prove the Turkishness of great civilisations through language, were short-lived and were soon discarded because of their extremely unrealistic character. What is more, after the Second World War, racially defined lineages were out of favour for their association with the Nazi regime. However, more implicit arguments that depicted Turks as the founders or close relatives to the founders of big civilisations can still be seen in more recent textbooks. As will be shown in detail below, the Anatolian Civilizations Museum can be best understood in this context of writing the history of the nascent Republic with domestic and international concerns in mind.

The Anatolian Civilizations Museum

The Anatolian Civilizations Museum was conceived as 'the apogee of the Turkish Historical Thesis' (Shaw 2011, 933). In the 1930s, Atatürk himself took the initiative to further archeological efforts in Turkey. A group of students were sent to European countries, mainly to France, Germany and Hungary in order to study archaeology. In addition, excavations were happening in full force in Turkey (Özdoğan 1998). Archaeology departments were opened at public universities (Gür 2007, 47). In line with the Turkish History Thesis, the Departments of Prehistory and Archaeology, as well as those of Hittitology and Sumerology were opened at Ankara University in 1935 and the latter two departments had no counterparts anywhere else in the world (Aydın 2010, 37). Atatürk also invited professors fleeing the Nazi regime to work at Turkish universities. As Özdoğan (1998) explains, most archaeology chairs were allocated to migrant German professors and this, coupled with the return of students educated abroad, increased the standards of archaeological research in Turkey significantly. Many excavations were started, particularly at Hittite sites in Central Anatolia. Hittites were significant because they had established the earliest known centralised authority in Central Anatolia (Gür 2007, 47).

The efforts to showcase the artefacts of the excavations in Ankara and its surroundings started early on, right after the proclamation of the Republic. In the process of realising the plan for an archaeology museum in Ankara, the site of the former Mahmud Pasha Bedesten (a covered market) and the Kurşunlu Han (a commercial inn) next to it were chosen in 1930. Plans for the restoration and renovation of this site to turn it into a museum were presented by the German urban planner Hermann Jansen, the Hittitologist Eckhard Unger and the Swiss architect Ernst Egli and the purchase was completed in 1933. The museum opened its doors to the public in 1945 as the Hittite Museum and was renamed as the Museum of Anatolian Civilizations in 1968 (Shaw 2007, 267–8).

As mentioned earlier, the initial Turkish History Thesis contained racial overtones. In texts such as Afet Inan's history books, it was claimed that Turks were from brachycephalic stock whose homeland was Central Asia and who moved to Asia and Europe and formed the Neolithic civilisations there. It was argued that the Turks belonged to the white rather than the yellow race, contrary to some European claims. According to the story, Sumerians and Hittites also migrated from Central Asia and possessed racial affinities with the Turks (Aydın 2010, 41). The interest in Sumerian and Hittite civilisations were very visible in some places, such as in the names of two Republican era organisations, the Eti (Hittite) Bank and the Sümer Bank.

As the racial tones of the Turkish History Thesis faded over time, a more cultural narrative dominated the scene. In parallel, the Anatolian Civilization Museum presents an evolutionary narrative line along the homogenous cultural unity of the peoples of Anatolia who are depicted as being part of 'a chain of civilizations that share a cultural essence starting from the Paleothic Age until the present' (Gür 2007, 48, 50). As Gür (2007, 52) argues, the museum narrates a story in which the visitor is assigned the role of a 'privileged actor situated at the endpoint of the developmental flow of history' who 'constructs contemporary Turkey as the achieved telos of a historical progress'. Based on her interviews with the visitors, Gür concludes that most visitors internalise this narrative of the museum.

The narration of the museum favours cultural unity through the geographical unity of Anatolia over the ethnic diversity of Anatolia. As Shaw (2011, 941) observes, the museum establishes a timeline for the growth of Anatolian civilisations from prehistory to antiquity presented as if Anatolia could be considered as a homogenous whole, downplaying the link of separate autochthone cultures such as the Urartu and Phoenicians to non-Turkish ethnicities such as the Armenian and Greek ones. In Shaw's (2007, 268) words:

At the Museum of Anatolian Civilizations [artefacts] are positioned . . . in a narrative of national unity. Following a trajectory from prehistory to the Hellenistic era, the visitor gets the sense of a uniform historical progression of peoples across all of Anatolia. . . . in the Museum of Anatolian Civilizations, a single geography moves across time, setting the groundwork for a national, rather than regional, prehistory.

Shaw (2007, 268) also notes that although in 1968 maps were added to the exhibit that showed excavation sites of the works, it would still take 'an exceedingly careful visitor to note that each people lived not in all of Anatolia, but in only a part of it, making of modern Anatolia what might be thought of as many separate countries constantly changing their borders and overlapping with much of modern Greece and Mesopotamia'.

While the Anatolian Civilizations Museum stresses the pre-Islamic roots of the Republic and presents the history of Anatolia in a unilinear teleological narrative that culminates into the homogenous body politic of the Republic, the Ethnography Museum draws the line between the *ancien régime* and modern times, which has significant political and social implications, as will be elaborated further below.

The Ethnography Museum

The project for the Ethnography Museum started in 1925 under the auspices of Atatürk (Tansuğ 1990, 659) and the museum opened its doors to the public in 1930 as the first museum of Ankara. The museum was surrounded by a cluster of new buildings which 'housed the novel cultural institutions' of the new Republic (Kezer 2000, 104). In the museum, visitors first see colourful artefacts such as 'exotic costumes, ornaments, and antique guns' (Kezer 2000, 104). While the items in the entrance of the museum also include objects from places such as North America, Australia and the Pacific Islands, the next sections start to focus more closely on domestic objects from Turkish village life and countryside as well as regional traditional handicrafts and religious artefacts (Kezer 2000, 104).

For the newly built Turkish state, cultural integration in the face of local and regional differences was essential. The founders wanted to build a homogenous nation at the expense of remaining particularisms and regional forms of communal allegiances. In order to achieve this, the nation builders utilised historiography, which was used to build a usable past and erase collective remembrances that challenged official history (Kezer 2000, 103). Given the scarcity of human and material capital, the attentions and resources devoted to the Ethnography Museum attest to its importance in the cultural life of the new Republic (Kezer 2000, 104). As Kezer (2000, 104) argues, the museum was intended to be a 'jarring separator between the past and the present'.

A detailed account of the museum can be found in a 1928 article written in the *Hayat* magazine, a weekly magazine published 1926–9 that supported the reforms of the new Republic (Akdağ and Davulcu 2016). That article, which was written as the museum was preparing to open its doors to the public, gives us a good sense of what the museum looked like in 1928, at the height of Kemalist reforms and the nation-building process. In this article, Halil (1928, 9) starts by writing that upon entering the museum, one finds ethnographic material belonging to 'primitive tribes'. He praises the showcasing of these materials and states that the museum guide, Mesaruş Bey, told him that it is necessary to know about the ethnography of the history of common civilisation (*umumî medeniyet tarihinin etnoğrafyası*) before learning about national ethnography. Among others, Halil mentions wooden, bone and stone items of Australian and Polynesian cultures and primitive items of 'African civilization' from the Iron Age, an 'Eskimo' collection gifted by the Danish government two years ago, and a statue of a native American tribal leader gifted by Theodore Roosevelt to (Sultan) Abdülhamid (II) (see Figure 2.1).

In the second chamber, which Halil (1928) says is 'entirely national'" Halil writes that respectively, household items, a ceramic collection, and folk decoration (*halk tezyinatı*) are showcased. Halil writes that the museum guide Mesaruş Bey told him that he finds the nexus between the metal household items demonstrated in the museum and those found in the ancient history of Anatolia very important. The third section is devoted to embroideries, Halil writes. Halil elaborates on these embroideries, which he argues are organised from primitive to more complex, in line with museology principles and science. 'At the end of this section, you encounter four mannequins', Halil describes, 'a Trabzon lad, an Amasya women, a type from Anatolian tribes (*aşiret*), and an Anatolian bride' (see Figure 2.2). He adds that the dresses of the mannequins carry local characteristics and that he believes that this part will be a source of reference for national social studies (*milli içtimaiyat tetkikleri*).

Halil then moves on to the fourth chamber, which he argues is the most important one in terms of 'our national and social history'. He writes that

Figure 2.1 Statue of an American tribe leader, gifted by American President Roosevelt to Sultan Abdülhamid II located in the Ethnography Museum. Source: Halil 1928.

Figure 2.2 Mannequins depicting 'a type of Anatolian women: Eastern Anatolian Women', and a 'Bektaşi (an unorthodox religious order) costume'. Source: Halil 1928.

these sections belong to an institution overthrown by the Revolution and that it is important to preserve the material from the closed religion dervish lodges for the sake of science. He states that the same scientific order has been followed in this section as well.

Scholars who work on the Ethnography Museum have also devoted special attention to the section displaying items from religious orders and dervish lodges due to its interventions into the cultural life of the society of its time. In the nation and state-building process, it was essential for the founders of the Republic to severe the ties to local allegiances, particularly religious and ethnic ones. As Kezer argues (2000, 103), the museum tried to define local religious allegiances as obsolete. A significant portion of the museum display was devoted to items that used to belong to religious orders and lodges that were banned by the new regime. When religious orders were closed in 1925 and their congregational spaces were outlawed, selected items from such places were put on display at the Ethnography Museum (Kezer 2000, 110). These objects were separated from the context of their daily use and from the functions they used to serve. The items were categorised by their types and put behind glass cases (Kezer 2000, 106). As Shaw (2011, 932) argues, 'the secularization of signs of religious devotion by shifting the act of the gaze from one of worship to one of aesthetic appreciation was part and parcel of the secularist ideology of the republican regime'.

The museum labelled items that were still familiar and part of everyday use as historical (Kezer 2000, 107). Not just religious heterogeneity but also ethnic heterogeneity and practices not in congruence with the modernising impetus of the regime were also deemed as museum material. In addition to being musealised and historicised, religious and ethnic differences were also reduced to regionalism (Shaw 2011, 940) as Halil's (1928) emphasis on different parts of Anatolia when talking about the costumes of the mannequins also demonstrate.

Just like the Anatolian Civilizations Museum, the Ethnography Museum also told a unilinear, evolutionary and teleological story according to which the Anatolian people moved in time to the modern nation state of the Turkish Republic. Kezer (2000, 108) summarises the implications of the story well:

the nation's history was a long single-minded journey towards modernity, the milestones of which were preserved in museum as relics as of the past to be

remembered but carefully kept at a safe distance. Accordingly, history and destiny were envisioned as the two ends of a single, unified and unifying path that
extended into eternity.

While the Ethnography Museum tells us the story of a nation with a long,
proud history that is moving up the stairs of progress in time, the First and
Second Parliaments of the Republic, which now serve as museums, tell us the
heroic story of the War of Independence as well as the founding era of the
Republic. The lively and nostalgic atmosphere of these museums stands in
stark contrast with the Ethnography Museum but complements its narrative
of progress very well.

The First and Second Parliamentary Buildings of the Republic

During the War of Independence, the resistance organised in the Anatolian
peninsula under the leadership of Atatürk. Ankara became the focal point of
this resistance. The first parliament was opened here to orchestrate the resistance effort and to serve as the new centre of authority of the newly established regime that refused to recognise the legitimacy of the Ottoman Sultan in
Istanbul, who collaborated with the invaders. The parliament was inaugurated
on 23 April 1920, which is commemorated every year as National Sovereignty
and Children's Day in Turkey, albeit the celebrations of this day have become
muted under AKP rule.

The first parliament building served between 23 April 1920 and 15
October 1924. It then became the headquarters of the CHP (Cumhuriyet
Halk Partisi) and later a law school. It was handed over to the Ministry of
Education in 1952 and it was turned into a museum in 1957, which opened
its doors to the public on the forty-first anniversary of the opening of the
First Assembly, on 23 April 1961 under the name 'Türkiye Büyük Millet
Meclisi Müzesi' (Turkish Grand National Assembly Museum; see T. C.
Kültür Bakanlığı). Upon renovations, the museum was turned into the
War of Independence Museum on 23 April 1981, the day of the sixty-first
anniversary of the opening of the First Assembly (Diken 2020).

The Second Parliament was built in 1923 and started to serve as the new
parliamentary building on 18 October 1924 since the first parliamentary
building was not able to accommodate the parliament anymore. This building

served as the parliamentary building of Turkey until 27 May 1960, the day of the first military coup in Turkey. In 1961, when the parliament moved into its new, bigger and more complex third building, the Second Parliament first served as the Central Treaty Organization (CENTO) headquarters. When CENTO, which was a mutual security organisation among Turkey, Iran, Pakistan and the United Kingdom, was dissolved, it was turned over to the Ministry of Culture in 1979. It was opened as the Republic Museum on 30 October 1981 (see Kültür Varliklari ve Müzeler Genel Müdürlüğü).

At the entry of the Republic Museum, the personal belongings of the first three presidents of the Turkish Republic and the economic and industrial developments of the early years of the Republic are showcased. Items from the time the building served as the parliament are also displayed. On the second floor, there are the prime minister's office, president's office, presidential reception hall, and the office of the speaker of the parliament. Across the museum entrance, there is the general assembly where Atatürk read the speech at the tenth anniversary of the Republic, and the periodical exhibition hall. The microphone Atatürk used during this speech is showcased in the Atatürk Principles and Revolutions room of the museum (Kültür Varliklari ve Müzeler Genel Müdürlüğü).

Even after they ceased to serve as parliamentary buildings, the First and Second Parliamentary Buildings continued to serve important missions for the Republican ideals, commemorating the War of Independence, the progress made during the Republic, as well as the steps of nation and state building. When we look at the years in which the museums received further attention, one can further elaborate on the implications of these museums for the statespeople of their eras: 1961 is the year following the first coup and 1981 is the year following the second coup, which are telling dates with regard to the instrumentalisation of the two previous parliamentary building in the valorisation of the juntas' own notions of Kemalism.

As Taraz (2021, 216) notes, both the War of Independence Museum and the Republic Museum provide an unmediated experience for the visitors as they preserve the original settings of the assemblies with minimal additions of glass cases displaying personal belongings of the statespeople and documents of the era. In the First Parliamentary Building, for example, the museum space is mostly organised in accordance with the former functions that the rooms of the buildings served when the building was used as the first parliament. As such, it retains original furniture, objects and documents of the era in addition to artwork commemorating key events of the War of Independence and the formative years of the Republic (Taraz 2021, 179). Taraz (2021, 216) gives the examples of the president room in the War of Independence Museum, which preserves the tools Atatürk used in this room as well as the General Assembly meeting room where the original wooden benches are accessible to visitors under the original inscription that reads, 'Sovereignty belongs to the nation'. Taraz sees similar elements in the Second Parliament in which the rooms are kept in relation to the former functions of the administrative spaces preserving the aura of the past while original materials document the steps taken toward modernisation and republicanism in the early years of the Republic.

One can argue that the atmosphere in these museums, bolstered by pictures of the time, public records of milestones of the Republic, and personal items characterising the ethos of the era, is full of nostalgia, pride and gratefulness.

Figure 2.3 The Second Parliamentary Building: photo of Atatürk exiting the building. Photo taken by the author.

Figure 2.4 The Second Parliamentary Building: Atatürk's speech on the tenth anniversary of the Republic accompanied by a picture from that date. Photo taken by the author.

Figure 2.5 The Second Parliamentary Building: the General Assembly. Photo taken by the author, March 2014.

Figure 2.6 The Second Parliamentary Building: Atatürk's pictures and personal belongings. Photo taken by the author.

The Republican Ulus

The Republican vision for the vicinity of Ulus, discussed with landmark examples, needs to be evaluated taking into consideration surrounding buildings such as the Ankara Palas, the modern building across from the assembly buildings in which Republican celebrations would take place, and other symbols such as the Atatürk statue at the centre of Ulus. The national holidays commemorated and the ceremonies in this region as well as the festivities such as balls at Ankara Palace stand in stark contrast with the image presented under Islamist governments, such as the Ramadan celebrations in Hamamönü, as will be elaborated in the next section. For the Republican elites, Ulus told a story of progress, embracing the past of the nation in a linear fashion and depicting this as something to be superseded. The Ottoman past was downplayed and a sharp rift was introduced between the *ancien régime* and the Republic. The images below from the 1938 commemoration of the fifteenth anniversary of the Republic, including images from Ulus, illustrate this point well. In these supplementary pages specifically prepared for the occasion by the pro-government *Cumhuriyet* (Republic) newspaper, old Ankara is juxtaposed

Figure 2.7 *Cumhuriyet* newspaper on 29 October 1938: Old Ankara.
Source: Koç University VEKAM Library and Archive, inventory no: LA008_16.

Figure 2.8 *Cumhuriyet* newspaper on 29 October 1938: New Ankara.
Source: Koç University VEKAM Library and Archive, inventory no: LA008_17.

Figure 2.9 Holiday celebration at the Ulus Square, 1930s.
Source: Koç University VEKAM Library and Archive, inventory no: 0936.

to the new one. If one were to only see the structures erected in the Republican era in Ulus, one would envision a nation that is heir to ancient civilisations, that is secular and Western-oriented and adheres to Republican values.

The Islamist Narrative Told through Ulus

With the rise of political Islam, the Kemalist hegemony faced a strong challenge. As in other parts of the country, this challenge presented itself vividly in Ankara. In 1994, one of the first actions of the new Ankara mayor Melih Gökçek – who was then elected from the predecessor of AKP, the Refah Partisi (Welfare Party, RP) and who later in his career joined the AKP upon its formation – was to change the logo of the Ankara Metropolitan Municipality. The new design, which replaced the Hittite sun disk, was composed of the shopping mall tower structure built in 1987 (Atakule) and the Kocatepe Mosque built between 1967 and 1987 which converged into a crescent and a star with three additional stars on top of them (Kilinç 2017, 3). Gökçek defended the change of the symbol of the city as follows: 'Turkish culture is uniform and the Islamic period constitutes its majority. The emblem that will symbolize Ankara is expected to reflect this reality' (Kilinç 2017, 18). This move openly demonstrated the attempt to counter the secular, world civilisational narrative of the Kemalist regime with one that presented Turks as inalienably Islamic. Such tendencies to insert Islam into the Turkish historical narrative started as early as in the 1970s, during the right-wing National Front governments. In school history textbooks, for example, more emphasis was put on the Islamic past of the Turks. In these stories, the Manzikert War (1071) of the Seljuks whereby Muslim Turks are believed to have made Anatolia their homeland as a result of the victory against the Byzantine Empire, played centre stage. Since then, interventions into the dominant historical narrative have been amplified significantly, particularly with the uninterrupted rule of the AKP since 2002. The AKP and its predecessors have been in charge of the Ankara Metropolitan Municipality from 1994 to 2019 and the Altındağ Municipality where Ulus is located has been ruled by Islamist parties since 1994 and by the AKP in particular since 2004. This shift in power provided the pro-Islamist rulers of Ulus with an opportunity to repaint the landscape so as to tell a different story of the Turkish nation, which stood in stark contrast to the Kemalist storyline as will be shown in the upcoming sections.

Ankara Intangible Heritage Museum

The Ankara Intangible Heritage Museum (Ankara Somut Olmayan Kültürel Miras Müzesi, SOKÜM) was founded by the work of members of the Gazi University,[2] Department of Turkish Folklore and the monetary support of the Ankara Development Agency on 15 June 2013. The process of building the museum started in 2011. SOKÜM is the first museum in Turkey in the field of intangible heritage. The founding president is Öcal Oğuz, the chair of Gazi University Folklore Department. The then Altındağ mayor Veysel Tiryaki sponsored this initiative by providing a *konak* (an Ottoman-era mansion) situated in the Hamamönü district for the museum (T. C. Kültür Bakanlığı). On the website of the Ministry of Culture, the essential purpose of the museum is explained as rescuing Ankara from the image of 'a city of bureaucrats/public officials', contributing to turning Ankara into a touristic centre, conducting field studies to reveal historical and cultural values and transferring the findings obtained from these studies to future generations by putting them into practice in the museum (T. C. Kültür Bakanlığı). The same website states that the activities in the museum consist of the presentation of the data derived from research in Ankara's provinces and villages in an applied manner. The website lists traditional plays and games, handicrafts, fairytale telling, folk songs, lullabies, traditional conversation meeting (*geleneksel sohbet toplantıları*), bride's henna nights and soldier's henna nights as some of the 'cultural values' that are kept alive in the museum through practices.

In the museum and on relevant websites and in writings, one is told that the notion of intangible heritage is inspired by UNESCO's emphasis on this concept in an attempt to protect cultural heritage from extinction. Çiğdem Şimşek, who served as the museum director, also wrote a Master's thesis in 2015 on the museum, which provides an important illustration of this claim. In the abstract of the thesis, Şimşek states that, in response to the loss of local and national cultures in the face of popular culture, the disappearance of the cultural diversity of humanity, and rising uniformity due to the destruction of culture, many countries are taking important steps towards preserving their culture. Şimşek cites the UNESCO 2003 convention on the protection of intangible cultural heritage and notes that Turkey signed the convention in 2006 and developed cultural protection policies so as to keep national heritage alive. She adds that this convention was prepared with the idea of protecting intangible cultural heritage products that are gradually disappearing as a result of globalisation and industrialisation (Şimşek 2015, 40). In the practices of the museum, however, one sees a selective application of intangible heritage, erasing the pluralism of the past and instead focusing on elements of the past that are politically pertinent and that are deemed estimable by the political stance of the AKP, as will be discussed in detail below.

In an interview featured on a state-operated TV channel, Şimşek states that the museum works mostly on the transmission of culture to new generations, and on reproduction and regeneration of culture (TRT Avaz 2015). In another speech featured in the pro-government *Yeni Safak* (2016) newspaper, Şimşek says that 'All there is in our culture (*öz kültürümüz*), we are trying to keep alive.' In her speech, she puts emphasis on 'reproducing our own cultural codes and transmitting them to new generations.' She also notes that it is vital that people can turn the things that they learn in the museum into life practices. To understand what she means by these activities that citizens were expected to put to practice in their own lives, one needs to look closer at the museum's exhibits and the narratives surrounding them.

I visited the museum and was given a guided tour in May 2022. While I was in the museum, a group of children (probably an organised school visit) were working on traditional handicrafts such as Ebru and Linden tree printing. When I was leaving the museum, these children were directed to playing 'traditional games' in the garden.

The tour guide, herself a student of folklore at the Hacıbayram University (a newly formed university created by the division of Gazi University), welcomed me at the entrance. She introduced the museum and told me that this museum is an applied (*uygulamalı*) museum and that nothing is put behind showcases here and that instead, visitors are encouraged to interact with the items. The statement that the museum is different in that it does not put collections behind showcases is a line used repeatedly by the staff of the museum. Şimşek, in her statement quoted in *Yeni Safak* (2016), also noted that this museum is an interactive one and that they do not put anything behind glasses.

In SOKÜM, the museum guide showed me and informed me about items which she referred to as elements of traditional Turkish theatre, traditional Turkish arts and handicraft. The tour was mostly structured around showing different rooms of the traditional Ottoman house, focusing on certain items situated in their daily use and on the discussion of idioms and sayings that are still used in daily lives today, in the context in which they are said to have originated in relation to the setting. The tour guide told me that they are 'showing the life-based roots of the idioms (*deyimlerin yaşamsal kökenleri*)', which she said were collected from Ankara and Central Anatolia. She added that especially visitors over the age of fifty often said, 'My memories are brought alive here.' When showing collected items, the museum guide frequently mentioned that most of them are still in use, particularly in villages.

In addition to (and in relation to) a strong emphasis on continuity with the past, gender plays a central role in the narrative of the museum. Şimşek (2015) discusses in her thesis the applied intangible heritage practices of the museum, such as performances of henna nights (women's wedding celebrations one day prior to the wedding) or the asking of the bride's family for permission for marriage (*kız isteme*) in which museum visitors are also asked to participate.

Figure 2.10 SOKÜM: kitchen photo 1. Taken by the author.

Figure 2.11 SOKÜM: kitchen photo 2. Taken by the author.

Figure 2.12 SOKÜM: guest room. Photo taken by the author.

Figure 2.13 SOKÜM: revolving cabinet between guest room and kitchen, where women would put the food to be served by the youngest male in the guest room so that women would not come in contact with strangers. Photo taken by the author.

In the museum tour, and in the structure of the display, a lot of emphasis is put on the gendered, segregated nature of the 'traditional life', which constituted an anathema to the Republican elite, and something that they have fought hard to overcome. The museum guide talked about the revolving cabinet between the kitchen and the guest room in which food from the kitchen would be put by women, to be served by the youngest male in the guest room by picking the food and other offerings from the cabinet. That way, men and women would not get into contact. The story of the cabinet is told in detail in which sometimes a girl who would like to marry this youngest male would leave a handcrafted handkerchief under the plate and if the male was not spoken for and was interested, he would take the handkerchief. I had the opportunity to watch numerous museums tours whose records are available on YouTube and I saw that this story was told by all of the museum guides in the same way.

In the museum, there is a room specifically designed to show the milestones and rites of passages of girls and boys during their life in such a house. The focus of the items on display changes from time to time particularly in relation to how the bed is decorated. When the room is decorated as a circumcision room (*sünnet odası*), in that case more emphasis is put on the boyhood of someone and his procession to adulthood. In the case when the room is decorated as a 'bride's room', then the display is mostly focused on the story of a bride who had just given birth to her child and is using the bed during her post-partum period (*lohusa odası*). When I was visiting the museum, the bed was decorated to depict the room as a circumcision room, denoting the celebrations that took place during the day the circumcision was performed. But as I will discuss below, items belonging to girls and boys were both presented in the room but through separate stories.

During my visit, the museum guide told me that the room was depicting important milestones of a boy's life, most prominently, circumcision and military service. The bed was decorated with handicrafts celebrating the rite of passage of the boy. There was a military uniform on the wall, a reproduction of a letter from a soldier along with pictures of young boys with costumes from circumcision days, and a bowl of henna, which is a substance applied at these ceremonies to the hands of the soldiers. The museum guide added that such traditions are still present in villages. At the other side of the room, she showed me a cradle and a dowry chest (*çeyiz sandığı*) next to it and told me about the saying 'the girl is in the cradle, her dowry is in the chest'. This, she explained,

Figure 2.14 The circumcision room. Photo taken by the author.

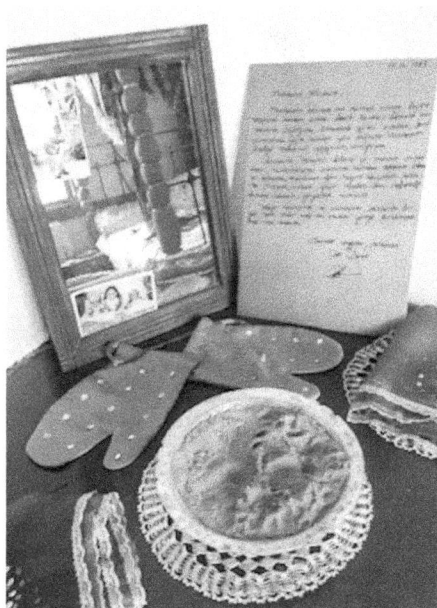

Figure 2.15 Memorabilia from circumcision ceremony and military service. Photo taken by the author.

Figure 2.16 Dowry chest and cradle. Photo taken by the author.

Figure 2.17 Mirrored broom in the dowry chest. Photo taken by the author.

meant that as soon as a girl is born, the mother would start making her dowry ready, in preparation of her wedding.

Another frequent set of characters that appeared in the stories told by my museum guide were the bride and her mother-in-law. For instance, she told me that the reason there were mirrors on the broom was because the mother-in-law decided that since the bride was so preoccupied looking at mirrors that she neglected housework, putting a mirror on the broom will ensure that she can look at herself while doing the housework. I was also told that the saying '*kulağına küpe etmek*' ('to make an earring to ones ear') – meaning, to remember advice – came from the fact that a mother would gift her son her earrings on the circumcision day, saying that these were gifted to her by her mother-in-law and that she had kept her advice all her life and that her son should gift these earrings to his future wife so that the new bride would also listen to the advice of her mother-in-law. In the living room, the guide showed me a cabinet on the wall called the 'lazy wife's cabinet' (*tembel avrat dolabı*) which, according to the guide, was prepared by the bride to put in all the things that the mother-in-law would ask for in one place (her medicine and other needs that she kept asking for from her daughter-in-law), for convenience (see Figure 2.18).

Figure 2.18 The 'lazy wife' cabinet. Photo taken by the author.

This very same room is also the place where children are told traditional fairy tales now. My museum guide mentioned that children knew stories such as Little Red Riding Hood but not the Anatolian fairy tales so they were telling children these Anatolian fairy tales in this room now, just as the children were told such stories in the past.

As mentioned above, the circumcision room is also sometimes presented as the bride's room (*gelin odası*). In that case, the main thing that changes in the room is how the bed and its surroundings are decorated. On YouTube, there are many videos available that show different presentations by different museum guides. In many of them, this room is presented with the artefacts of a traditional Ottoman newlywed bride's room, who comes into the house of the extended family of her husband upon getting married. In one of those, a female museum guide talks about the bride room telling stories about the life of the bride in the house, her childbirth, the dialogues she has with her unmarried female friends regarding their future prospects of marriage, and so on (Tin Medya 2018).

In her analysis of the narrative construction of identity of undocumented Mexican immigrants in the United States, De Fina (2003) demonstrates how identities are built, represented and negotiated in narrative form by paying special attention to different linguistic elements such as pronoun switches. Such linguistic elements in the storytelling of museum guides are also very indicative of how individual and collective identities are constructed through narratives. In another video recording, the male museum guide talks about the bride room in which he tells the visitors about the 'traditional' roles and practices. As he tells the stories, he moves between the past and present and he uses the words 'we, us, our' frequently. He also tells gendered stories in relation to the past, referring to women as wives and to men as 'the son of the house' (*evin oğlu*). Military service is also mentioned in relation to the life events of the son. The guide makes statements such as 'Of course, we are the Turkish community, we come from a conservative structure (*muhafazakar yapıdan geliyoruz*). Men and women would not mingle.' Or, he would say things such as 'our people (*bizim insanlarımız*)'. When talking about the revolving cabinet connecting the kitchen to the guest room, he says: 'women won't enter the guest room, men won't enter the kitchen. However, women have to serve in some way (*bir şekilde kadın da hizmet etmek zorunda*).'

While giving the tour of the guest room, the tour guide says things such as 'we are a sensitive society (*hassas bir toplumuz*)', 'wall tapestry is very important for us because we are a nomadic society (*yörük bir toplumuz*)'. In the bride room, explaining the saying on dowry and little baby girls mentioned above, he says, 'In our case (*bizde*), dowry is always prepared.' Continuing along the gendered storyline discussed above, he notes that postpartum women are never left without their male relatives (father, brother or husband) against the folk belief called *albasması* (the belief that a bad spirit will harm the mother and the child after childbirth) but if the men must leave the room, they will hang their jackets on the side of the bed to ensure male presence (Her Sey 2014).

In the museum, one witnesses the blurring of things that the Republican founders deliberately would want to keep separated. While the stories of the early Republic want to put an important distinction between the modern and the traditional, the old and the new, science and superstition, the museum deliberately blurs these boundaries and tries to ensure a continuity between the Ottoman past and the present while at the same time drawing the picture of what a 'common Turk' would look like. Moreover, as the depictions of the museum show, this Turk is gendered. Men are associated with public life, protection, military service, while women are discussed as brides and mothers, and in the context of their domestic household duties.

What is more, the narratives used blur the distinction between not only the past and the present but also between the individual and the communal. As Brockmeier (2002) argues, narratives are essential in linking individual memory to collective memory. Relatedly, Geoffrey M. White (1999) demonstrates the intertwined nature of personal and national narratives through his research at the Pearl Harbor memorial with military survivors of the attack who told their stories at the memorial on a regular basis. White examines the links between collective representation and personal cognition and emotion by focusing on acts of public remembrance. By doing this, White wants to complicate the boundaries that have been created between the 'psychological' and the 'cultural', and between the 'individual' and the 'collective' by modern paradigms. He analyses the discourse of 'survivors' who present personal stories in the context of the national memorial for Pearl Harbor. He argues that the acts of remembrance at the memorial by the 'survivors' represent and enact national identity in performative acts that are at once individual and collective, personal and national. White holds that narrative performance forms social and emotional identifications. White considers two discursive means used to interpolate personal narrative and national history: the use of pronouns (I and we), and other indexical signs to link personal and collective perspective in narrative performance and the use of personal stories as allegories to embody and emotionalise national histories. The stories we witness at SOKÜM show how the stories of the past collected and presented at the museum are intertwined with the stories of the tour guides, the visitors and the nation at large. The next museum follows on this trend to tell the story of current Turkey in relation to the Ottoman and Islamic past.

Ankara Mehmet Akif Ersoy Museum House

Across the street from SOKÜM, after a three- to four-minute walk, you reach the House of Mehmet Akif Ersoy. Mehmet Akif Ersoy is the author of the Turkish national anthem (1921) and the house is the place where he stayed when he was in Ankara. It is also the place where he wrote the national anthem. In the latter years of the Republic, Mehmet Akif fell into disagreement with the ruling elites over secularism and moved to Egypt in 1926. He returned in 1936 but died of natural causes six months later. He remains a prominent figure among the Islamists to this day.

The Mehmet Akif Museum is situated in the religious lodge of Taceddin, which was active until the ban on religious orders and lodges. Mehmet Akif was invited to stay at this house by the members of the lodge during the War of Independence. As we discussed earlier, such organisations were banned and left to oblivion under the Republican regime. Yet for the pro-Islamist rulers, putting the religious tones of the past in the limelight is key. This also applies to the case of Mehmet Akif. The writings, pictures and items surrounding the house are framed within a religious narrative. The fact that this place was part of the Taceddin Lodge is written everywhere in the museum. The place is also presented as a religious place, a shrine, a cemetery, and a mosque. The backyard of the house is a graveyard with Ottoman-era inscribed tombstones. Muhsin Yazıcıoğlu, the far-right youth leader of the 1970s, who later identified himself more and more with Islam, and even founded a more religious version of the ultranationalist party he participated in in the 1970s, is buried in the backyard of this house, next to old graveyards dating back to the Ottoman Empire. Most of the visiting times, there are at least a couple of people around Yazıcıoğlu's grave, praying for him.

While nearing the building, there is a park named after Mehmet Akif. In this park, a monument was installed in order to commemorate Mehmet Akif, as part of the 2011 'Year of Mehmet Akif' initiative of the Ministry of Culture and Tourism. All of the ten stanzas of the national anthem are inscribed on stone blocks of a monument erected for Mehmet Akif, which was opened on the ninetieth anniversary of the adoption of the national anthem, on 12 March 2011.

Figure 2.19 The Mehmet Akif Ersoy monument. Photo taken by the author.

In front of the building, there is a long line of photos of Mehmet Akif along with biographical notes regarding his life. There are also placards that provide information about the mosques near the museum.

Once you enter the house, you are welcomed by an overwhelming number of pictures of Mehmet Akif and by a recorded, mystical voice that constantly recites Mehmet Akif's poems. Similar to museums that want to commemorate

Figure 2.20 The exterior of the Mehmet Akif Ersoy Museum. Photo taken by the author.

the secular origins of the Republic, but in a mirror image fashion, wax statues have been put in place and artefacts such as handwritten texts and photos of the past are showcased throughout the museum. In the kitchen, wax statues of the dervish lodge are shown in their daily practices and Mehmet Akif is depicted as conversing with his guests in the guest room. Information about the Taceddin Lodge is provided on a placard. Mehmet Akif's personal items such as ID card, letters, and the bed he used to sleep in are also presented in the museum.

The Mehmet Akif Ersoy Museum is another perfect illustration of how the AKP continues its political struggle with the founding ideals of the Republic in the cultural realm. While the Republican reforms aimed at leaving the remnants of the archaic regime such as the religious orders and the Ottoman script behind, the AKP has brought them back to the limelight through the way it presented the commemoration of Mehmet Akif. The storyline of continuity with the Ottoman past, deliberately cut by the revolutionary secular elites, is reinstated by the governing party using techniques similar to the ones used during the early Republican era. Museums, with the artefacts in them and

Figure 2.21 Wax statues in the Mehmet Akif Ersoy Museum I. Photo taken by the author.

Figure 2.22 Wax statues in the Mehmet Akif Ersoy Museum II. Photo taken by the author.

the way they are installed, play a key role in this process as will also be seen in the next case below. In addition, the environment surrounding the museums is also utilised to reinforce the aura of the museum as seen in the case of the Mehmet Akif Museum. When I was visiting, groups of school children were also there, suggesting that this place, like SOKÜM, is also used for pedagogical purposes by the AKP-controlled education system.

The Ulucanlar Prison Museum

While SOKÜM and the Mehmet Akif Ersoy Museum tell stories from the Ottoman era to the early Republican era, the next landmark, the Ulucanlar Prison Museum attempts to tell the story of the entire Turkish Republic culminating in the AKP rule, which is presented as the saviour of the nation from the oppression of the establishment. As I have discussed elsewhere (Ugur-Cinar and Altınok 2021), the Ulucanlar museum plays a crucial role in the AKP's efforts to further its populist cause. It is a focal point of the historical narrative of the AKP that presents itself as the voice and liberator of the people against the oppressive and aloof elites of the secular establishment. The Ulucanlar prison is significant because it was the place where high-level political prisoners were held and some of them were executed either at the hands of the Independence Courts (Istiklal Mahkemeleri) of the early years of the Republic or during the recurring military juntas.

The prison museum turned into a medium through which the AKP told a narrative that divided the community into the homogenous body of righteous people on the one hand, and the oppressive elite on the other. In this story, the AKP, and Erdoğan in particular, appeared to be the authentic voice of the people, the saviour of the victims. In what was framed as 'coming to terms with the past', the AKP found an instrument to expand its power and to silence dissent (Ugur-Cinar and Altınok 2021). It was this motivation that led to the current form of the 'museumification' of Ulucanlar.

Ulucanlar was turned into a museum between the years 2009 and 2011, at the height of the AKP's struggle with the military and judicial establishment.[3] The Ulucanlar prison was built in 1925 and served as the first prison complex of Turkey. Since it was a remand prison, prisoners would either stay for a short amount of time and then be transferred elsewhere or they would be executed at Ulucanlar. The prison housed many notable political prisoners across the political spectrum including politicians, public intellectuals, poets and journalists. In total, eighteen people were executed in the prison, seventeen of which were political prisoners, including revolutionary youth leaders Deniz Gezmiş, Yusuf Aslan and Hüseyin Inan, who were executed after the 1971 military intervention, as well as Erdal Eren, whose age was increased to eighteen by the 1980 military junta so they could execute him. Iskilipli Atıf Hoca, a religious figure who challenged the Republic's reforms, was hanged in the Ulus square, not inside the prison in 1926, but was also counted amongst those executed here by the museum (Batuman 2011). Far-right militants Fikri Arıkan and Ali Bülent Orhan were also among the executed at Ulucanlar following the 1980 coup.

The museum thus provided an invaluable opportunity for the AKP rulers to project the Republican past as one of oppression and brutality while situating themselves as saviours and democrats. As will be exemplified below, despite the heterogeneity of the inmates, the prison museum narrative collapses this plurality to an oppressor–victim dichotomy in which the victim is stripped away from its political context. With the homogenising storyline and the ending of the story with the arrival of the AKP in a triumphalist fashion, the museum hinders the possibility for the contemplation of contemporary injustices and wrongdoings of the AKP's authoritarian rule (Ugur-Cinar and Altınok 2021, 1111).

Most of the displays in the museum are focused on the human rights violations of the past, such as torture and capital punishment. The innocence and victimhood of the inmates are a focal point of the museum narrative. The stories of the inmates are made familiar and relatable to the audience through the display of their personal items, their pictures and their farewell letters to their families. Those items on display belong to diverse political figures ranging from Iskilipli to Deniz Gezmiş and Fikri Arıkan, who are presented as a homogenous mélange of victims in the museum narrative. The theme of execution takes centre stage, with the exhibition of the personal belongings of the executed and the original materials directly linked to their execution, such as the placards hung on their necks during the execution explaining which panel code they violated.

Through the display of familiar, domestic and folkloric items (such as hand-knitted sweaters or a prayer rug) and the reliance on family tropes, the museum also attempts to create a personal connection between the stories of the visitors and the former inmates. This identification extends the victimisation of the inmates to the visitors, turning the AKP into the saviour of not only the inmates but also the visitors. To this end, wax sculptures recreate the scenes in the common wards in which inmates are presented in their daily lives, reciting the Qur'an, playing backgammon and drinking tea or playing the folk instrument, the *saz*. Torture sounds accompany wax sculptures shown in agony in prison cells. The sensory experience of the populist narrative of the museum reaches its climax at the end of the tour where one finds original gallows and hangman's knot put behind bars. Under these, there is a caption stating 'Death Penalty in Turkey was removed entirely by the Decree no: 5218 of National Assembly in 14.07.2004' without reference to the process that started the removal of the death penalty before the AKP came to power due to EU negotiations, and neglecting to give the information that the last execution in Turkey had taken place in 1984.

The fact that the original gallows and hangman's knot are located as the finale of the tour is not a natural occurrence but is instead curated intentionally. There is a specific route visitors are expected to follow in the museum, which leaves the gallows to the end even though, in actuality, this area is close to the entrance of the museum. Visitors are expected to 'see the isolation cells with the sounds of torture, the wards exhibiting wax sculptures and personal items of inmates, and historical newspaper clips covering coup d'états' (Ugur-Cinar and Altınok 2021, 1114) before reaching this happy ending, which signals a closure in the AKP's narrative of the Republic.

What is striking here is that in this narrative, all political particularities are erased in favour of the populist storyline that narrates the past as the story between the oppressor and the oppressed until the saviour and the true representative of the people comes in and saves 'the people'. As such, 'the victims in the museum become synonymous with the people at large, memorializing a shared experience that molds different segments of society into one totality in which remembrance is only possible through a shared victimhood' (Ugur-Cinar and Altınok 2021, 1117). The omissions of the museum are manifold. First, we do not learn about the specific political ideas of the prisoners except for very brief biographical sketches and some brief information regarding which years the prisoners stayed at Ulucanlar and the penal code they breached. As Aysu (2015, 37) also observes:

> Display of kitchen utensils, music instruments, backgammon and the like, on the one hand, offers a 'humanized' representation. That is, the inmates are given life, but this life is a specific form of life. They eat, play, make, and listen to music. However, on the other hand, such representation deprives them of their political content.

Second, inmates who stayed at the Ulucanlar Prison in different time frames are collapsed together time-wise. The museum shop puts mugs of the revolutionary poet Nazim Hikmet and the far-right youth leader Muhsin Yazıcıoğlu next to each other and the bunk beds in the wards depict them as though they slept side by side in the museum. As Batuman (2011) argues, judging by the way the museum was curated, visitors could easily come to think that the communist poet Nazim Hikmet and the Islamist political icon Necip Fazil stayed together in the same ward, sleeping next to each other on adjacent bunk beds.

What is more, the contemporary history of Turkey that would link the prison to the time of the AKP's rule is deliberately left out of the museum narrative. The infamous 'Return to Life' Operations of December 2000 that resulted in the death of thirty-one prisoners and the torture of many more are conspicuously absent, aside from a couple of newspaper clips, all narrated from the official line (Aysu 2015). The role that right-wing political leaders, particularly Süleyman Demirel, played in the executions of Deniz Gezmiş, Hüseyin Inan and Yusuf Aslan are also omitted. In addition, political figures, when deemed to be opponents of the AKP rule, are also erased from the museum, as was the case with Sırrı Süreyya Önder whose biography and picture were removed from the museum upon his participation at the forefront of the Gezi protests and his political actions under the Peoples' Democracy Party (HDP) (Ugur-Cinar and Altınok 2021).

One of the most important issues with the museum narrative that is based on the oppression of the people at the hand of political, bureaucratic and military elites and on the role of the AKP as the saviour of the people, is that it does not open opportunities for conversations regarding current malpractices and human rights abuses in prisons and beyond. The museum presents such occurrences as a thing of the past which the AKP has dealt with. As reiterated by the Ulucanlar Prison Museum curator Merve Bayıksel during an interview, the AKP line is that 'people are no longer imprisoned for their views in Turkey' despite Turkey's current record showing otherwise (Ugur-Cinar and Altınok 2021, 1122). The Ulucanlar Museum contributes to the master narrative woven together by the AKP by depicting the Republican elites as part of a brutal regime that would go against the values and will of its people, and which is presented as a situation remedied by the AKP that reconnected the state with its people and the people with their own culture and community. Even behind the façade of a democratic rhetoric surrounding the years of the founding of Ulucanlar discussed in detail elsewhere (Ugur-Cinar and Altınok 2021), it is possible to discern the homogenising, univocal tone of the AKP via strategic omissions and absences through the analysis of the museumification of the Ulucanlar prison.

The Ulus of the AKP Era

As was the case with the Kemalist landmarks, the SOKÜM, Mehment Akif Ersoy Museum and the Ulucanlar Prison Museum need to be understood in the broader landscape in which they are situated. This area houses the renovated Hamamönü buildings of the Ottoman era most of which were actually built from scratch perhaps because they were too old to rescue. The central role they play in current-day Ulus differs strongly from the role they played in the Kemalist era. One can see in Figure 2.7, for example, that the old houses are depicted as a thing of the past. In the Ulus of the AKP, this place constitutes the centre of gravity. It is an attraction for locals and tourists alike and the municipal government organises festivities in this area, particularly during the holy month of Ramadan. When you walk through the streets of the renovated Hamamönü district, you will see the efforts of Ottoman revival.

Similarly, the Hacı Bayram Mosque and its surroundings have also been renovated during the AKP era and are made very visible with signposts and posters. There are 'traditional Ottoman houses' converted into restaurants that also offer traditional Henna Night celebrations, where the bride celebrates her upcoming marriage with female friends and relatives, usually one day prior to the wedding. Cafes, restaurants and kiosks sell items connoting the Ottoman era, such as the *Osmanlı Macunu* (Ottoman Paste). These consumption practices create a very different atmosphere from the one aspired to

Figure 2.23 The historical Hamam of Ulus renovated with the inscription 'since 1440'. Photo taken by the author.

Figure 2.24 Entrance to the Taceddin mosque and lodge in Hamamönü. Photo taken by the author.

Figure 2.25 Street in Hamamönü. Photo taken by the author.

by the Republican elites, who attended Western style restaurants and patisseries newly built in their era. This new image of Ulus, systematically built since the transfer of municipal authority to the Islamist parties, further intensified during the AKP regime, tells a very different story from the secular Republican one through the buildings discussed earlier, in addition to the Atatürk Statue erected in 1927, the Ankara Palas, or the Little Theatre.

In contrast to the founding stories of the Republic, these new stories deliberately try to blur the link between the Ottoman past and the present. While these new additions to the area can be seen as sources of pluralism, as I tried to show in this chapter, they serve a homogenising role both in terms of an envisioned nationhood and community as well as the gender roles and ideal notions of the youth.

The case of Ulus shows us that stories are not always told in written form. Most of the built environment discussed in this chapter certainly relies on written materials, such as brochures, written explanations or biographies. Yet the organisation of items within a place, the way they are presented, the cluster of buildings and the attention given to or the neglect shown to certain structures also have an important role to play in alternative historical narratives and national storylines. Where the story begins, how it unfolds and what the trajectory drawn for a nation consists of comprises elements that are written as well as expressed in non-written form. They draw on performances, commemorations and consumption items, and on the material culture more generally. What is to be renovated, what is to be excavated, and what is to be left as ruins is also affected by the storyline politicians hope to tell. What is more, in a hegemonic battle such as the one between Kemalists and Islamists there is a dialogical attempt that is visible. In this case, the Islamists mirror the practices of the early Republican elites in their attempt to make their own image of the nation dominant as seen in the examples of museum artefacts and wax statues.

In the next chapter, we will move from historical narratives to economic narratives, in order to demonstrate the role economic narratives play in politics, particularly in their role in enabling those in power to thwart dissent, suppress pluralism, and evade accountability and checks and balances, all of which are crucial aspects of democracy.

Notes

1. This quote was used in the following history textbooks: Mercil, Tarhan and Gunal 1990, 18; Uğurlu and Balcı 1989–92, 14; Sümer and Yüksel 1986. All translations are by the author unless otherwise stated.
2. Gazi University is traditionally known for being dominated by right-wing academics, administrators and students. In the clashes between the right and the left, it has been known as the stronghold for the far right.
3. For more on the details of this period in relation to the Ulucanlar Museum and for more details on the museumification process, see Ugur-Cinar and Altınok 2021.

3

CAN MONEY BUY FREEDOM? NARRATIVES OF ECONOMIC DEVELOPMENT AND DEMOCRACY IN TURKEY

This chapter focuses on the relationship between narratives of economic development and prospects for democracy. It does so by tracing the political speeches of high-ranking Turkish government officials and journalists close to them to show how they use narratives of economic development as a tool to politically legitimise interventions to liberal democracy. The chapter first illustrates the dangers caused by these stories of economic development to democracy by looking at the Gezi protests of summer 2013. It shows how demands for pluralism and respect of different lifestyles – which are indeed crucial aspects of a liberal democracy – were instead framed by the government as chaos created by agents of the so called 'interest rate lobby' and provocations caused by those who want to stop Turkey's economic development from within and from without.

The chapter analyses the Gezi case in comparative perspective with presidentialism debates and the corruption scandal of December 2013. It detects a similar pattern in these cases as well, such that demands for democracy, transparency, checks and balances are pitted against economic development. Citizens are made to choose vaguely defined promises of economic development over demands for democratisation. The chapter thus tries to shed light on the impacts of economic development narratives on democratic backsliding, which is a serious threat not only valid for Turkey but for other developing countries as well. The chapter also delves into the question of how institutional settings and structural conjectures provide opportunities for certain political narratives to thrive. In particular, it shows how the economic, social and political transformations that led to the rise of neopopulism were also greatly responsible for the expansion of economic narratives at the expense of democracy and human rights.

Narratives of Economic Development

In understanding the role economic development narratives play in the fate of democracy, a refreshment of our discussion of public narratives and meta-narrativity will be useful. These concepts will help us situate individual economic development narratives into the broader context in which they are utilised. Somers (1994, 619) defines public narratives as 'narratives attached to cultural and institutional formations larger than the single individual, to intersubjective networks or institutions, however local or grand, micro or macro'. Meta-narratives, or master narratives run even deeper than public narratives. They refer to narratives in which we are historically and socially embedded (Somers 1994, 619). In Patterson and Monroe's (1998, 325) words, 'Meta-narratives are so ingrained in our common understanding that they are difficult to recognize and are often uncritically adopted . . . Meta-narratives . . . appear as abstractions and universals, erasing their own history and particularity.' As Bamberg argues, master narratives 'permeate the petit narratives of our everyday talk' (Bamberg 2004, 361). These master narratives are also the narratives that politicians rely on when they speak publicly in narrative form as is demonstrated throughout this book. Public narratives told by politicians are thus embedded in meta-narratives and politicians try to appeal to individuals by weaving together individual narratives of citizens with the broader narratives they tell.

In conjunction with global narratives regarding capitalism, progress and the like mentioned by Somers (1994), or security narratives which are discussed by Wibben (2010, 43) as grand narratives, local contexts also provide centres of gravity for deeply embedded unique meta stories. In fact, Somers (1994, 630) herself notes that 'the extent and nature of any given repertoire of narratives available for appropriation is always historically and culturally specific; the particular plots that give meanings to those narratives cannot be determined in advance.' Localising such deeply running narratives, Wertsch

(2004, 56) talks about 'a generalized narrative form' that 'underlies a range of specific narratives in a cultural tradition'. Wertsch (2008) follows this discussion with his conceptualisation of 'schematic narrative templates', which, in contrast to 'specific narratives', are more generalised structures used to generate multiple specific narratives with the same basic plot and, due to their abstract nature, are unnoticed and especially 'transparent' to those who employ them.

Relatedly, when we talk about narratives, we do not simply mean the narration of singular events but we refer to 'narrative networks' that provide meaning to particular narratives within this network (Andrews, Kinnvall and Monroe 2015, 142; Somers 1995). Similarly, Polletta and Chen (2012, 495, 501) argue that hegemony operates not by the identical repetition of a single story over and over again but rather by the 'promotion of stories that thematize familiar oppositions'. As such, in the Turkish case, narratives related to gender, economic development, and collective memory are anchored in narrative networks in which they resonate. This is not to say that they evoke the same sentiment across all listeners but they resonate in the sense that they provide intelligibility and common understanding across the community. They become the hub of a 'system of signification' (Wedeen 2002). It is around this understanding that consent and contention are built as explicated in this book.

As discussed in the introduction, the three types of narratives covered in this book, namely stories of development, historical narratives and patriarchal narratives, are deeply embedded in the cultural terrain that contains global as well as local elements. Gendered narratives are closely embedded in patriarchy. Economic development narratives are bound by capitalism, particularly neoliberalism, as well as the drive for modernisation. Historical narratives are closely tied to the predominance of nation states and nationalism. Among these narrative types, this chapter focuses on economic development narratives considering both their global and local dynamics. The chapter focuses on what political purposes these economic development narratives serve and what their implications for democracy are. Before focusing on the potentially disruptive effects of economic development narratives on democracy, I first discuss the central role economic development narratives play in Turkish politics. I then proceed with the conceptualisation of democracy accepted in this book, which is not confined to free and fair elections but also entails basic political rights, rule of law and societal pluralism.

The Predominance of Economic Development Narratives in Turkey

Patterson and Monroe (1998, 325) point at narratives of mastery and progress, including economic development narratives as part of meta-narratives, or grand narratives. By economic development narratives, we mean narratives that promise citizens more economic security and/or more economic accumulation. While economic development narratives become useful tools for politicians, they cannot be regarded as completely autonomous forces operating in the political realm. They are meaningful within the political and social context in which they are used. As Somers (1994, 616) argues, narratives are 'constellations of relationships (connected parts) embedded in time and space, constituted by causal emplotment'. In this context, meta-narratives, particularly narratives of development intertwined with neoliberalism, interact with commonplace public narratives in Turkey on modernisation and development and serve as the web of narratives on which members of the AKP build their narratives of economic development.

So why is it that narratives of development can become important tools in weakening democratic mechanisms and leading to authoritarianism? How can a party like the AKP, which neglects issues of social security and economic redistribution and embraces neoliberal policies, give so much weight to economic narratives? It would not be correct to attribute the central role of economic development narratives to a single reason. Multiple forces are at play here. Narratives of development play a central role, particularly in countries such as Turkey, which are eager to catch up with more developed countries. The literature on Turkey has pointed at the central role of development and state-led developmentalism (Adaman and Arsel 2012; Keyman and Gümüşçü 2014). Since the early years of the Republic in Turkey, modernisation has played a very important role in legitimising the state's own existence and facilitating obedience (Adaman *et al.* 2014). Accordingly, the state has defined itself as *the* source of economic development and it claimed that through top-down accelerated modernisation and industrialisation the society would be transformed into a modern, industrialised and civilised totality. This notion of development impeded the accountability of the state to a great extent (Keyman and Öniş 2010).

While development was always a key goal of Turkish politicians, starting with the late Ottoman years and accelerating in the early Republican era, the nature of the quest for development has changed considerably. Modernity and development have come to mean different things to different groups in the history of the Turkish Republic (Özyürek 2006, 19). Especially from the first years of the Republic, development, intertwined with modernisation, was very much understood in conjunction with Westernisation and was deemed inseparable from cultural modernisation (Buğra and Savaşkan 2014, 30; Kasaba 2008, 2). Political groups that did not accept this definition of modernity and opposed Westernisation aspired to define development separate from Western civilisation. With the rise of the right-wing governments starting in the 1950s, the meaning of development in the Turkish context has started to be dissociated from Westernisation and 'goals to reach civilized nations' and has come to be defined more and more in terms of economic development. In this regard, modernity was equated with economic development and industrialisation (Göle 1993, 201) and even full-blown neoliberalism (Cinar and Ugur Cinar 2018, 20).

This trend of equating modernisation with economic development gained speed with the rise of political Islam in Turkey. With the increase in the visibility of political Islam, alternative development approaches started to be expressed more loudly (Göle 1997, 47). Among the educated, urban Islamists (among which engineers have occupied an important place; Göle 1997, 55), the understanding of development of the modernist elite has been replaced by an understanding of development based on industry and economy. In post-1980s Turkey, cultural modernisation has been replaced by economic development (Göle 1993, 201) to a great extent.

While political Islam sought to distinguish between modernisation and Westernisation, it continued to emphasise the role the state would play in development and modernisation. Beyond that, political Islamist parties put economic development at the centre of their politics. As Akbulut and Adaman (2013, 2) point out, even though alternative political movements have questioned secularism and unitary nationalism, which are the foundations of the modern Republic, the idea of rapid economic development as an indispensable condition for progress maintained its dominance and even increased.

Considering that AKP stands for Adalet ve Kalkınma Partisi (Party of Justice and Development), it can already be seen how development is considered a key part of the AKP's branding. As will be made evident in this chapter, the AKP made economic development one of its main talking points. The emphasis put on the construction sector during the AKP period is a good illustration of the AKP's synthesising of its own understanding of modernity with the '90-year dream of development and contemporaneousness' (Çavuşoğlu 2011, 13). The AKP continued the developmentalist discourse emphasised by the right-wing politicians before it and developed a definition of modernity and civilisation similar to them, revealing a 'material reductionism' in this respect (Türk 2014, 437).

In addition to the long-term historical process, the AKP's own past and, in parallel, Turkey's recent past play important roles in the prominence of economic narratives in the politics of the AKP. When the AKP came to power in 2002, the economic depressions of the nineties were still fresh in memories of the electorate. Likewise, the effects of the economic crisis in Turkey in 2001 had spread to society. The AKP grew and was strengthened in response to such a recent past (Çarkoğlu and Hinich 2006, 373; Özbudun 2013, 83). All of the political parties active in the parliament during the 2001 economic crisis remained below the 10 per cent threshold after the 2002 election, and as a result, the AKP disproportionately gained 66 per cent of the seats in parliament with 34 per cent of the votes (Cinar 2016, 1222). For the AKP, which came to power in this atmosphere, economic performance played a key role in maintaining its vote share (Gürkaynak and Sayek-Böke 2013, 64). In fact, a positive correlation exists between the AKP's economic performance and its electoral performance (Cinar 2016; Çarkoğlu 2008. 339; Kalaycıoğlu 2010, 39). Therefore, the AKP's shaping of politics through economic narratives was important in terms of both maintaining its own power and neutralising the opposition.

In addition to factors specific to Turkish politics, neoliberalism and ensuing neopopulism also play central roles in the predominance of economic development narratives deployed by politicians. Neoliberalism, with its disdain for organised societal actors (Harvey 2007, 26, 32; Weyland 1996, 9), and its belief that such actors will reduce economic efficiency (Palley 2005, 23), leads to the individualisation and atomisation of the society rather than, for instance, the organisational empowerment of labour (Cooper and Ellem 2008; Roberts 1995, 90). On the other hand, to prevent social explosion, neoliberal governments allow the poorest segments of society to reach minimal assistance in an unorganised way (Candaş and Buğra 2010, 300) while such governments simultaneously advocate the dismantling of the welfare state. The aid provided by these governments is mostly carried out through the informal sector and civil society (Bozkurt 2013, 384; Buğra and Candaş 2011; Zencirci 2015).

Considering the depoliticisation of the post-1980 coup period, neoliberalism has found a very convenient place in Turkey. Neoliberalism, which gradually became the dominant ideology in Turkey with the 1980 coup and tightened its grip under AKP rule, shaped the political scene considerably. Former prime minister (1983–9) and president (1989–93) Turgut Özal played a major role in Turkey's neoliberal transformation (Öniş 2004, 129). In the early 2000s, neoliberal transformation was seen as a way out of economic crises, and finally, the AKP also adopted the neoliberal framework and the economic policies it brought (Bozkurt 2013, 373).

The Turkish workers' movement, which was historically not very strong to begin with, was further weakened by the neoliberal transformation programme initiated after the 1980 coup which brought policies such as strike bans, restrictions on social rights and on the union structure (Aytaç and Öniş 2014, 53–4). As a result, unions and organised society have weakened (Eder 2016, 880). To illustrate, trade union membership dropped from 2.5 million in 1980 to 650,000 in 2010, despite population growth (*Milliyet* 2010, cited in Aytaç and Öniş 2014, 54). In addition, considering that political parties were uprooted due to both internal party discipline and the effects of coups and party closures, there was not much of an institution to look up to in terms of seeking justice and economic prosperity for society.

This is where neopopulism comes into play. Neoliberalism and populism were previously thought of as contradictory to each other (Roberts 1995, 89) due to the assumption that the state would shrink and rationalise with neoliberalism and therefore would implement fiscal discipline and follow more programmatic policies instead of following populist policies (Weyland 1996). However, neoliberal policies have fed neopopulism in many ways.

Both neoliberalism and neopopulism oppose social organisation (Weyland 1996, 9). With neoliberalism destroying organised interest groups and ways of institutional representation, populist leaders can reach atomised masses directly (Roberts 1995, 90).

Neopopulism follows a different path in making material distributions to the masses compared to populism. High salaries and other policies that we were accustomed to seeing under traditional populism are not possible under neoliberal conditions given budgetary restrictions. Hence, neopopulism provides its supporters with other means of economic satisfaction. For example, by reducing high inflation, it can relieve the poorer segments a bit, while providing direct clientelist economic benefits to designated groups. This type of aid is less costly and strengthens the neopopulist style of politics by establishing more visible ties between the leader and the aid recipients (Roberts 1995, 91).

As can be understood from the discussion above, with the weakening of institutions and the organisational structure in Turkey, coupled with the weakening of welfare policies, leaders in the political arena have become the centre of economic expectations. This is valid both for the clientelistic meeting of daily needs and for longer-term macroeconomic policies. Aid to the poor and similar social policies are either tied to more non-institutional formulas or are transferred from state responsibility to foundations and aid organisations (Bozkurt 2013, 384). While the unions, which are in close relations with the government, increase their membership numbers, the existence of unions as a meaningful and organised group for workers' rights is prevented (for details, see Yıldırım 2009). This paves the way for the political leader to be seen as the only source of economic recovery and social security, especially for the unorganised segments of society. In this case, political leaders who see themselves as the providers of economic welfare increase their power with economic narratives as evident in the case of Recep Tayyip Erdoğan, the president of Turkey.

What is more, as Aytaç and Öniş (2014, 43) argue, populist leaders generally emerge after severe economic crises, and their fate largely depends on their economic performance. Therefore, emphasising economic development in Turkey aims to revive bad memories of the past while at the same time making citizens look at the present with gratitude and thereby ensuring that the leader maintains popularity.

As will be discussed in this chapter, economic narratives are not only used to bolster popularity but they offer an important discursive tool to leaders who want to expand their authority at the expense of democracy. As will be elaborated on further below, according to this narrative, the political leader works for the economic welfare of the citizens, but certain sections of the elite and the internal and external groups allied with them undermine this well-intentioned effort of the leader. With this narrative formula, the leader expects to deflect the responsibility of the cost of possible economic losses on others. As such, economic development narratives emerge as an invaluable political tool for leaders who want to expand their power field.

Democracy and Economic Development Narratives

Before delving into the discussion of the current state of democracy in Turkey, a conceptualisation of democracy will be in order. Scholars of democracy have convincingly shown that equating democracy with elections is problematic (Schmitter and Karl 1991, 78) and that such a conceptualisation fails to understand the degradations of democracy (Diamond 2008, 38). Dahl (1982, 11), in his widely accepted framework of democracy, lays out the essential elements of democratic regimes. In addition to free and fair elections, he stresses the importance of freedom of expression, free and pluralistic media, and freedom of association. To these, we also need to add the importance of checks and balances and the lack of domination of one government branch over another (Kapstein and Converse 2008, 57–8; Cinar and Ugur-Cinar 2015). As Diamond (2008, 38) explains, with illustrations from Nigeria and Russia, the expansion of the executive power vis-à-vis other branches of government and the opposition forces has 'extinguished even the most basic form of electoral democracy'. As this short overview suggests, we need to pay close attention to pluralism, civil rights and checks and balances in addition to free and fair elections if we want to grasp the state of democracy in a country.

The relationship between democracy and economic development has been discussed from various angles in the comparative politics and political economy literature. While some focus on the role of economic development on democratisation, others look at its impact on the survival of democracy.[1] Further, other studies look at the relationship in reverse, focusing on how democracy affects economic development. Others, such as Polanyi (1957

[1944]) point out the negative effects of economic development, particularly focusing on the inequalities and feeling of insecurity created by capitalist economic development, which can lead to sacrificing rights, among other things. In this chapter, I focus on a related but significantly distinct aspect of the relationship between democracy and economic development. I trace the dangers caused by the narratives surrounding economic development to democracy. I detect this as a serious threat particularly for developing countries, including Turkey, the focal case of this chapter. The current discussion of hybrid regimes and democratic backsliding reveal the imminent threat caused by executives in chipping away elements of democracy (Levitsky and Way 2010; Bermeo 2016; Waldner and Lust 2018). Understanding the role that narratives in general, and economic development narratives in particular, play in this process is thus crucial in highlighting a main element through which democracy is eroded in the hands of those in power.

The three cases selected in this chapter, namely debates regarding presidentialism, the Gezi movement, and the recent corruption scandal in Turkey, are emblematic in understanding the current state of democracy in Turkey. They also provide critical junctures in the sense that all three of them have resulted in severe democratic backsliding in Turkey. We can explain this in the chronological order of the events. First, the version of presidentialism proposed by the AKP has constituted a major threat to checks and balances in Turkish democracy. While presidentialism is not in itself undemocratic, it can lead to erosion of democracy if proper checks and balances, such as bicameralism, mutual veto powers, and federalism are not institutionalised, which was the case in the AKP's formulation of presidentialism. The approach of the government to the Gezi protests and the suppression of the movement by the government constitute major blows to freedom of expression, association, and civil rights and liberties in Turkey. Finally, the government's condemnation and its attempt to stop the prosecution of corruption starting in December 2013 exemplify both efforts for immunity from accountability as well as the encroachment of the executive upon the judiciary. The government's response to the corruption investigations, which included the then prime minister Erdoğan, other ministers of the government, and their children and relatives, was to remove police and public prosecutors who initiated the investigation from office.

Having shown why these three instances constitute a milestone in the erosion of the state of democracy in Turkey, I will now turn to the closer discussion of these cases. I will show how instead of the threats posed to democracy in each case; the government narrated each case as an attack on Turkish economic development, thereby attempting to legitimate their expansion of power.

Presidentialism Debates in Turkey

Turkey switched to presidentialism with the referendum on 16 April 2017 that was held under the emergency law established after the failed coup attempt of July 2016. This new presidential system granted the president unchecked power over other branches of government (Esen and Gümüşçü 2017). Before this switch, Turkey was categorised as a parliamentary regime even though it deviated from pure parliamentarism primarily due to the legacies of military regimes. The leaders of military regimes, who transformed themselves to presidents after transition to democracy, allocated stronger powers to the presidency, which made presidents more than symbolic actors in Turkish politics contrary to the ideal typical parliamentary regime type.

Even though debates of presidentialism started earlier,[2] the government started to take more tangible steps in 2013, officially proposing to switch from a parliamentary system to a presidential one. AKP's proposals for presidentialism aimed to strengthen the executive at the expense of other governmental branches by granting the president powers such as issuing decrees having the force of law, the dissolving of the parliament, appointing cabinet members without the approval of the parliament, appointing the majority of the justices in the higher courts and making the parliament ineffective (Barobirlik 2017; Kalaycıoğlu 2013; Kalaycıoğlu 2016; Öniş 2013; Özbudun 2014). Cameron (1998, 125) expresses the dangers of such a system succinctly in the paragraph below:

In presidential self-coups, or *autogolpes*, presidents may suspend the constitution, fire the supreme court, close congress, and rule by decree until a plebiscite or a new election is held to ratify a new regime with wider executive powers. In less extreme cases, presidents may stack courts, abdicate their authority over the military in cases of human rights violations, abuse executive decree authority, refuse to accept legislative oversight, limit freedom of the press, or use public resources to undermine the development of political parties and local governments.

Yet, instead of focusing on the repercussions of such a presidential regime for Turkish democracy, the AKP government tried to appeal to economic incentives, arguing that presidentialism will ensure faster economic growth in Turkey. Even though there is not an established relationship between presidentialism and economic development in the relevant literature, Prime Minister Erdoğan reiterated his view on a positive relationship between these two concepts on numerous occasions, which found wide publicity in the media. In April 2013, he maintained that a presidential system would ensure political stability and contribute to economic development. To endorse presidentialism, Erdoğan (Anadolu Ajansi, 8 April 2013) also made the following statement:

Among the G20 member countries, almost 80 percent are ruled by a presidential system. This is the picture. We need to see the realities of the world. In the world economy, the G20 constitutes 90 percent of the economic weight. We need to make some inferences from that. We need to derive lessons. Where are we, where are we heading? If we really want to get intense, practical results, we need to revise the system. We need to acquire opportunities that enable us to make much faster production within the system.[3]

Setting aside the incorrect statement that most of the G20 member countries are ruled by presidentialism, this statement is illustrative in showing the role economic development narratives have played in the presidentialism debates.

Burhan Kuzu, who at the time was an AKP MP and the head of the Parliamentary Constitutional Commission, similarly complained about the dispersion of power within the context of presidentialism. In support of presidentialism, he allegorically stated that 'whoever holds the drum should also hold the stick' (*Radikal* 2013). What is more, in a meeting organised to advocate presidentialism, Kuzu warned Turkish citizens about a potential economic crisis unless presidentialism is adopted. He maintained that 'if Turkey does not switch to presidentialism, Turkey will again meet the God damned coalition government. In that case, forget about 2023 and 2071. We will see the same economic crises that we now see in European countries' (*Aksam* 2013).

Journalists close to the government used a similar rhetorical strategy. An important example in this regard is the then columnist Yiğit Bulut, who is now among Erdoğan's advisors. Without necessarily elaborating on the causal mechanism at work here, Bulut argued that the presidential system is key to economic growth, sustainable development and stability (*Star* 2013b). Bulut (*Star* 2013a) even went so far as to state that:

> If Turkey's economy is to grow three times in size in ten years . . . and if every citizen's wealth is to triple in size as a result of this, I say the PRESI-DENTIAL SYSTEM IS A SINE QUA NON . . . As a result, if we switch to presidentialism . . . I assure you that whatever wealth you have will triple in size . . . If you want a country whose economy flies, who shares wealth equally and who possesses the real values of Turkey, work for PRESIDENTIALISM with all your energy! [capital letters in original]

These arguments cannot be taken at face value, especially considering the mounting evidence that suggests otherwise. In addition to there not being an established relationship between economic development and presidentialism, on the contrary, there is strong scholarly evidence that suggests that the kind of presidentialism proposed by the AKP, which does not protect separation of power and pluralism, could actually work against economic development. Existing research has shown that checks and balances reduce political volatility as they 'minimize the ability of politicians to respond to short-term political or social incentives to favor one group over another or transfer resources from society to the public sector' (Henisz 2004, 6). Deterioration in the checks and balances leads citizens to refrain from committing to contractual, investment, or other types of economic decisions (Daley, Haider-Markel and Whitford 2007, 696–7; see also Keefer and Knack 2007, 567). Having said that, it would not matter even if there were a positive relationship between presidentialism and economic development since the fact that economic narratives are used against pluralism and thereby hurt democracy would still hold in this context.

As is the case with Erdoğan's stories, Yiğit Bulut's story also tries to put forward an easily digestible link between a proposed political alternative (presidentialism) and the economic benefits that are expected to follow from that alternative. Like other stories, it reduces the alternative ways of talking about separate events by emplotting them into a single storyline. According to this story, presidentialism is what is good for the people as it will lead to economic development. Other alternatives will slow down growth and even lead to economic crises. Thus, everyone who wants what is best for the country will support presidentialism. This one-dimensional storyline hinders the discussion of presidentialism from various angles in the media and other public platforms, especially in relation to its repercussions for the durability of democracy. Further research can tell how influential this strategy was in the AKP's success in getting presidentialism approved in the referendum of 2017, albeit with a small margin (51.41% 'yes' vs. 48.59% 'no'), by looking at the demand side of the story to see how such narratives were received and to what extent they were adopted by the voters.

The Gezi Movement

The protests that spread throughout Turkey in the summer of 2013 started at Taksim Square in Istanbul in the last days of May. The government planned to uproot trees in the Gezi Park to rebuild the demolished Topçu Barracks from the Ottoman Empire and to construct a new shopping mall on the site. Concerned with the diminishing sources of oxygen and gathering places in Istanbul, environmentalist protests started in the park, which faced brutal police intervention. To the surprise of the government, police brutality increased the sympathy for the movement and within days protests reached other parts of the country. In addition to common concerns about public recreational areas and forests getting demolished as a result of the arrangements between the government and clientelistic deals with some members of the construction sector, the protesters were also voicing their discontent about the governments growing authoritarianism and interference in the lifestyles of the citizens. Aside from the long-term impact, the movement also had immediate legal and political consequences. The head of the Constitutional Court, Haşim Kılıç, stated that state interference in the lifestyles of citizens is unacceptable. The Sixth Administration Court of Istanbul, in response to a motion from Taksim Gezi Park Preservation and Embellishment Association, suspended the Topçu Barracks Project.

One reason why the Gezi movement was so phenomenal is the rarity – even complete lack – of such large social movements in Turkish history. Particularly as a result of the depoliticising atmosphere of the 1980 intervention, social protests were not undertaken often and the wider public tended to see such occurrences as the act of marginal groups. The Gezi movement, on the other hand, managed to include people from all classes, ethnicities and religious convictions. While the Gezi event could have served as an important opportunity for soul-searching for the government, the government instead preferred to delegitimise the movement and blame it on forces that wanted to see the demise of the Turkish economy. The government called these forces '*faiz lobbisi*', which is translated as 'interest rate lobby', and sometimes as 'forex lobby' or 'stock market lobby'. The basic idea behind this accusation is that, allegedly, the Gezi protests were organised and provoked by profiteer capitalists with external ties. The government kept such accusations deliberately vague. It did not clearly identify who the actors were and it did not back such accusations with evidence.

Erdoğan (*Hürriyet* 2013a) blamed the 'interest rate lobbies' for losses at the stock exchange. He asserted that 'lobbies think that they could threaten the government by making speculations in the stock exchange' and vowed not to 'waste the efforts of the people on interest rate lobbies'. 'Who won as a result of the protests going on for three weeks?' Erdoğan asked. He provided his own answer: 'The interest lobby won. Turkey's enemies won, the rentier lobby won. To a limited degree, Turkish economy lost . . . Young people have been victims of this plot' (NTV 2013b). In another statement, this time in July 2013, Erdoğan maintained that those who are disturbed by Turkey's persistently growing economy prepared traps to hurt Turkey's economy because they did not want a powerful Turkey in the region (*Hürriyet* 2013c).

As was the case with the presidentialism debate, columnists close to the government echoed Erdoğan's arguments. Yasar Süngü (2013), from the pro-government *Yeni Şafak* newspaper, wrote a piece in his column which was titled '"The interest lobby" and what does the Gezi youth do?' In this piece he described the 'interest lobby' as follows:

> The fact that the prime minister has pointed at the interest lobby has brought to mind our worries on whether, once again, internal and external forces are preparing a proxy coup against Turkey. The interest lobby, which the prime

minister says has a role in the Gezi Park resistance, always pursues high profit. To ensure this profit, it desires high interest rates and high exchange rates. It does not care about the impoverishment of the country while it enriches itself. It is wrong to analyze these events just by looking at the youth because in the background we can clearly see international capital owners, along with their media and politicians.

Such arguments, which were plenty on the government side, did not cease even when the official Banking Regulation and Supervision Agency (BDDK) absolved Gezi Park protesters of having ties to any interest or foreign exchange lobby. After a close scrutiny of the foreign currency transactions of banks during the Gezi protests, the BDDK found no reasonable correlation that would prove the existence of a plot to profit from forex trade or traces of a lobby. The BDDK concluded that all banking transactions were within the framework of routine trade (*Hürriyet Daily News* 2013b; BBC 2013). The same was true for other inspection agencies of the state. Upon the then Prime Minister Erdoğan's remarks, the Capital Markets Board (SPK), the BDDK and the Finance Ministr''' Financial Crimes Investigation Board (MASAK) initiated separate investigations. None of them found any evidence to support Erdoğan's accusations. The investigations found that the foreign exchange transactions were all routine operations defined in banking law as normal trade (Kanal B 2013; *Hürriyet* 2013d; *Cumhuriyet* 2015). Be that as it may, the government brought up similar accusations on future occasions. As we will show in our next case, the rhetoric of an 'interest rate lobby' in the Gezi protests turned into an important tool in the government's toolkit in framing political discussions.

The attempt of the government side to reduce the Gezi events to an economic storyline, discrediting the political claims it made, continues to this day. For example, on the third anniversary of Gezi, the governmentally controlled public news agency Anadolu Ajansı (27 May 2016) put Gezi-related news under the tab 'economy'. Their news coverage titled 'Gezi's biggest harm was to economy' reads: 'The demonstrations that started on 28 May 2013 at Istanbul Gezi Park created a widespread chaotic atmosphere that lasted about 15 days and resulted in economic costs amounting to billion dollars for Turkey.' The same news coverage talks about huge economic damages in depth and attributes stock market losses and the rise in interest rates, unemployment and inflation to the Gezi protests.

Corruption, Accountability and the Rule of Law

The final illustration of this chapter will be the economic development narratives deployed by the AKP government in response to the corruption investigations that started in December 2013. The government not only condemned the investigations and took measures to stop the prosecution, it also used this opportunity to tighten the grip of the executive over the judiciary. These steps harmed democracy in two ways: the executive gained immunity from being held accountable for its acts and the executive branch encroached upon the judiciary.

The corruption scandal involved ministers of the government and their children and relatives as well as some top-level bureaucrats. In response to the corruption inquiry, the government purged hundreds of police members and judiciary members (Croft and Coşkun 2014). Police and public prosecutors who initiated the investigation were removed from their offices. Not confining itself to this case, the government also attempted to use this case to gain tighter control over the judiciary. The AKP drafted a bill to give the executive more control over the appointment of judges and prosecutors (Croft and Coşkun 2014). Law experts, business circles (including the biggest business association of Turkey, TÜSIAD), as well as the EU raised concerns over the expansion of the executive at the expense of the judiciary. Erdoğan did not seem to be concerned with the warnings regarding separation of powers. He averred that 'if we consider the judiciary as a separate power, then this would lead to a country of judicial rule and not democracy' (Croft and Coşkun 2014).

In the heated debates regarding the shape of the judiciary and the fate of the corruption investigations, the government once more resorted to economic narratives to restrict the scope of discussions and to stifle dissent. For instance, bringing up economic growth in Turkey Erdoğan asked: 'if there were corruption in our government, would we be able to triple the size of our national wealth in ten years?' (*Hürriyet* 2014). Even though there is concrete evidence, including tapes of some of the accused, Erdoğan narrated the issue in economic terms, putting forward a plot based on economic conspiracy that involved both internal and external actors. Erdoğan presented these corruption investigations as a continuation of the Gezi protests and as another episode of economic conspiracy. This time, the same actors tried to succeed in their efforts, which they had failed to do in the summer. Erdoğan (*Sabah* 2013b) summed up the reasons for the corruption investigation under nine headings:

1. In Istanbul, we implemented the 46 billion dollar airport project. This has disturbed some groups.
2. We have hosted the Japanese prime minister. They might try to do something to prevent positive developments about this any time.
3 We have started the construction of the third bridge in Istanbul. They have done everything to prevent this.
4. The Istanbul stock market has reached a record with going above 93 thousand. Hence, interventions to the stock market have started.
5. In May, the Central Bank reserves reached a record of 135 billion dollars.
6. We took over the basic interest rate as 63 percent. In May it fell as low as 4.6. If it could continue that way, it would even fall under 2.5. [read: blame on the Gezi protests in May-June.]
7. Four credit rating agencies have increased Turkey's grade.
8. We saw historical developments in our relationships with the IMF. We paid our debts and international forces went into play; because who accepts loans also accepts commands.
9. We broke new record in inflation, foreign trade, and industrial production.

As one can see, Erdoğan depicted the motivation of the corruption investigations as purely economic. We can find the recurrent melody in this case, just like in the previous two cases analysed in this chapter.

Other members of the AKP and columnists close to the government echoed Erdoğan's statements. A case in point is the then AKP MP and vice-premier Ali Babacan whose first reaction toward the corruption investigations was to discuss the fall in the stock market along with other damages caused to the economy by the investigations (NTVMSNBC 2013; Dünya 2013). Likewise, another AKP MP Mehmet Metiner (2013) claimed that the reason behind these operations was the fact that the profits of the interest lobby were hurt due to the government's decision to decrease interest rates. Metiner concluded by stating that even though national wealth increased from 230 billion dollars to 800 billion dollars 'some shameless people still have the nerve to say that public money is stolen and that there is corruption'. Another article in *Yeni Şafak* (3 January 2014) also associated the investigations with the 'interest rate lobby' and with the Gezi movement:

> The increase of foreign exchange rates in the aftermath of the Istanbul operations has once again brought to the agenda the demands of the interest rate lobby. The interest lobby, which has tried every means to ensure its financial interests during the Gezi incidents, is now voicing its expectations for increase in interest rates.

With this storyline, the government and its associates make it explicit that every attempt to check and balance the government through horizontal accountability mechanisms will be perceived as a threat to the government and to the economic well-being of the country. This attitude puts Turkish democracy in a difficult position. O'Donnell (1999, 38), who coined the term 'horizontal accountability' defines the term as 'the existence of state agencies that are legally enabled and empowered, and factually willing and able, to take actions that span from routine oversight to criminal sanctions or impeachment in relation to actions or omissions by other agents or agencies of the state that may be qualified as unlawful'. O'Donnell (1999, 122) holds that the violation of horizontal accountability through encroachment of one state agency upon the lawful authority of another intrinsically threatens to eliminate polyarchy.

What is more, like in our previous case, in this one we also need to remember that the relationship between democracy and economic development is not one of a trade-off. For example, supervision over economic policy, which is an essential aspect of democracy, serves against rulers enriching themselves. It prevents elites from exploiting societies and it can prevent corruption, thereby leaving more tax money to be spent on development (North 1990; de Mesquita *et al.* 2001). As La Porta *et al.* (2004, 446–7) show, 'judicial independence promotes both economic and political freedom, the former by resisting the state's attempts to take property, the latter by resisting its attempts to suppress dissent'. It is essential to conserve these two functions of the judiciary so as to 'counter the tyranny of the majority, to secure political and human rights, and to preserve democracy'. In a similar vein and regarding the Turkish context, as Öniş (2004, 130) observed, neopopulist leaders such as Özal ve Menem have actually prevented the development of sustainable economic performance by leaving issues such as the consolidation of democracy to the distant future and thus bypassing democratic institutions and legal norms in the name of economic reforms.

Conclusion

In this chapter, I traced the speeches of high-ranking government officials and journalists close to them to show how they deployed economic development narratives at critical junctures of Turkey's recent history to chip away key aspects of Turkish democracy. I demonstrated how these actors have used economic development narratives to politically legitimise interferences into liberal democracy. By first looking at economic development narratives surrounding the Gezi protests of summer 2013, I illustrated how demands for pluralism and respect for different lifestyles – which are indeed crucial aspects of a liberal democracy – were instead framed by the government as chaos created by agents of the so called 'interest lobby' and provocations caused by those who want to stop Turkey's economic development from within and from without.

I tried to make strong parallels between the Gezi case, presidentialism debates and the corruption scandal of December 2013. In all three cases, demands for democracy, transparency, checks and balances were pitted against economic development. Citizens were made to choose a vaguely defined economic development narrative over demands for democratisation.

The observations of this chapter outline a serious threat that is not only valid for Turkey but for other countries as well, particularly developing countries. The potentially disruptive effects of economic development narratives to democracy can shed new light to our understanding of the relationship between democracy and economic development. We know how arguments for security have in the past increased the tolerance of citizens toward undemocratic means and to the loss of freedom. The question now is whether economic development narratives play the same role. If that is the case, we might need to rethink our approach to economic development not only from the angle of the backlash neoliberalism and austerity measures have caused in countries like Greece but also from a perspective that takes the problematic relationship between pressures of economic development and democracy seriously. Being alert to how narratives contribute to the repertoire of politicians will also further enable us to disentangle separate phenomena that are meshed together in the plots narrated by politicians.

The observations discussed for the critical cases covered in this chapter multiplied over the last decade. The concrete reflections of the authoritarian aspirations justified by economic development narratives have become even more clear over time. Increasing authoritarianism in Turkey in the recent period manifests itself with symptoms such as the restriction of freedom of expression, the complete loss of the independence of the judiciary and the media, the overpowering of the executive and the intolerance to opposition (Aytaç and Öniş 2014, 56). The Homeland Security Act, Internet prohibitions, and amendments to the HSYK (Turkey's Council of Judges and Prosecutors) are some of the concrete examples. According to Freedom House data, media freedom in Turkey declined from 'semi-free' to 'non-free' (Freedom House 2013; Freedom House 2016a), and Turkey has also started a downward trend in the democracy index (Freedom House 2016b; Economist Intelligence 2015). Likewise, in terms of checks and balances (ninety-fifth out of 102 countries) and fundamental rights (ninety-sixth out of 102) Turkey is also following a downward trend (World Justice Project 2015). In this process, Erdoğan has also increased his reliance on economic development narratives as evident in an analysis that observed Erdoğan used keywords such as 'investment, production, growth' at record levels in the year 2021 (T24 2021).

In the case of contemporary Turkish politics, economic development narratives offer convincing arguments for the unorganized masses who do not feel safe in terms of social rights, as well as for those for whom the economic instability of the previous decades is still fresh in their minds, and for those who equate modernity with economic development. Even though most of the promises made in the economic development narratives of government officials are impossible to deliver, the fact that these narratives feature scapegoats ('internal and external enemies') ensures that in the event of failure to deliver the promises, the blame is placed on these scapegoats thereby absolving those in power from responsibility. Thus, economic development narratives are useful tools both for gaining widespread support and for avoiding criticism and accountability.

It is of course possible to use economic development narratives in support of democracy. A case in point is the statement of Selin Sayek-Böke, the CHP deputy and then CHP's Chairman of the Economy: 'The rule of law and democracy are indispensable for development' (Business HT 2015). However, contrary to scholarly evidence and to a limited number of dissenting voices, the prevailing economic narratives in Turkey pit pluralism and liberal democracy against economic development. Especially for those who are in power, such narratives are used to expand their power and to weaken the basic components of democracy. What is more, such economic development narratives put a straightjacket on political events, attempting to prevent them from being viewed from perspectives other than the economic one put forward by the government.

In the next chapter, we will delve into how narratives of the past, of development and of patriarchy are used by populist leaders with illustrations from Turkey, Austria and Hungary.

Notes

1. On the former, see Lipset 1959, and on the latter, see Przeworski and Limongi 1997. For reviews of the relevant literature, see for example Bunce 2000, Geddes 1999 and 2007.

2. See, for instance, Erdoğan's speech on his preference for presidentialism in 2011 (*Sabah* 2011).

3. It is actually not new that Erdogan pits checks and balances and pluralism against socio-economic development. Earlier in 2012, for instance, he complained about separation of power claiming that it slowed down development. Regarding a hospital project called Şehir Hastaneleri (City Hospitals) that was stopped by the Council of State following the complaints of the Turkish Medical Association (Türk Tabipleri Birliği), Erdoğan said that separation of powers stands as an impediment in front of the government. Erdoğan suggested that by delaying their projects, the judiciary harmed the interests of the country and that members of the judiciary would need to answer to Turkish history and ancestors (*Milliyet* 2012; *Radikal* 2012).

4

THE POPULIST REPERTOIRE: STORIES OF DEVELOPMENT, PATRIARCHY AND HISTORY IN AUSTRIA, HUNGARY AND TURKEY

It has been a good century for the populists so far. As populism has become a spectre haunting not only Europe but also the world (LSE IDEAS 2018), the Cambridge dictionary coined it as the word of the year in 2017 (Cambridge University 2017). The impact of populism has been felt vividly in events such as Brexit and the election of Trump as well as the astonishing levels of democratic backsliding observed around the world.

Understanding the appeal of such a phenomenon that came to hold a central place in contemporary politics thus becomes crucial. While the existing literature discusses underlying structural reasons such as cultural backlash or economic anxiety (see, for example, Mudde and Rovira Kaltwasser 2018) one also needs to examine political agency, including narrative strategies that frame the past as well as the currently existing conditions in particular ways. It is through narrative strategies that populist leaders exploit social facts such as existing social cleavages, economic crises, neoliberalism or immigration.

This chapter discusses how political narratives reinforce populism by instigating a certain sense of peoplehood and depicting the leader as the embodiment of the people as well as urging the leader to act unilaterally on behalf of the people at the expense of societal pluralism and institutional checks on the executive. Using contemporary Turkey, Hungary and Austria as cases studies, it demonstrates how stories of history, development and patriarchy are deployed by populist leaders Recep Tayyip Erdoğan (AKP), Viktor Orban (Fidesz) and Heinz-Christian Strache (Freedom Party – FPÖ).

Comparing the aforementioned cases provides sufficient variation to see how narratives operate within a wide spectrum of right-wing populism. AKP and Fidesz have been ruling their countries for a significant period of time (2002–today and 2002, 1998–2002 then 2010–today, respectively). The FPÖ remained mostly in opposition, having joined ruling coalitions as a minor partner multiple times and recently as a partner of the conservative Austrian People's Party (Österreichische Volkspartei – ÖVP), and having held key ministerial positions. The party is in opposition now, after a political scandal brought down the government in 2019, which also led to the expulsion of Strache from the FPÖ. Strache founded Team HC Strache – Alliance for Austria in 2020, another populist movement.

The three cases covered in the chapter also provide significant variation in terms of economic and political development. At 51,900 US dollars GDP per capita, Austria is economically more advanced than the other two cases. Austria ranks twenty-fifth in terms of GPD per capita (PPP), while Hungary is sixty-third with 31,000 dollars and Turkey sixty-eighth with 28,400 dollars. In terms of economic equality, Austria is the most economically equal (Gini index of 29.7) while Turkey (Gini 41.9) is economically the least equal and Hungary is in between (Gini 30.06). In terms of net migration rate,[1] Austria ranks thirty-third (3.57), Hungary fifty-seventh (1.24) and Turkey 158th (-1.55) (Central Intelligence Agency – World Factbook n.d.a). With regard to political development, their levels of democracy also vary: Austria ranks eighteenth (full democracy), Hungary fifty-fifth (flawed democracy) and Turkey 104th (hybrid regime) (Economist Intelligence 2020). This chapter will show the appeal narratives hold in all three cases despite their differences, while these differences influence the content of the stories in various ways as will be shown. In all three cases, the populist leaders tell a story of us and them, and they define the self and the other in particular ways.

As we will see in the discussions below, in all the stories, economic, historical and patriarchal agency is attributed to the populist leader with the (historical) mission to save 'the people' and fulfil their needs and desires. While agency is attributed to the leaders, political opponents and 'the people' are constructed in particular ways. The political opponents are constructed as threatening, alien and aloof to the interests and values of 'the people'. 'The people' are also constructed, this time as objects of threats, as static, timeless and homogenous communities.

The Appeal of Populist Narratives

Populism's defining features can be summarised as a leader who claims to be the embodiment of 'the people', a Manichean anti-establishment discourse, and a mass support base.[2] Populism divides society into an imaginary 'pure people' and 'the corrupt elite' and claims that politics should be the expression of 'the will of the people' (Mudde and Rovira Kaltwasser 2018).

Applying insights from Goffman (1974), who defines frames as 'schemata of interpretation' that enable individuals 'to locate, perceive, identify, and label' occurrences within their life space and the world at large, Aslanidis (2016, 100) proposes to see populism as a discursive frame that 'diagnoses reality as problematic because "corrupt elites" have unjustly usurped the sovereign authority of the "noble People" and maintains that the solution to the problem resides in the righteous political mobilization of the latter in order to regain power'. While this conceptualisation acknowledges the need for populist leaders to create discursive frames that resonate with the people at large, approaching populism from a narrative perspective would further help us understand the appeal of successful populist strategies due to the peculiar characteristics of narratives. As Polletta (1998, 139), who studies the 1960 student sit-ins in the US, argues, narratives have a 'temporally configurative capacity' that equips them 'to integrate past, present, and future events and to align individual and collective identities'. The fact that narratives, as opposed to frames, have a chronological character, automatically makes them conductive for identity building and gives them an action-oriented character since 'story's chronological end is also its end in the sense of moral, purpose or telos, they project a future' (Polletta 1998, 140).

In addition to the time dimension underlying narratives, the fact that narratives rely on emplotment instead of explanation makes them especially powerful. While the success of frames depends on how credible, logical and explanatory they are, narratives rely on 'emotional identification and familiar plots rather than on testing or adjudication of truth claims'. While frames combine a richly developed and interconnected, and empirically credible 'diagnosis of the social condition in need of remedy, a prognosis for how to do that, and a rationale for action' (Snow and Benford 1988; Benford and Hunt 1992), narratives tend to be more vague, leaving room for personal interpretation and actually requiring our interpretative participation to 'fill the gaps and resolve the ambiguities' (Polletta 1998, 141).

Narratives' distinct characteristics that make them conducive for politics have been studied in various social science and humanities disciplines. Narratives give coherence to our daily lives, help us make sense of separate events, tie our past, present and future. Narratives attribute separate, objective facts, the continuity of a subject (Balibar 1990, 338) and present to us 'a formal coherency that we ourselves lack' (White 1980, 24). According to Alasdair MacIntyre (2007), we understand what a good, or virtuous, life is through narratives about our lives. Thus, narratives prove to be important interpretive and rhetorical resources as they affect the meanings attributed to events (Bridger and Maines 1998). Narratives are also crucial for the formation of social identity (Somers 1994) and in the formation of envisioned forms of peoplehood (Smith 2003; 2015). They are influential in the constitution of the basic premises of nationalist ideologies (Moreno and Perez Garzon 2002) and citizenship policies (Ugur Cinar 2015a). When used by populists, narratives not only serve to consolidate a sense of unity among certain members of the society but they also sharply define the limits of inclusion (Ugur-Cinar and Altınok 2021).

Narratives can thus help us understand the wide appeal of populism as we zoom in to the way populist narratives are constructed and propagated for political purposes. Such purposes include winning elections, expanding the power of the executive, rallying people around political causes, as well as subverting extant political institutions. We will now turn to see such narratives in action with illustrations from Erdoğan, Orban and Strache, who have used historical narratives, economic development narratives and patriarchal narratives to advance their populist movements and to make gains for their causes.

The Past Reloaded

As discussed in detail in Chapter 2, identity, both at the individual and collective level, is constructed through a narrative understanding of the past. As Taylor (1989, 47) argues 'in order to have a sense of who we are, we have to have a notion of how we have become, and of where we are going', which we reach with narratives. Historical narratives assure the existence of a people in the past and in the present and demand a commitment to carry out a future plan (Moreno and Perez Garzon 2002, 276). While historical narratives are planned to provide a cohesive, homogenous history of the nation in order to bolster unity, compliance and solidarity, such narratives prove to be very divisive in the hands of populists. By providing an envisioned sense of peoplehood and depicting the leader as the embodiment of the people such narratives also define the limits of inclusion and exclusion and seek to mobilise the power bases of populist leaders. Roediger and Wertsch (2008, 14) find that a great deal more remains to be explored when it comes to the power of the 'lessons of history' to shape political thought and decisions. As Olick and Robbins (1998, 134) and Art (2006) have also noted, collective memory is mostly treated as a dependent variable rather than an independent variable that affects other political or social phenomena. Populism provides a fruitful area through which one can study how collective memory can be utilised to bolster political causes. In the populist historical narratives, politicians choose critical junctures in the history of the nation, in which they narrate the struggle between them and their political opponents as a continuation of past struggles. 'The people', in whose name they speak, are chosen as actors who serve to bolster the legitimacy of the struggles of the populists, as the discussions below will illustrate.

Turkey

The Turkish Republic was founded on the ruins of the Ottoman Empire in 1923 as a result of a two-fold war against the Allied occupation and the Ottoman Empire, led by Mustafa Kemal Atatürk. Once this new force consolidated its power, an extensive history-writing project was undertaken in order to erase both Ottoman legacy and Western stereotypes as discussed in Chapter 2. The Ottoman history was seen as an *ancien régime*, whose religion-dominated, multiethnic structure and monarchical rule were antithetical to the newly founded Republican nation state. Hence, state institutions were put to work in order to popularise a Turkish history that was pro-Western and saw the Ottoman state as one among many Turkish states established. This new history acknowledged the early success of the empire but claimed that it became archaic and dysfunctional toward its latter part (Ugur Cinar 2015a).

With the AKP in power for the last twenty years, we see the presentation of the past in an entirely different way from that of the founders of the Republic, evident in political speeches as well as in commemorative practices, renaming of places, renovation and rebranding of Ottoman related spaces and so on. Such attempts, initiated by the Islamist predecessors of AKP during their municipal rule (Cinar 2005), accelerated once AKP came to office ruling the country solo and possessing unchecked control over the rewriting of Turkish history.

In Erdoğan's populist rhetoric, secular elites and Westernisation are the key existential opponents. Erdoğan projects himself as the representative of the authentic Turkish people against these elites and their allies. Though it is common for right-wing populism in Turkey to exploit the secular–religious divide (Aytaç and Elçi 2018, 90–1), Erdoğan made this binary the cornerstone of his political strategy throughout his political career (Bakiner 2018, 9–10).

Erdoğan's populist struggle with the Kemalist, secular elite situates itself all the way back to the last decades of the Ottoman Empire. The nostalgia of an Ottoman past that has never really existed serves as an anti-establishment, anti-elite discourse, which is essential for populism. It thus does not come as a surprise that Erdoğan, being extremely dissatisfied with the depiction of Ottoman sultans in the TV series of private television (Zalewski 2012), endorsed the production of Ottoman-themed TV series at TRT, the public TV channel in Turkey.

The struggle, depicted to be one between the Western-oriented, 'culturally alienated' ones (Young Turks) and those who support the genuine values of Turkishness and Islam, is especially focused on the reign of Sultan Abdülhamid II. Abdülhamid II, an autocrat who ruled the Ottoman Empire between 1876 and 1909, is seen as the protector of religion and culture against the fervent Westernisation of his opponents.[3] TRT produced two TV series on Abdülhamid in recent years (*Payitaht Abdülhamid* 2017; *Daily Sabah* 2016), among other series produced on the Ottoman sultans. In one of his rallies, referring to the TV series *Payitaht Abdülhamid* (Capital City: Abdülhamid) Erdoğan, directly asked the supporters 'Are you watching Payitaht?' He continued by arguing that his supporters should be watching it because 'foreign powers are still seeking concessions from us'. His response to such powers, he exclaimed, was: 'Never!' (Bloomberg 2018). As opposed to the

Republican representation of Abdülhamid as an autocrat with an extensive spy network and extreme press censorship, Erdoğan popularised Abdülhamid. Under Erdoğan's rule, a series of events were held to mark the 100th anniversary of Abdülhamid's death. In one such event Erdoğan stated that 'Too many Turks, misled by the West, have cut the country off from its Ottoman roots' adding, 'history isn't just a nation's past, it's the compass for its future' (Bloomberg 2018).

Erdoğan's narrative and the narratives propagated by his party, also attempt to fill the gap of over a hundred years between Abdülhamid and Erdoğan by selectively borrowing from the history of the Turkish Republic. Accordingly, Erdoğan is grouped together with other populist right-wing leaders such as Menderes, Özal and Erbakan. Erdoğan is depicted to be the one who will finally bring well-deserved success to the people. This way, Erdoğan is again activating the secular–religious dichotomy, this time strictly tying his constituency with democracy and his opponents with autocracy, deceit and crime. Menderes was the prime minister during the 1950s once the regime had been opened up to multiparty elections. He expanded his power, repressed the opposition, and clashed with the Kemalist establishment, particularly the bureaucracy and the military. He was executed after the 1960 military coup. Özal, on the other hand, was the first prime minister after the 1980 military coup. The military was not favourable to his candidacy because of his links to political Islam earlier but they did not veto his candidacy probably because they did not think he stood a chance in the elections. To everybody's surprise, Özal won the elections and became prime minister. Erbakan was Erdoğan's mentor and the first openly Islamist prime minister in Turkish history. He had to step down as prime minister following the 28 February 1997 memorandum of the military.

A mouthpiece media source, *Sabah*, which also broadcasts in English as *Sabah Daily News*, put together a video that depicted Menderes, Özal, Erbakan and Erdoğan as 'Milletin Adamları' (Men of the Nation) (*Sabah* 2016). In this video, the right-wing leaders of Turkish contemporary history are shown to have worked for a 'Great Turkey' and they are depicted as having been stopped by other elites or by bigger conspiracies in their effort to serve the country. The video depicts Erdoğan as the leader who took over where these leaders left off and who was able to finally fulfil the needs of the people against all odds.

Another case in point is a poster that initially originated as a reaction to Gezi protests. This poster was used both by AKP-dominated municipalities and by Erdoğan's own campaign. The poster, which also became popular on social media, brought together Menderes, Özal and Erdoğan. It has the pictures of all three leaders on it and has the following words written under each leader, respectively: *astınız, zehirlediniz, yedirmeyiz* (you hanged him, you poisoned him, we won't let you have him).[4]

Bringing these figures of more contemporary history together with Abdülhamid II, Erdoğan claimed, for example, that by criticising him, the *New York Times* was continuing a smear campaign, which it had been following for over 100 years. Erdoğan claimed the following:

> The job of the New York Times is not new. They did the same thing to Abdülhamid, to Menderes, to Özal and to me. We know what source is behind this. They did the same during the Gezi incidents. Their purpose it to divide Turkey, to tear it apart and to swallow it. But we will not allow this. (*Sabah* 2015)

Erdoğan is trying to achieve multiple things with such narratives. First, he is urging his followers to situate his political opponents in a broader context. Instead of perceiving political opposition as a natural part of politics, Erdoğan is turning mundane criticisms into existential struggles that are linked to historical missions. Against such threats, which are not only addressed to him, but to the people in general, he is stating that he will fight tirelessly and that he will protect his people from such threats. Similar to Orban, who will be discussed below, Erdoğan also finds a way to escape criticism of his growing authoritarianism by arguing that he is just working for the good of his people and that this is why those who are the enemies of the people are targeting him.

Erdoğan's reference to history is prominent among his cultural and educational policy efforts, which are vital in his hegemonic struggle against the secular power blocs he sees as his enemy. In his call to radically revise the education system, for instance, Erdoğan juxtaposes two youth figures from the Ottoman era: Haluk and Asım. Haluk was the son of the famous poet Tevfik Fikret (1867–1915). Fikret, a dissident of Abdülhamid, was a humanist, Westernised Ottoman intellectual whose son Haluk went abroad to study and ended up converting to Christianity and becoming a Presbyterian priest. Fikret saw

Haluk as the future ideal citizen of the country during Haluk's childhood and youth and wrote many poems addressed to Haluk, which included progressive, secular and humanistic messages. Asım, on the other hand, was a fictional figure in the works of Mehmet Akif (1873–1936), a prominent Islamist poet discussed in detail in Chapter 2. Asım is depicted as the representative of ideal youth by Mehmet Akif. Juxtaposing Asım to Haluk, Erdoğan maintains:

> On the one hand there is Asım, who wanted to understand the West without turning his back to the East. On the other hand, there is Haluk, who first went to Scotland and then to the USA and had his last breath in a church. We are still face to face with the living symbols of Asım and Haluk today. A sick form of westernization is still with us. I believe that we need to take this into consideration during our works in the field of education.

Erdoğan also added that 'every step we have taken has faced fierce resistance but this resistance did not come from the people but from a minority that defended Haluk-style westernization' (T24 2016). Erdoğan ended by stating that his government may take radical steps in their education policies to remedy the problems.

The overall historical narrative propagated by the Erdoğan rule then goes as follows: Erdoğan is the authentic representative of the people in a historical struggle against those who are alien or hostile to the will of the people. Those who are working against the true will of the people are either external forces or internal enemies who lost touch with the people. Erdoğan is the one who will finally bring the people what they want and what they deserve. He is willing to do whatever it takes to reach this goal and, significantly, in this process, ends justify means.

By writing history in a distinctly different fashion than the founders of Turkey, the AKP is also refashioning membership to the national community. Who are the people? Who is a deserving citizen? What do 'the people' need and want? All these questions are answered on the basis of a history that is rewritten. The 'people' in populism, thus, do not include all citizens but only those who comply with the norm that is based on a selective reading of history. In the case of Erdoğan, they include those who are in line with the historical figures favoured in Erdoğan's speeches.

Hungary

In his effort to shape Hungarian politics his own way by subverting existing institutions and silencing dissent, Orban also resorted to historical narratives to widen his populist appeal. Orban borrowed liberally from Hungarian history and turned commemorations of historical milestones into opportunities for his political propaganda. On the anniversary of the 1848 Revolutions, for instance, Orban turned the commemorations into a campaign speech for the elections a few weeks ahead (Hungarian Government 2018b):

> Today we must talk to each other about . . . matters just as serious as those which had to be dealt with 170 years ago. We are the heirs of the 1848 revolutionaries and freedom fighters, because, just as 170 years ago, today we must speak honestly and directly . . . Petőfi and his associates expressed it clearly: 'Shall we be slaves, or we shall be free?' . . . Together we have fought many great fights and memorable battles. But . . . the greatest battle that we could fight together is still ahead of us . . . The situation, Dear Friends, is that there are those who want to take our country from us. Not with the stroke of a pen, as happened one hundred years ago at Trianon; now they want us to voluntarily hand our country over to others, over a period of a few decades. They want us to hand it over to foreigners coming from other continents, who do not speak our language, and who do not respect our culture, our laws or our way of life: people who want to replace what is ours with what is theirs. What they want is that henceforward it will increasingly not be we and our descendants who live here, but others . . . External forces and international powers want to force all this upon us, with the help of their allies here in our country. And they see our upcoming election as a good opportunity for this.

In one paragraph, Orban revokes two important milestones in Hungarian history, the 1848 revolutions and the Trianon Treaty signed after the defeat in World War I. His depiction of Hungarian history puts winners and freedom fighters on his side while allocating defeat and surrender to the opposition whom Orban himself calls 'accomplices of external forces':

> We, the millions with national feelings, are on one side; the elite 'citizens of the world' are on the other side. We who believe in nation states, the defence of borders, the family and the value of work are on one side. And opposing

us are those who want open society, a world without borders or nations, new forms of family, devalued work and cheap workers – all ruled over by an army of shadowy and unaccountable bureaucrats. On one side, national and democratic forces; and on the other side, supranational and anti-democratic forces.

In his David versus Goliath type of war, the following constitute the enemies for Orban: 'media outlets maintained by foreign concerns and domestic oligarchs, professional hired activists, troublemaking protest organisers, and a chain of NGOs financed by an international speculator, summed up by and embodied in the name "George Soros".'

These 'enemies' are likened to the enemies of the past by Orban not just in 1848 or during World War I. In one election speech (Hungarian Government 2018d), Orban draws parallels between 1990 and today:

Freedom or oppression? Independence or foreign military occupation? Eventually we sent the Soviets packing, torpedoed and sank communism, reconquered our country; and a free Hungary was born. Today, twenty-eight years later, others want to take our country from us. They want to install in government opposition parties which serve outside interests. They want to give power to opposition politicians in the pay of outsiders who will then dismantle the border fence and accept the mandatory resettlement quotas handed down from Brussels – thereby turning Hungary into an immigrant country, and exposing us to the financial and power interests of their patrons.

At the anniversary of the 1956 revolution, after talking about the horrors of the Soviet occupation and Hungarian heroism in detail, Orban likens the current affairs with Brussels, particularly the immigration discussions, to Soviet and other forms of imperialism.

National Socialism and international socialism, fascism and communism all chased imperial dreams: supranational concepts; new forms of human created in melting pots; commercial profits on an unprecedented scale; and the global – imperial – governance to guarantee all this. This has been – and still seems to be – the great temptation that implants itself in the souls of the powerful in Europe. Today in Brussels imperial marches are being played again. (Hungarian Government 2018f; see also Hungarian Government 2018e)

Similar messages are echoed in other speeches as well: 'Brussels must not turn against the European people. The EU must not be a kind of Soviet Union reloaded.' (See also Hungarian Government 2016c; 2017b.)

The EU and its domestic allies are seen by Orban as opposing the genuine interest of the people:

> The way I see it, in Brussels and some European capitals the political and intellectual elite see themselves as citizens of the world – in contrast to the majority of people, who have a strong sense of nationhood. The way I see it, the political leaders are also aware of this. And while there is no chance of them agreeing with their own peoples, they would rather turn their backs on them. (Hungarian Government 2016a)

Likening recent protests in Europe to the 1848 revolutions and claiming that 'nations have rebelled against the hypocritical alliance of Brussels bureaucrats, the global liberal media and international capital, with its insatiable appetite', Orban puts himself at the forefront of the battle for the Hungarian people:

> Perhaps neither the past nor the future of the Hungarian nation matters to Brussels and international capital – but they matter to us. Perhaps the security of the European people does not matter to Brussels and international capital – but it matters to us. Perhaps whether or not we remain Hungarian does not matter to Brussels and international capital – but it matters to us . . . In defence of our independence and national sovereignty, we must bravely fight the battles that lie ahead of us.'" (Hungarian Government 2017a)

Elections, which are about determining the next government in power turn into existential struggles in light of the lessons of the past in the hands of populists such as Orban:

> In 1956 we salvaged the honour of the nation. In 1990 we regained our freedom. And in 2010 we embarked on the path of national unification. No one can tell us that something is impossible . . . The stakes are high, and we must not treat anything casually. Our strength today must not lead us into complacency or inactivity. We must never underestimate the power of the dark side. We are strong favourites to win the next election, but we have yet to earn it, and

we have yet to complete the fight for victory. We will need everyone. We will therefore make our preparations in the months ahead. In March we will start anew, and then in April we will win again. (Hungarian Government 2017b)

The message of the story is clear: the situation throughout history is fragile, Hungary faces a siege of globalist elites collaborating with domestic allies as was the case during 1848 and the Soviet occupation, Fidesz and Orban are the authentic representatives of the people and fight an existential battle for them. The historical narratives told by Orban serve important purposes in this regard. Orban moves freely between centuries, selecting separate events and weaving them into a master storyline in which friends and enemies are used interchangeably in order to align history with the goals of Orban and in order to represent him as the sole embodiment of the historical struggle of his people.

Austria

Similar to the Hungarian case, the party programme of the FPÖ makes reference to the 1848 revolution and argues that since these historical revolutions 'we have dedicated ourselves to the struggle for freedom, and to defend it wherever necessary if what we have achieved comes under threat' (Freedom Party of Austria 2011). However, the Turkish sieges of Vienna constitute the centre of gravity of the historical narratives deployed by the FPÖ. A case in point is the FPÖ's slogan for the 333rd anniversary of the end of the Siege of Vienna: 'Protect the Occident. At that time as today.' During his speech at the anniversary event, the party leader Strache states, 'Protecting our West was not just a mission in the past, but also a mission for the future.' Furthermore, Strache maintains that they have an obligation vis-à-vis children and grandchildren to do justice to and preserve the Christian-Jewish tradition of the European Occident culture (Freedom Party of Austria 2016).

A comic book prepared and sent to the addresses of voters (Sedlaczek 2010) by the FPÖ for the 2010 Vienna mayoral elections elaborates further on the parallels between the past and the present as well as the urgency for action for which only FPÖ and its leader Strache are deemed fit. The cartoon book is named 'Legends from Vienna' and according to Strache it intends to raise historical consciousness among the people (*The Guardian* 2011). The cartoon book depicts Strache as a knight defending Vienna against the

Turks. A poem opens the book which is recited by Strache, who is drawn arm-in-arm with Prince Eugen, the war hero of the Second Siege of Vienna: 'Always keep in mind while reading, much of this can still be true today', the poem warns the readers. The cartoon book keeps drawing parallels, both implicit and explicit between the past sieges and the present situation of Austria. For example, in one carton about the Second Siege of Vienna, an Ottoman sultan is shown with a project for turning the Stefansdom Cathedral into a mosque. An Ottoman soldier shouts that even if they are not victorious this time, their successors will succeed by entering the EU. An Austrian voice responds: 'Turkey does not belong to Europe. Neither today, nor in a couple of centuries.'

Strache and the FPÖ are situated in a position to best fight the 'Turkish offensive' which is allegedly played out in different forms today as far as the book claims. Political opponents are criticised for not being cut out for this job. One cartoon depicts the incumbent social democratic mayor as indifferent to the invasion (which is said to bring minarets, muezzins and compulsory headscarves). While Strache is trying to defend his country with his sword, the mayor claims that all the defenders are nuts. After all, the mayor is depicted to say, 'I am a man of the world and not a racist.' Other 'lefties', as they call themselves in the cartoon, are also indifferent to the struggle. They are lying around lazily and do not identify with the plight of the nation. Here, Strache and the FPÖ are responding to the allegations that they are racist by claiming that they are merely protecting their homeland as opposed to the self-alienated, opportunistic left. By letting Turks in, Austrian political elites and intellectuals are said to be betraying history and are being naïve against the dangers. Among the Austrian political actors, only the FPÖ can see this historical problem, the narrative goes, and it is the only party that can correct for it.

Stories of Economy and Development

Economic development narratives play central roles in politics and particularly so for populist politics. In addition to the personal utility expected by voters out of economic development, economic development narratives also serve as meta-narratives or grand narratives as narratives of mastery and progress (Patterson and Monroe 1998, 325). The capitalist system and the triumph of neoliberalism as well as the drive for modernisation (particularly visible in the

Turkish case) can also be counted as reasons for the prominence of economic development narratives as discussed in further detail in Chapter 3.

Turkey

In the Turkish case, the economic development story told by Erdoğan and the AKP tells us about a leader who is tirelessly working for the economic well-being of its people but is slowed down by the elitist institutions established before Erdoğan came to power. The predecessors, especially the secularist and leftists, are not good fits for this job, as we are told in the narrative. For example, Erdoğan claims that the Republican People's Party is the cause of the economic ills of the country in the past (*Gazetevatan* 2018) and that the party could not even comprehend what it means to build a national car company (*Gerçek Gündem* 2018).

In Erdoğan's economic development story, checks and balances mechanisms are depicted as ways of slowing down the efforts of the leader to serve its people (Cinar and Ugur Cinar 2015). For example, Erdoğan, while talking about one of his projects halted by the Council of State, maintained that 'The thing called separation of powers stands as an impediment in front of us . . . The legislature, executive and judiciary need to think first and foremost about the interests of the nation and then of the state. It is only that way we can become strong' (*Radikal* 2012). Similarly, Erdoğan criticised the opposition, particularly the RPP for slowing down legislation:

> What would have taken an hour takes two hours as a result. What would have taken only one day, takes two days. Of course, they do not have a problem with wasting time . . . *We* have responsibility. They neither have such responsibility, nor do they have love. We care and we are in love with this nation. This makes us different. (*Posta* 2012)

The same storyline holds for the corruption scandal and the presidentialism debate both of which were framed as attempts at holding the leader back in his effort to serve the people as discussed in detail in the previous chapter. For example, Erdoğan defined the corruption investigations against his government as the outcome of a conspiracy involving local and foreign actors and as a continuation of the Gezi incidences. Erdoğan counted nine reasons for these investigations: the initiation of the third airport in Istanbul, the hosting of the Japanese prime minister, the launching of the construction of the third bridge in Istanbul, the record of the Turkish stock market, the new records of the Central Bank's dollar reserves, the fall of the indicator interest to 4.6 per cent, the fact that four credit rating agencies raised Turkey's ratings, the fact that they paid Turkey's IMF debts and the new records in the areas of inflation, foreign trade and industrial production. Erdoğan maintained that these positive developments in Turkey's economy had led to an offensive against Turkey by those who do not want it to prosper (*Sabah* 2013b).

Regarding presidentialism debates, which finally resulted with the presidential system being adopted after a close and controversial referendum, Erdoğan pushed for a majoritarian and unchecked presidential system, making economic arguments for it. Alleging that almost 80 per cent of the G20 countries are ruled by a presidential system, and claiming that 90 per cent of the world's economy comprised the G20, Erdoğan argued that Turkey needed to take lessons from this. He said 'Where are we and where are we headed at? If we really want to get practical and intense results, we need to revise the system so that we can reach the opportunity to produce more quickly' (*turkiyegazetesi.com.tr* 2013).

Hungary

As we have seen in the Turkish case, populists use arguments for economic development as tools to politically legitimise interventions to liberal democracy. All sorts of challenges to their rule are also seen as economic plots against them. Demands for pluralism and respect to different lifestyles are instead narrated as acts of those internal and external agents and provocateurs who want to stop the country's economic development from within and without. Citizens are made to choose a vaguely defined economic development over demands for democratisation.

In line with the argument, in the Hungarian case, Orban argues that it was their government that brought economic independence to Hungary by sending 'the muzzle back to Brussels and the dog lead to the IMF' (Hungarian Government 2018a). Orban claimed that they were able to 'rescue an economy plummeting into bankruptcy', something that was a battle that seemed to be unwinnable because others had failed time and again as 'forces on the other side seemed bigger, richer or more powerful than we Hungarians' and 'we had to fight against a headwind which simply blew others off the field' (Hungarian Government 2018d). Orban insists that administrative affairs, including the national economy, be arranged by the Hungarians themselves so that they serve them the best (Hungarian Government 2015a).

As part of the populist economic narrative, Orban is depicted as the sole force capable of fighting the 'new economic battlefields' (Hungarian Government 2018c). Orban blames the problems of the European economy on the European political elite who, he claims, refuse to recognise the issues that cause such problems (Hungarian Government 2014b). For him, left wing parties are also a long way away from establishing a Left that is 'based on Hungarian national values, a desire to preserve the Hungarian nation culturally, to defend its economic interests and political sovereignty in the international world' (Hungarian Government 2015b). Like the Turkish case, liberal elements of the regime are to be done away with so as to create an economy that will 'serve the people'. A case in point are Orban's ideas on the restructuring of the economy, including what Orban coins the 'illiberal state' for the economic benefit of Hungarian people (Hungarian Government 2014a).

Austria

In electoral campaigns, the FPÖ puts emphasis on what it calls 'fairness'. According to the FPÖ, so far, especially the social democratic and conservative party coalitions have been too lenient on immigration and have used the state budget in an unfair manner to benefit the so-called 'economic immigrants' instead of the deserving Austrians. The FPÖ claims that Austria will solve this 'fairness crisis' with its leader Strache (FPÖ TV 2017).

In a striking example, the FPÖ initiated its election campaign with a poster that reads, 'Austrians deserve fairness – The red and black fat must go' alluding to the Social Democrat–Conservative coalition. It shows a tandem bike steered by a cycler in a red-white-red jersey. Only the one in the front seat powers the bike, struggling, while in the rear seat we see an overweight man who is eating and drinking greedily and wearing a T-shirt with the inscription: 'SPÖ-ÖVP Refugees Welcome' (*Heute* 2017). SPÖ is the social democratic party of Austria (Sozialdemokratische Partei Österreichs) while ÖVP is the conservative party (Österreichische Volkspartei), which was refered to earlier above. This poster, which was shown during the election campaign by Strache and posted on his social media websites, is accompanied by a video, distributed on various Internet channels. This video shows an Austrian cyclist competing with other cyclists. Despite all the effort he puts in, he is overtaken by the other ones, including cyclists from Switzerland, Hungary and Slovakia. Later in the video, we see that this is because the cyclist is carrying the same overweight man from the poster in the back seat (*Heute* 2017).

In its party programme and economic programme the FPÖ echoes similar messages and elaborates on them. Playing on the fears of the citizens, the FPÖ claims to be the only party, and Strache the only leader, who will work for the Austrian people. For example, in the economic programme of the party, which is also organised around the concept of fairness, a worst-case scenario is written in which Austria will be the Greece of the Alps (Alpenhellas) since Austria is falling behind other member states economically because of the 'red-black cartel', referring to the social democratic–conservative coalition. The programme states that the country is characterised by the inability to reform and the failure to integrate existing migrants, while at the same time increasing immigration into the social system, which increases fears and gives rise to islands of prosperity and poverty. This, according to the story, can be corrected only with the FPÖ in power, since the FPÖ is the only party that works for the Austrian people (Freedom Party of Austria 2017, 11; see also Freedom Party of Austria 2011; *Neue Freie Zeitung* 2017) whereas the SPÖ and ÖVP have 'sold and betrayed the country' and help bankers and speculators instead of the people as the electoral campaign poster maintains (*Oe24* 2013).

Even though its economic programme is dependent on stigmatising immigrants, the FPÖ also, from time to time, reverts to Nazi-style anti-Semitic conspiracy theories. One infamous cartoon for example, depicts bankers in a stereotypically Jewish manner with Stars of David on their cufflinks. In this cartoon, the banker is eating greedily while another person, who has the words 'the government' inscribed on him, pours the drink of the banker. The people (*das Volk*) are drawn as a poor man with only a bone on his plate sitting at the same table as the banker (*Die Presse* 2012).

The differences in the three cases can be attributed to the variation in their economic and political development level as well as the fact that the FPÖ has not (yet) enjoyed the advantages of an incumbent with major powers. While the Turkish case demonstrates most clearly how the urge for economic development can be used for populist purposes, this emphasis is less in the Hungarian case and even less so in the Austrian case. The FPÖ, instead of focusing on raising the economic development level of the country, is more focused on keeping Austria's standing and enhancing the economic position of native Austrians at the expense of immigrants. Unlike the other two cases, the FPÖ is not yet talking about curbing democratic institutions to reach these goals.

Patriarchal Stories

Despite many affinities between populism and patriarchy, the relationship between gender and populism remains understudied (Abi-Hassan 2017; Mudde and Rovira Kaltwasser 2015). The study of this link needs to go beyond the focus on descriptive representation of women in terms of numbers and policy positions of women. What is more, patriarchy operates as a narrative tool in politics, which cannot just be seen as the domination of women by men. Patriarchal narratives depict the people as objects in need of protection that can only be provided by the leaders. Some leaders are more explicit in situating themselves as husbands and fathers of the people, while others do this more implicitly, focusing only on the message of protection without openly using familial terms.

In her analysis of the relationship between nationalism and gender, McClintock argues that family tropes help naturalise the hierarchy between members of the nation, who, as far as the nationalism ideology is concerned, need in fact to be equals: 'Since the subordination of woman to man and child to adult was deemed a natural fact, hierarchies within the nation could be depicted in familial terms to guarantee social difference as a category of nature (McClintock 1995, 357–8).' The patriarchal discourse helps naturalise political hierarchies. This point is amplified in the case of populism which valorises 'the people' and talks about the leader as 'one of them', while at the same time justifying overly personalistic and hierarchical rule. The leader, who is the embodiment of 'the people', justifies hierarchy with familial references since there are already assumed roles and obligations about family members that are culturally embedded. As fathers and husbands, state authorities are to be esteemed as natural sources of authority (to be obeyed no matter how irrational their demands and actions might be). At times as children and at times as wives, citizens are expected to follow the lead of the all-knowing leader who will bring happiness and fortune to the rest. In some cases, as will be seen in the cases of Austria and Hungary, the references to paternal authority are less direct. Yet they are still visible in the situation of citizens as objects of protection and in the emphasis on familial and reproductive duties of citizens.

Turkey

In the patriarchal stories he tells, Erdoğan includes constant references to 'his children' (*yavrularımız*) (Bianet 2013), daughters (*Hürriyet* 2013b) and 'sisters' (*bacılarım*) (NTV 2013a) when talking about his constituency. He projects himself as the saviour and protector of 'the people'. This vision of peoplehood does not extend to the entire community but instead only encapsulates those whom he deems as the deserving ones (Kandiyoti 2014).

In Erdoğan's stories, he is the all-knowing patriarchy who knows what is best for his people, including quitting smoking, having at least three children, not living in mixed-sex dorms, avoiding C-sections, and so on (Ugur-Cinar 2017). Erdoğan plays the role of the father who works tirelessly for the people. In these stories, it is claimed that it is Erdoğan's responsibility to educate, guide and discipline the populace, when necessary, as will be further elaborated on in Chapter 5.

Merging historical narratives with patriarchal ones, Erdoğan presents himself as the saviour of the 'family' narrating a story that ties the past with the present as part of a broader mission. At a wedding ceremony he attended, Erdoğan, for example, complains about birth control, arguing that 'for years they have committed the treason of birth control in this country and they have sought to extinguish us . . . I believe in you' (Oda TV 2014). What he means here is that, his youth (including the newlywed couple) will join his effort to end the plot against the people and have plenty of children.

Erdoğan's patriarchal narrative bolstering his populist image is perhaps most evident in his approach to the headscarf issue in Turkey. Erdoğan maintains that until he and his party came to power his veiled 'daughters' had to endure great ordeals.

Erdoğan's patriarchal plotline does not consist of women and children alone. In his battle with current politicians, he uses this storyline quite often, accusing his opponent of being the source of suffering while presenting himself as the saviour of the victims (Ahaber 2018). In the patriarchal storyline followed by Erdoğan, he is presented as 'the father of the nation'. A case in point is an AKP poster in which Erdoğan is shown along with a quote from him stating 'We have never left the oppressed to the cruelty of the oppressor.' This story is not confined to domestic politics alone as Erdoğan is also presented as 'the savior of all oppressed nations', which is a role he frequently adopts in his speeches in the international arena, such as the UN meetings or the meeting of the World Economic Forum.

Hungary

Compared to the Turkish case, familial references are less direct in the Hungarian and Austrian cases. There are some similarities however. For instance, both Fidesz and the FPÖ have proposed family and gender policies that attempt to regulate the lives of women (and men) so that 'the traditional heterosexual multi-child family becomes dominant again' (Hungarian Government 2018c) Nevertheless, in the latter two cases, we see the protection of Hungary and Austria, as well as more broadly, the protection of Europe, as the dominant format as opposed to constant references to sisters, brothers or daughters. Such narratives are not less patriarchal however, since they still put political figures at the position of a protector figure while interpellating the people as victims and as those who need protection.

Fully understanding the gendered and patriarchal nature of power requires us to understand patriarchy in a way that goes beyond 'male domination'. As Iris Marion Young (2003) notes, the masculinist logic goes beyond a distinction between men and women and instead takes its source of legitimacy from the role of the protector that is attributed to the masculinist power. The logic of masculinism associates 'the position of male head of household as a protector of the family, and, by extension, with masculine leaders and risk takers as protectors of a population' (Young 2003, 4). As such, it is the position of the protector and the protector that carry the patriarchal logic and this logic does not necessarily have to be employed along gender lines, even though in our cases the gender of the leader further reinforces the patriarchal tone.

Orban portrays a grave picture showing Hungary almost under siege. He talks about the wars to the east of Hungary and the threat of trade wars between the EU and the US. The biggest threat for him, however, is posed 'by the millions of immigrants coming from the South'. Orban claims that if resettlement commences, Hungary will face decline in economic growth and security, rise in terrorism and women will be in danger of violent attacks (Hungarian Government 2018d).

In the case of immigration, Orban argues that the danger 'comes from politicians in Brussels, Berlin and Paris', as well as 'the forces opposing us, George Soros's network and the international bureaucrats'. Orban argues, 'We have prevented the Muslim world from inundating us from the south. Facing that direction, we are the last country in Latin – or Western – Christianity. We are standing firm. Our defence lines are sufficient to hold back the largest flows' (Hungarian Government 2018a). As the only source of protection against the grave danger allegedly posed by immigration, Fidesz is presented as the only viable address for the votes of the people: 'Everyone who wants to preserve Hungary as a Hungarian country must go out and vote, and must cast both their votes for Fidesz. Only this is safe. Everything else is a gamble, and may sweep our future into danger' (Hungarian Government 2018d).

Fidesz is claimed to protect not just Hungary but also Europe at large. Orban claims that Europe is under invasion and its political leadership lacks the will to protect Europe (Hungarian Government 2018b): 'Hungary is protecting the Germans' Orban claims, 'along with the Swedes, the Dutch and all its other European partners' (Hungarian Government 2016b). As per the patriarchal narratives of Orban, the protection of the spiritual and cultural life of Hungarians and Europeans are as essential as the physical protection of the Hungarian people. Orban, for example, argues that his party works for the protection of traditional forms of family which, he argues, were neither protected by the EU leadership nor by the previous Hungarian 'liberal' governments (Hungarian Government 2018c; 2014a).

More recently, Orban has also stressed his role in protecting Hungarian families against 'attacks'. Similar to Erdoğan, who recently withdrew from the Istanbul Convention on the grounds that its gender equality commitments were pro-LGBT and would harm the youth and the family in Turkey, Orban also raised criticism against the treaty and against attempts to create equality of gender and sexual orientation as promoting 'destructive gender ideologies' (Politico 2021). To this day, the Hungarian parliament has not ratified the Istanbul Convention. The government explained its refusal to sign the treaty as follows: 'We have the right to defend our country, our culture, our laws, traditions and national values, which should not be threatened by . . . gender theory that goes against the beliefs of the majority of the population.' Orban's government has also changed the constitution to solely recognise heterosexual marriages defending this decision as follows: 'Hungary protects the institution of marriage as a union of man and woman . . . and the family as the basis for the survival of the nation' (*Deutsche Welle* 2020).

Erdoğan and Orban's narratives, which situate the two populist men as strongmen who work tirelessly in order to protect their citizens, families, children and culture, among other things, show us that patriarchy is a key ingredient in the stories of populists.

Austria

The FPÖ storyline has many parallels with the Hungarian one. In addition to Strache's depiction as a knight protecting both Austria and Europe in the cartoon book *Legends of Vienna*, we see multiple examples in which Strache takes on the role of the saviour of the Austrian people. One election poster posted on Strache's Facebook page maintains that Strache and the FPÖ serve as protection mechanisms against the further sale of Austria to Brussels (Facebook 2012). In addition, the party programme states that the party is 'prepared to put up a resolute defence' of European values (Freedom Party of Austria 2011). In a typical Strache speech calling citizens to defend and protect their homeland (Freedom Party of Austria. 2015), Strache claims that European governments (including the Austrian government) want to impose asylum regulations on the European and Austrian citizens 'against the majority of their own population'. Strache also adds that Austria and Europe need to be protected against Islamisation and terrorism, which he calls fatal developments and against which he sees the FPÖ as the only solution (see also (*Wiener Zeitung Online* 2018).

In a mirror image to Erdoğan, the FPÖ and Strache claim to protect women and girls, especially against Islam and oppression. Strache maintains, for example, that the ban on veiling in Elementary schools is a policy to protects the girls (*Oe24* 2018) while an election poster shows an Austrian women wearing a burka who looks stunned accompanied by the poster title 'Should this be our Future?: Austria says no.' Another election poster states: 'We protect free women' (*Der Standard* 2010). Those who are worthy of protection are clearly designated in these posters. Free women, in the case of the FPÖ, refer to those women who do not wear headscarves and are of native Austrian origin (*Der Standard* 2010).

Conclusion

As the cases above have shown, populism relies on stories that are told over and over by leaders who adhere to it. In the form of historical narratives, citizens are told the story of a nation moving through history with the leader furthering historical struggles that rhyme with the past. The populist leaders are mostly depicted as the ones who will ensure that the country does not fall into the traps of the past and that the nation fulfils its destiny despite enemies working against this. In these stories, current opponents to the populists are depicted to have counterparts in the country's past. These 'enemies of the people' are sometimes presented as the descendants of people who in the past desperately wanted bad things for the country or they can be the ones who are historically alienated from their own people and do not know what is best for 'the people'.

In economic stories, again, the leaders are depicted to work for the prosperity and fairness of their people against obstacles presented by internal and external forces. These obstacles also include the democratic checks and balance mechanism or civil society organisations. These institutions and organisations become further targets of intensified attacks by the populists once these populists have served sufficient time in power to institutionalise themselves and when they enjoy comfortable majorities in government.

In patriarchal stories, the leader justifies vertical decision-making despite supposed comradeship with the people by assuming the role of the protector of the people. Patriarchal stories can be overt, speaking directly to the people with the voice of a father, for example. They can also be covert, without familial references yet stressing the wisdom, will, strength and protection of a father vis-à-vis the childlike citizen in constant need of protection.

In all these forms of stories, which are among the most common but not exclusive forms of populist stories, people are defined and redefined in particular ways. The exclusion of certain citizens from 'the people' is justified on historical, economic or patriarchal grounds as the examples have shown. This chapter tried to also show that in addition to the specific content of stories, which can vary depending on the political, historical and social context of the countries, the overarching storylines or meta-narratives and their implications cut across cases.

Leaving out exact details and selectively quoting from empirical facts (or distorting them deliberatively) populist stories create both a common understanding among supporters as well as creating an urgency for action which populist leaders usually use to extend their power, silence dissent and criminalise opposition – all of which are detrimental for pluralism and liberal democracy. A future set of research can complement the current one by engaging further with those at the receiving end of populist stories to see how their stories dovetail with the ones of their leaders and to what extent the supporters of populist leaders internalise such stories.

Of course, populist stories are not the only ones told in societies. As we will discuss in Chapter 5, the Gezi movement has shown, for instance, that protestors can get into a Bakhtinian dialogue (Bakhtin 2013) with such stories. They can pick them up and subvert their message and in an ironic tone negate 'on the figurative level what is positively affirmed on the literal level' (White 1973, 34). As a result, while political phenomena can be reproduced by familial stories, they can also be subverted by alluding to familiar stories. Alternatively, populist stories of economic development, for example, can be countered by telling alternative stories on development that value constitutional constraints on the executive or emphasise the positive role immigrants have played in the economy (as European Green parties do, for example), even though such stories appear to be harder to sell than those of scapegoating. Historically, one could focus on eras of pluralism and cooperation to counter the binary and exclusivist stories told by populist leaders.

In addition to the predisposition of human beings to comprehend and evaluate reality through stories, one could also talk about the cultural and institutional settings under which these narratives operate. Culturally, patriarchal stories appear to strike a chord for the supporters of populist leaders. As long as familial hierarchies are taken for granted, populist leaders will have a comparative advantage. Or in Eisenstein's (1994, 31) words, 'as long as feminism, however it is defined, is thought of as "dada" by leaders . . . the struggle toward real democracy will be much more difficult'. Institutionally, the rise of neoliberalism is also responsible for the expansion of economic narratives at the expense of democracy and human rights while the dislike for organisation and universal welfare benefits paves the way for stories of populist leaders as rescuers (Weyland 1996). Though its reasons are multiple, populism is here to stay with us in politics, at least for a while, with detrimental results for democracy and pluralism. Thus, understanding it as well as thinking about alternative ways of countering it, with alternative stories or otherwise, appears to be crucial. These will be some of the questions addressed in the next two chapters.

Notes

1. 'Net migration rate compares the difference between the number of persons entering and leaving a country during the year per 1,000 persons (based on midyear population)' (Central Intelligence Agency – The World Factbook n.d.b).
2. On defining features of populism, see Weyland 1996; Mudde 2004; Filc 2010; Gidron and Bonikowski 2013; Mudde and Rovira Kaltwasser 2018; Aslanidis 2016; and Barr 2009.
3. Abdülhamid was dethroned and put under house arrest until his death in 1918.
4. There are allegations that Özal was poisoned even though there is no decisive evidence for it.

5

NARRATIVES, POWER AND RESISTANCE: GEZI AS A COUNTER-NARRATIVE

This chapter turns the attention to the relationship between master narratives and counter-narratives. It shows the ramification of the interaction between these two types of narratives through the analysis of the case of the Gezi movement. The Gezi movement started with the protests at the Taksim Square in Istanbul in the last days of May. The protests were a reaction to the government plan to uproot trees in Gezi Park to rebuild the demolished Topçu Barracks from the Ottoman Empire and to construct a new shopping mall. In response to police violence against the peaceful protesters at Gezi Park, the movement grew and spread throughout Turkey in the summer of 2013. Protests in continuation of Gezi were reported in every province in Turkey, except for the predominantly ultraconservative small northeast Anatolian province of Bayburt.

The interactions of Gezi protesters with the dominant narratives of those in power open multiple entry points in the discussion of counter-narratives and their political implications. For example, Bamberg (2004, 362–3) argues against seeing master and counter-narratives as being entirely separate, oppositional narratives. In his discussion of how counter-narratives interact with dominant narratives, he shows how sometimes counter-narratives can appropriate and transform dominant narratives by keeping the plotline more or less intact but introducing 'counter characters' or otherwise reshaping or reconfiguring certain aspects of dominant narratives. Existing studies on counter-narratives mostly focus on how personal counter-narratives interact with dominant narratives. (See, for instance, the set of studies introduced by Andrews (2004) as well as Squire *et al.* (2014).) The goal of this chapter is to trace this interaction at the collective level.

Recognising the dialogical character of narratives is a productive starting point to understand how dominant and counter-narratives operate. As Wertsch (2002, 517) argues, 'the meaning and form of one narrative may be understood in terms of being a dialogic response to another, previous one, in terms of anticipating another, subsequent narrative, and so forth'. Utilising Bakhtinian dialogicality (Bakhtin 2013), the chapter takes a close look at the slogans, graffiti and other forms of expression at Gezi to illustrate its point.

To understand the interaction between the protesters and the political authority, Bakhtin's concept of 'hidden dialogue' is very useful. According to Bakhtin (1986 [1953], 92), 'our thoughts and verbal expressions of them are born and shaped in the process of interaction and struggle with that of others' and each utterance is a response to what has been said before about a given topic. What makes a dialogue hidden is that the addressee is not immediately present yet 'the other's words actively influence the author's speech, forcing it to alter itself accordingly under their influence and initiative' (Bakhtin 2013, 199). Bakhtin (1986 [1953], 95) also emphasises the significance of the addressivity of an utterance whereby the utterance creates the position of the addressee in a particular way. As we will see in the Gezi case, the protesters entered into a hidden dialogue with the political authority and they created their subject position in relation to this authority as the addressee of their dialogue. This then generated the possibility of the use of such subject positions in subversive ways by the addressees.

As the analysis of Gezi will reveal, a narrative inquiry into the dynamics between narratives and counter-narratives needs to pay attention to the interaction between these narratives by not only seeking entire narratives, but also by being attuned to narrative components that intersect. As Lueg, Bager and Lundholt (2021, 2–3) argue, while looking for elements of narratives, namely temporal order, a teller and emplotment, will help researchers to a certain extent, we need to extend our approach to narrative to a 'more processual understanding'. As a result, the authors suggest, in addition to narratives that are clearly structurally cognisable, research should also 'investigate narratives in the making, narratives that are being planned and constructed, and fragments of narratives'. As Freistein and Gadinger (2020, 224) also argue, 'narratives can take shortcuts to recipients without addressing issues in their full complexity, particularly in their use of imagery and metaphorical language'.

Polletta and Callahan (2017) also give us important cues regarding how narratives are presented:

> if stories' power comes from their allusiveness, then the most powerful stories may not even need to be told. They can simply be referred to, often by way of their protagonist. For example, to refer to the 'welfare queen' calls up a story, or stories, of women on welfare taking advantage of the system to live in the lap of luxury.

The shorthand forms of narratives are not only valid in the case of the perpetuation of a story but also in order to challenge or subvert such dominant stories. Gezi protesters' reference to 'three kids', 'motherhood' and the like are examples of them entering into a dialogue with the dominant patriarchal narratives only to subvert them and the authority which they serve. Dominant narratives and their counter-narratives, in this case, can be best understood as part of a 'semiotic community' as it is through them that people engage in 'mutually comprehensible symbolic action' (Wedeen 2002, 722).

Discussing Gezi by integrating the theoretical insights discussed in this chapter will help us gain a well-rounded understanding of its politics as well its potential longstanding legacy. As Özyürek (2006, 7, 19) argues, new fields of inquiry and updated methods of analysis are necessary to understand contemporary politics in Turkey and beyond as politics is blurring more and more the conventional distinctions between the private and the public and the political and the apolitical. If we do not pay attention to what is told between the lines, what dialogues are created with those in power and how narratives are used to redefine identities, hierarchies and possible futures, we risk treating movements, their messages or their participants as apolitical or we miss what is really at stake in them. The narrative engagements of Gezi enable us to rethink the possibilities of alternative notions of Turkish citizenship that is inclusive, nonhierarchical and nonpaternalistic, while at the same time helping us observe narratives at work.

The Counter-narratives of Gezi

In all its elements, Gezi can best be understood as a counter-narrative against not only AKP's authoritarian, populist narrative but also against some of the most established narratives of the Turkish Republic. Among the narratives that Gezi destabilises, we can count, for instance, the understanding of Turkish citizenship as an organicist unity in which the visibility of non-Turkish elements is seen as a threat (Ugur Cinar 2015a). As per this dominant narrative, Turkey has been established throughout history with the unification of various groups under the leadership of Turkish identity and these groups lose their distinct identities in the narration of Turkish history once they have become part of the Turkish community (Ugur Cinar 2015a). This historical narrative suggests a citizenship that is inclusive but only as long as ethnic diversity is left behind. One attempt of the deliberate subversion of the pre-given ethnic divides as well as the dominant citizenship narrative is visible in the Gezi slogan '*Biji Serok Atatürk*', which means 'Long live Leader Atatürk' in Kurdish. The inclusion of '*biji serok*', which most of Turkish society has only heard in the context of Kurdish separatism, if they have heard it at all, constitutes an important element of a counter-narrative of peoplehood that is hitherto not envisioned by the majority of society.

In addition, Gezi also subverts religious cleavage stories that are mostly taken for granted in Turkish politics. In these narratives, for the staunchly secularists people, Islam is associated with backwardness and with unquestioned loyalty to Islamist political authority. On the other hand, for political Islam, secular themes, especially alcohol, are anathema. During the Gezi protest, in an emblematic example that subverts the narratives of both camps, a woman with a headscarf held a banner that reads 'You are unbearable when I am sober.'

Against the militaristic tones of some groups of Kemalists who see themselves as literal guardians of the Republic and use the slogan 'We are the soldiers of Mustafa Kemal Atatürk', the Gezi protesters responded in graffiti featuring slogans such as 'We are the soldiers of Mustafa Keser' (a folk song singer) or 'We are the verses of Turgut Uyar' (a famous poet). These iconic examples illustrate how the protestors creatively responded to an increasingly authoritarian political system and opened to negotiation the main societal dividing lines on which the government strategy relied in keeping its constituency intact.

In addition to these two deepest social cleavages of the country, secularist versus Islamist and the Kurdish–Turkish divide, the protesters also subverted the political–apolitical dichotomy by using terms and figures that would have been deemed apolitical by many. Irony was very visible in the tones of the protesters. For irony to reach its goal, there needs to be a common ground of understanding for the protestors and larger groups to whom the messages are conveyed. In White's (1973, 37) words: 'the Ironic statement . . . presupposes that the reader or auditor already knows, or is capable of recognizing, the absurdity of the characterization of the thing designated in the Metaphor, Metonymy, or Synecdoche used to give form to it'. This common ground at Gezi is created by humour and with the aid of common popular cultural elements such as references to computer games, social media, popular TV series, Hollywood movies and soccer, most of which would formerly be deemed as apolitical. Some such slogans, written on the walls and on banners include, for example, 'You messed with the generation that beats the police in Grand Theft Auto', and 'Tayyip, who always picks Barça at Pro Evolution Soccer'. Other slogans such as 'Tayyip winter is coming' made reference to Game of Thrones and references to soccer players offered 'solutions' to the current problems of the country. A case in point is '*Çare Drogba*' (the solution is Drogba), which is a word play on earlier political slogans that proposed certain political leaders as saviours of the nation.

As Polletta (2009, ix) argues, 'although narrative's ambiguity, or, as I prefer to say, its openness to interpretation, can make for confusion, it can also generate political resources'. Gezi's appeal can also be seen in part in the open space it left in the stories it told. Gezi is striking because it builds some common ground but deliberately refuses to fill the content of subjectivity with a fixed meaning. Totalising projects are faced with ridicule in Gezi. The certainty of old modernist projects are mixed with humour to relativise them and make them inconclusive and open-ended as is the case with the play on the old revolutionary slogans of the 1970s: 'Revolution party! All are welcome. Pilaf will be served', 'Chocolate is the only way out'. Similar world plays are made on Islamist slogans such as 'Peace is in Islam', which is turned to 'Peace is in

Rebellion' (*Isyan*). Given the context, it is not surprising that Ikinci Yeni (Second New), a literary movement that emerged in Turkey in the 1950s and is known for its abstract, esoteric, multilayered imaginary and an experimentalist and existential exploration of the self (Günay-Erkol 2013; Halman 2012), became the most popular artistic point of reference for the movement. Turgut Uyar, who was mentioned above, is also part of this artistic community.

As opposed to the certainty or binary operation of previous social movements, such as the Republican rallies in Turkey, Gezi's narrative engagements are thus inherently non-binary, ambiguous and open to interpretation. Being open to interpretation became an important political asset of narratives in the Gezi case in many ways. It was through the deliberately ambiguous message of Gezi that it was able to embrace different groups by making it possible for the participants to fill the movement with different meanings that appealed to them.

Ahıska (2019, 141), in her discussion of memory, protest, and politics in Turkey, focuses on the importance of connotation. She states that 'connotation becomes an effective mechanism for crossing the thresholds of concealment through the activation of multiple meanings'. Ahıska concentrates on the Saturday Mothers, who meet every Saturday at Galatasaray, Istanbul in protest of the forced disappearances and political violence. She maintains that in the context of the Saturday Mothers, 'the connotations are triggered by the embodied performance of collective memories that creates a space-time with conative power'. The observation of Ahıska with regard to the Saturday Mothers applies perfectly to the Gezi protesters. The connotations of the poems, social media and popular culture references, childhood nostalgias and the like, worked very well in creating a communality among the protesters that is based on a common understanding without necessitating fixed, binary meanings.

The fact that Gezi protesters engaged with one another and with the wider audience with humour further reinforced the sense of commonality not entirely dependent on a fixed content. As Wedeen (2013, 870) argues, laughter requires the participation of others and presumes a community. In the spirit of Hayden White (1973, 1987), the prominence of humour at Gezi thus reinforces the finding that when it comes to narratives the form is as important as the content (see also Ugur Cinar 2015a; Ugur-Cinar and Smith 2015).

The main hub of the protests relied on the subversion of the asymmetry between the rulers and the ruled, which is based on a hegemonic patriarchal narrative as discussed in the previous chapter. According to the patriarchal narrative, as fathers and husbands, state authorities are to be esteemed as natural sources of authority and citizens are expected to follow the lead of the leader. Before delving more deeply into the ways in which Gezi protesters engaged with and subverted patriarchal narratives in order to problematise the very foundations on which state–citizen relations were built in Turkey, I will first discuss the relevant theoretical framework to delineate the relationship between patriarchy, legitimacy and political authority.

Patriarchal Narratives and Power

State formation is an ongoing process and legitimacy is one of its key components. This legitimacy is negotiated on a daily basis between the state and the citizens and it is communicated through narratives. The extant literature on state formation approaches state formation mostly as a historical episode. For social contract theories, the issue of legitimacy is mostly tacit. For scholars of state formation like Tilly, legitimacy is strongly associated with domination. Tilly (1985, 171) is aware that what differentiates racketeers from states is the fact that they operate 'without the sanctity of governments'. Where then does the sanctity of governments come from? According to Tilly, the distinction between 'legitimate' and 'illegitimate' force as an abstract ideal does not cause a difference here. With Stinchcombe (1968, 150), Tilly argues that legitimacy depends little on the assent of the governed but relies instead on 'the probability that other authorities will act to confirm the decisions of a given authority' (1985, 171–2). He believes that the tendency of other authorities to recognise state authority will be enhanced the more the state monopolises the means of violence and thereby 'makes a government's claim to provide protection, in either the comforting or the ominous sense of the word, more credible and more difficult to resist'. Olson (1993, 568) acknowledges that 'autocrats of all kinds usually claim that their subjects want them to rule and thereby nourish the unhistorical assumption that government arose out of some kind of voluntary choice', yet he does not delve into the mechanism of how such legitimation is achieved either.

We cannot leave the issue of legitimation unexplored if we want to understand the functioning of the state and the relationship between state and society. As Pierson (2011, 17) suggests, issues of authority and legitimacy are central to the modern state:

> No state can survive for very long exclusively through its power to coerce. Even where power is most unequally distributed and the possibilities for coercion are at their greatest – for example, in a prisoner-of-war camp – the subordinated can always exercise some level of non-compliance, and, across time, the maintenance of social order is 'negotiated'. How much more is this the case for a state governing many millions of subjects in a comparatively open society? A stable state requires that, for whatever reason, most of the people most of the time will accept its rule.

In order for us to understand the legitimating storylines of states, we can utilise theories informed by feminist and gender studies. State-formation theories have hitherto not made sufficient use of the findings of that body of literature. As Adams (2005, 32) argues 'sociological theories of state formation have remained remarkably resistant to specifically feminist concepts, observations, and insights'. As Adams (2005, 33) also maintains, the same can be said for the other side of the story as feminist theory 'has failed to address and incorporate sociological theories of state formation'. With these insights in mind, we need to focus on how the gendered narratives of the state serve as legitimation tools for its existence as well as the actions of those who claim to act on its behalf.

Adams (2005, 200) argues that 'the early modern patrimonial state and its sovereign arms or extensions would not have existed without the concept of father rule and associated patriarchal practices of power'. This observation can also be extended to today's states even though the association between patriarchy and power is less literal nowadays. In states' legitimating mechanisms, patriarchal stories play an important role. As a storyline learnt from childhood, normalised through socialising institutions and everyday practices, patriarchal narratives create an economy of politics: by providing shortcuts in the minds of citizens, politicians are able to gain more with less. Politicians rely on already assumed roles and obligations about family members that are culturally embedded. As fathers and husbands, state authorities are to be esteemed as natural sources of authority. At times as children and at times as wives, citizens are expected to follow the lead of the all-knowing leader who will bring happiness and fortune to the rest (Ugur-Cinar 2017, 328).[1]

In my own work (Ugur-Cinar 2017), I have demonstrated that patriarchal justifications play a central role in the endorsement of and compliance to neopatrimonial political authority. I have found that the patriarchal language legitimising male domination, state domination, paternalism and hierarchy plays an enabling role in neopatrimonialism. By doing so, I have tried to restore the organic link between patrimonialism and patriarchy, thereby challenging the current predominant notion that neopatrimonialism (unlike traditional patrimonialism) can be solely understood as a material exchange between the ruler and the ruled for political support. I have substantiated the theoretical framework with illustrative examples from the Turkish case that show how neopatrimonial acts of political leadership are justified with patriarchal narratives that are equally paternalistic and male dominant. These narratives, naturalise hierarchies between the ruler and the ruled, reduce citizens to a position of submissiveness in which personal favours replace legal entitlements of citizens and thereby serve to reinforce personalistic rule, delegitimise opposition, and suppress pluralism:

> As the all-knowing patriarch who knows what is best, the neopatrimonial leader becomes the bearer of national interest and the embodiment of the nation. Institutions still exist, but they are auxiliary to the rule of the leader. They can be bent according to his will and they can be constantly undermined in a populist fashion. In this system, the people are depicted as in need of help, guidance and protection. They are infantilized and seen as naive and vulnerable at best, being open to manipulation at worst. (Ugur-Cinar 2017, 337)

Patriarchal stories rely on assumed gender and familial roles, which have a highly hegemonic standing considering how they seem to seamlessly function in Turkey as well as in many other countries. As such, they are assumed to unproblematically create ties between the ruler and the ruled, normalising hierarchies and demanding consent. One could thus approach patriarchy in light of Somers' conceptualisation of meta-narratives or Wibben's (2010) conceptualisation of grand narratives. Most of the research on grand narratives of patriarchy focuses on individual level stories. For example, Squire *et al.* (2014,

61–2), focus on 'how the grand narratives of gender, women's sexuality and regulations were deployed and contested' in the sexual narratives of educated young women and their mothers in Turkey within the context of the role the Turkish modernisation project assigned to women. This chapter expands the analysis further into the realm of collective political action.

Among the literature on the state, society and citizenship, two scholars deserve special praise for analysing the link between gender tropes and state legitimation. One is Schatzberg (1993, 446), who in his studies of sub-Saharan African regimes has pointed at how gendered understandings of the state and society have influenced citizens' views of the state. Schatzberg (1993, 446) believes that we need to examine political language, including metaphors and other images used, to understand the cultural components of political legitimacy. These cultural components consist of what Schatzberg calls 'moral matrices'. These matrices 'form a culturally rooted template against which people come to understand the political legitimacy, or "thinkability", of institutions, ideas, policies, and procedures' (Schatzberg 2001, 1).

Among those, Schatzberg (1993, 455) argues that 'the tacit normative idea that government stands in the same relationship to its citizens as a father does to his children' is the most profound in sub-Saharan Africa and contributes to the implicit 'infantilization' of the population (Schatzberg 2001, 25). This depiction of the father chief has important consequences for the political opposition:

> The unstated yet potent political logic of this rhetoric is insidious. In the first place, even if the political opposition places an altogether different accent on the paternal and familial language, they have still let the state dictate the ideological terrain of the political debate. Furthermore, if Presidents Moi, Mobutu, Biya, or Houphouet are (or were) the 'fathers' of their respective national 'family', their people are reduced to the role of his children. The regimes can present, therefore, any political protest as the work of 'ungrateful' or 'misguided' or 'wayward' children. They are all brothers and sisters, and like siblings who squabble over inconsequential matters, citizens do also. Important political questions, such as ethnic competition for scarce resources, may thus be presented as the petty sibling rivalries of those lacking in maturity. And . . . the 'father' must occasionally 'discipline' naughty and immature children for their own good.

As Schatzberg (2001, 24–5) explains, 'the father chief' has two different sides with different political implications attached to each of them:

> On the first side there is the loving, kind, understanding, always solicitous, and caring paternal – and occasionally maternal – figure . . . The second side of the coin is less loving, less nurturing, and less paternal. If the father smiles and forgives, the chief snarls and punishes. This harsh and repressive visage has confronted many middle Africans when they have protested their lot. Occasional and 'necessary' parental discipline – of course undertaken only with the good of the child in mind – can be transformed into vicious and nasty repression when the political 'children' repeatedly fail to toe the political line or are insufficiently grateful for all that their father chief does, and has done, for them. The benevolent father thus gives way to the malevolent chief whom people expect to command both the forces of coercion and the forces of the occult, deploying them as arms of governance. These are part of his strength, power, and legitimacy.

Claiming that the failure to analyse the continuing use of familial beliefs to justify political authority limits our understanding of the complex processes through which governments maintain and lose their political legitimacy, Thomas (2011b, 71) also provides sharp insights into the relationship between familial discourse and political legitimacy in her analysis of the Chilean case. Thomas (2011a, 4) finds that 'idealized relationships among families and between families and other institutions provide important symbolic and discursive resources for political actors'. Political leaders and mobilised citizens use such familial beliefs 'to provide the language, metaphors, symbols, and images that framed their political appeals, justified their political actions, and made sense of larger political events' (Thomas 2011a, 5). Based on her study, Thomas (2011b, 85) concludes that 'powerful ideological beliefs about the relationship between the state and family continued to operate even in a modern democratic political system that did not fit the traditional definitions of either patrimonialism or patriarchalism'.

While the formulations of patriarchy by Schatzberg and Thomas give us important insights, the authors are focusing on how all sides in a community accept the patriarchal discourse, even if the patriarchal discourse is employed by different actors for different political ends. For instance, Schatzberg argues, 'even if the political opposition places an altogether different accent on the paternal and familial language, they have still let the state dictate the ideological terrain of the political debate'. In parallel, Thomas (2011b) shows how both proponents and opponents of Allende drew on embedded beliefs about the relationship between families and politics to discuss the legitimacy of Allende's rule in Chile. Thomas' article looks at how the opposition reproduces the same gendered tropes as the ones used by the proponents of those in power.

These formulations of the role of patriarchy in society give us important insights. Yet, at the same time, they provide a holistic approach to patriarchy that assumes its acceptance and reproduction by the entire society. While patriarchal narratives provide the basis of political allegiance, compliance and legitimacy across the political spectrum, they can also serve to unsettle the political system and question its legitimacy when mobilised in narrative form, which is a point so far left unexplored in the literature. With this in mind, in this chapter, I try to demonstrate how opposition actors can challenge dominant patriarchal tropes at their core instead of merely reproducing them.

In its discussion of gendered narratives, this chapter will borrow insights from discussions of political culture that problematise seeing a discursive construct as holistic and all-encompassing. Lisa Wedeen's (2002, 719) criticism of Geertz and his followers on the grounds that their conceptualisation of culture insists on coherence, depicts culture as a reified, frozen system of meaning and is blind to multiple significations within social groups is an important insight with significant implications for the topic under study in this chapter. In place of such an approach to culture, Wedeen (2002, 720) proposes a dialectical understanding of culture that 'allows us to view meaning-making activities as being both stable and changeable, both a single system and internally various and conflicted, an aspect of both structure and agency'. In her analysis, Wedeen (2002, 723) provides a blueprint as to how to treat culture as 'the dialectical relationship between people's practices and systems of signification' which is open to being 'created, reproduced, and subverted'. In a similar vein, we need to develop an understanding of the patriarchy–state nexus that is both aware of the patriarchal basis of the system but is also attentive to the dynamic possibilities opened up through narratives.

Narratives provide room for subversion and resistance within the same community and not just cultural resonance that leads to the continuity of dominant political discourse. Citizens reproduce, internalise and reinforce but also negotiate, resist and subvert culturally embedded narratives. As Polletta (2009, 16–7) argues, stories can be used for transgressive effect or they can be used to 'redefine people's interests and identities in ways that can create entirely new lines of contention'.

Citizens are not passive subjects who just accept or reproduce patriarchal stories. Instead, such stories are quite dynamic and citizens react to them in creative ways. Just as some families and marriages do not necessarily comply with the patriarchal and domineering cast in which they were originally preconceived, citizens also can and do envision non-patriarchal relationship between the state and citizens. The patriarchal contract in which the ruler and the ruled adhere to the same storyline can very well continue to be the basis of societal and political order. Yet, societal actors can and do also target the very basis of this consent, which can happen at different levels. Especially participants of social movements, when trying to attack the citizen–state patriarchal relationship, can do this by simultaneously attacking the very core of the assumption of this relationship by attacking the gendered structure, which has been taken for granted until then.

The analysis of the Gezi protests in relation to patriarchal narratives in Turkey serves as the platform that demonstrates the dynamic, semiotic and interactive relationship among the state, its citizens and patriarchy. In the case of Gezi, instead of assuming the traditional roles assigned to them as members of families and as citizens, protesters tried to unsettle the patriarchal premises of authority by severing the patriarchal ties that claim to bind them to the state. Gezi is not the only incidence in which citizens and collectives reject the patriarchal interpellation of the state. For example, during the headscarf debates, Peoples' Democracy Party (Hakların Demokratik Partisi – HDP) female MPs explicitly stated that they were not the daughters, sisters or otherwise relatives of politicians but they, as women were citizens of the regime in demand of their constitutional rights. Yet the counter-narrative against the government's patriarchal narratives was most visible and most expansive in the Gezi protests as will be elaborated on in this chapter.

Counter-narratives: Pluralism, Solidarity and Egalitarianism against Patriarchal Narratives

The state as a father figure has a long and uninterrupted history in the Turkish case. As Mardin (1973, 169–90) has demonstrated, the Turkish power centre has maintained its asymmetrical power over the periphery and it has seen itself as the top-down moderniser and bearer of wisdom.[2] As the AKP example shows, even actors entering politics from the periphery have quickly positioned themselves in the centre and have situated themselves as all-knowing fathers of the country.

As the previous chapter has detailed, Erdoğan benefits immensely from patriarchal narratives. He presents himself as the all-knowing patriarch who is selflessly devoted to his people but who never hesitates to punish those who stand in his way to fulfil his historical mission. In addition to broadly patriarchal narratives based on the protector and protected, or victim and saviour, detailed in Chapter 4, Erdoğan also relied on both paternal and male dominant notions of patriarchy.

The paternal power assumed by the state is evident in many political statements. For instance, Erdoğan deemed it the state's duty to raise pious generations and he stated that they were working toward this goal (*Hürriyet* 2012). Erdoğan's frequent use of phrases such as '*benim başörtülü kızlarım*' (my headscarved daughters) is another case in point (e.g. *Hürriyet* 2013b). Yet another example is his statement during his verbal attack on mixed-gender housing (private dorms as well as apartments): 'It is unknown what is going on there. All kinds of messy things are happening. Parents are crying out, "Where is the state?" We have to show where the state is' (Cengiz 2013). In agreement with Erdoğan, the then Minister of Interior Muammer Güler also stated that it was the duty of the state to protect the youth (*Sabah* 2013a).

In addition to patriarchy as paternal power, Turkey is also full of examples of patriarchy as male domination. Ironically, at a speech he gave at the Women and Justice Summit, Recep Tayyip Erdoğan declared that 'you cannot bring women and men to equal conditions, it is against their nature' (CNN Turk 2014b). This was not the first time he made such statements. Earlier, he had announced that he did 'not believe in the equality of men and women' (Hogg and Pamuk 2014; Steinvorth 2012). Erdoğan defended his latest speech on subsequent occasions (Bianet 2014). Such statements have been accompanied by actions and policies of the government that attempted to regulate the lives of women by the patriarchal state. Erdoğan, for instance urged women to give birth to a minimum of three children, accused birth control as treason, and condemned Caesarean section and abortion (*Radikal* 2014; *The Economist* 2013).

By situating citizens in a certain position (as children and/or wives) through patriarchal narratives, the then prime minister (now president) Erdoğan created the space for a language of protest that followed the trope of a rebellious teenager protesting against his/her parents, or wives who became sick of their husbands. One way the protesters deployed such a language was by building on preexisting narrative plots (particularly patriarchal narratives) to undermine the very essence of such narratives. This was the case, for example, in the slogans such as 'We are young Tayyip, bear with us', or 'Tayyip, I want a divorce'. To the authority, that insisted on women having at least three children, the protestors asked (on numerous posters and in graffiti): 'Are you sure you want three children like us?'

The familial references of the protestors are not to be taken at face value. An explicit irony is at the centre of the Gezi protests in which the protesters negated 'on the figurative level what is positively affirmed on the literal level' (White 1973, 34). Instead of reproducing the dominant familial discourse then, the overarching message of Gezi is ironic in the sense that it is very aware of the constructed nature of the family tropes mobilised by the AKP. The movement is also highly subversive because it speaks with the same words of the hegemon yet destabilises these words and problematises the very foundations they rest upon. The movement tells the political power that it is resisting the political outlook of the government and it is refusing their political categories and cleavages upon which they build their political strategy.

The patriarchal narrative of Erdoğan intensified during Gezi, which caused further engagement of Gezi protesters with patriarchy in order to subvert Erdoğan's rule. During the protests Erdoğan addressed the 'young kids' (genç yavrularımız) in Gezi Park: 'Please do not fall prey to the games of illegal organizations. We have maintained our patience but we are reaching its end. I am warning you for the last time. I am saying "mothers, fathers take care of your children" [yavrularınıza sahip çıkın] (Bianet 2013).'

The formulation of Gezi protestors as youth and kids is not self-evident. According to KONDA's Gezi survey (KONDA 2014, 8), the average age of the respondents was twenty-eight. KONDA has also observed that the protesters were representative of Turkish society in terms of average age since according to their datasets the average age is 30.3 in Turkey and 30.1 in Istanbul. The report proceeds with the following findings: only 22 per cent of the Gezi Park protesters were twenty years old or younger, the majority of the protesters who were twenty years old or younger were between the ages of eighteen and twenty, only 5.5 per cent of the protesters in Gezi Park were seventeen years old or younger, while 16.5 per cent of the protesters were between the ages of eighteen and twenty, the majority of protesters did not comprise of high school students or college students in their freshman or sophomore year (KONDA 2014, 9). Engaging with the protesters as children and youth was a choice Erdoğan made that enabled him to present the protestors as naive and lacking agency, thereby being prone to become buttresses of evil forces (CNN Turk 2014a). Erdoğan's retrospections on Gezi in the aftermath, including statements claiming that the enemies of Turkey profited by the protests whereas 'young people became victims of this plot', further support this point. An illustrative statement by him goes as follows: 'You participated as voluntary soldiers in a game that you could not understand; young people, you were used and deceived' (T24 2013).

The fact that Erdoğan addressed parents, particularly mothers, instead of the protestors and asked them to control their children brought unintended consequences. Coupled with the Istanbul governor Hüseyin Avni Mutlu's call to mothers of the protestors to come to Gezi Park and remove their children from the park, the patriarchal attitude of those in power was turned into an opportunity for the renunciation of pre-given roles by the protestors. The motherhood trope exploded among the material created and disseminated by the activists. In response to the governor's call, mothers gathered at Gezi and created a circle around their children to protect them from the police. These women, dancing in the dark, in a public space and at the centre of Turkey's largest public protest, challenged the established notion of motherhood, womanhood, and their perceived relation to the state. Instead of pulling their children from the protests, mothers declared solidarity with their children. Motherhood tropes, instead of serving the patriarchal cause, this time served to present the Gezi cause as genuinely approved by mothers, further authenticating and endorsing the cause.

Conclusion

Despite the power asymmetries and the deeply polarised social cleavages of the Turkish political atmosphere, Gezi protesters found creative ways to engage with the wider audience and to present an alternative vision for Turkish politics. Gezi can be understood as a movement that deliberately left its message ambiguous. The secret of the fact that it has embraced such different groups lies in this intentional ambiguity, which made it possible for the participants to fill it with different meanings. Gezi's refusal to fill the meaning of citizenship and membership with concrete characteristics has a lot to say to us with regard to citizenship and nationalism as well as populism. As discussed in Chapters 2 and 4, populism also reinforces homogenous notions of citizenship according to which 'the people' are envisioned in their totality and are reflected in the populist leader's image. As de la Torre (2019, 68) argues, populists target democratic institutions and attack pluralism as 'under populism the people and the nation speak with one voice, that of a small clique of politicians and ultimately the voice of the leader'. Müller (2016) also addresses the anti-pluralist nature of populism and its claim to exclusively represent a homogenously envisioned 'people' through their embodiment by the leader. Such monist accounts of citizenship are detrimental to democracy as they are ready to crush pluralism and multivocality in the society. Movements such as Gezi that try to envision solidarity by keeping the very pluralism of the people intact can help us open new ways in thinking about political alternatives to populism. Like the creation of populist movements, the struggle against them will have patriarchal narratives at its core. But this time, to subvert them instead of reproducing them.

What do the findings of this chapter tell us about patriarchy? They show us that the Gezi protesters invite us to a more horizontal political understanding and a more horizontal gender notion simultaneously. This proposal does not just mean equality among men and women but also a total rethinking of the very foundations of the relationship between the ruler and the ruled. Gezi proved that while political phenomena can be reproduced by familial stories, it can also be subverted by alluding to familial stories. Gezi's deliberative attempt to support a free and horizontal imaginary of citizenship relies on its subversion of patriarchal power narratives.

From the angle of political opportunity structure literature (McAdam 1982) and Kuran's (1991, 7–48) prediction of tipping points of social movements, one can say that the state has made it much more costly for protestors to take to the streets in the future. Those killed, the ones who lost their eyes as a result of police violence, those who received lifetime prison sentences, and the ones who got fired from their jobs, made it more difficult for people to participate in such movements. The fact that Erdoğan stood behind the violence by stating that he gave the orders (*Hürriyet Daily News* 2013a) and the legislation passed by the AKP[3] further stifled the prospects of social movements in Turkey. However, we now know that even the seemingly most apolitical aspects of popular culture such as computer games and sit coms can provide a common language and a repertoire for alternative narratives that can make future political protest waves possible.

Taking stock of the long-term impact of Gezi, one needs to look at the ways in which Gezi has problematised the relationship between state and citizen, which so far has mostly been taken as granted. Gezi is an expression of a call for a new polity in which people are not categorised in binaries and are not treated paternalistically as children or wives of the state but are instead seen as equal, worthy participants of the political community. Gezi has achieved this call for a more horizontal polity through a deliberate subversion of given dichotomies. It has created a novel repertoire of protests (Tilly 1977) and a commemorative vantage point upon which future movements can build.

In the next chapter, we will switch gears and look at political narratives in global perspective to trace their role in exclusionary, homogenising and authoritarian politics and in restrictive citizenship and immigration policies. We will also delve into the potential role narratives can play against such politics and policies.

Notes

1. On the role of family tropes in naturalising the hierarchy between members of the nation, see McClintock 1991.
2. Heper's (1992) depiction of the Turkish state as a strong state that situates itself above the society as an isolated and superior actor is also a case in point.
3. On the details of the Internal Security Package, see Gürsel 2015.

6

POLITICAL NARRATIVES AND POLITICAL REGIMES IN GLOBAL PERSPECTIVE

So far, in this book, the role of political narratives in politics has mostly been studied through the Turkish case, except for Chapter 4, which discusses the Turkish case in comparison with Austria and Hungary. The aim of the current chapter is to broaden the focus and to discuss the role of narratives in other contexts and to further the possibilities of future research of key issues of politics through the analysis of political narratives. In showing how political narratives can be used in understanding political dynamics not limited to the Turkish case, it will particularly focus on the discussion of the crucial role political narratives can play in countering populism and the way studies of democratic backsliding can incorporate the study of political narratives.

The relationship between political narratives and political regimes is a key issue that needs to be tackled. This, we can understand in multiple ways. The most prominent concerns seem to be the relationship between political narratives and the political system on the one hand, and the relationship of such narratives with the citizenship regime of the country, on the other. Both points, though analytically distinct, need to be thought of in conjunction however, as most authoritarian leaders, and in its most current form, right-wing populism, attack liberal democracy and the more inclusive and pluralistic aspects of citizenship simultaneously. I will first briefly discuss how political narratives influence institutions and policies, which is relevant to the prospects of not only the characteristics of the political regime, but also to the future of the citizenship and identity policies of the countries. I will then move on to the discussion of illustrative examples in the rise of political narratives that aim to justify exclusionary and authoritarian institutions and policies, and even politically motivated violence. I will particularly focus on the most popular far-right narrative, especially in the West, namely the political narrative called 'The Great Replacement Theory'. The remainder of the section will lay out debates with regards to how to best tackle such narratives and the role narratives can play in this struggle.

Political Narratives, Political Institutions and Political Regimes

As I have tried to demonstrate in my previous book through the cases of Austria and Turkey (Ugur Cinar 2015a), political narratives have far-reaching, path-dependent effects on citizenship regimes. In the aforementioned work, I looked at how different forms of historical narratives institutionalised in a country's formative years have long-reaching consequences for citizenship policies. Taking two post-imperial core countries as my main cases, I examined how historical narratives institutionalised in school curricula and trough commemorative practices play crucial roles during critical junctures of citizenship policies. One novelty of this study was to create a typology of forms of historical narratives and then trace the way in which these forms influence policy outcomes. Complementing existing studies that hitherto focused on the historical trajectory followed by a country, the study showed that we also need to understand the way history is narrated and institutionalised to make sense of the variation across citizenship regimes.

We have further extended this line of research with Rogers Smith, by expanding our empirical scope to also include Israel and the US in addition to Austria and Turkey and by deepening our theoretical scope regarding the relationship between political narratives and citizenship and immigration policies by combining Rogers Smith's previous (Smith 2003) focus on the content themes (economic, political power and constitutive) and my own focus on the structure of themes (mechanistic, organicist and contextual). Through the discussion of similarities and differences between the cases, we demonstrated that political narratives institutionalised at the formative years of countries have far-reaching effects that become especially visible during critical junctures of citizenship and national identity policies (Ugur-Cinar and Smith 2014; 2015).

We maintained that though this process is not entirely top-down, power asymmetries in the process are clearly visible. We were also able to lay out what type of political narratives would lead to what type of citizenship policies, which is a point I will not further elaborate on here in order to keep the discussion more focused on the current cases in hand.

Given the current political context both in terms of the domestic setting of most countries, as well as the overall global climate under which most pluralistic and liberal democratic institutions are under threat, the study of the role of political narratives gains further importance. As will be elaborated with examples, by telling particular stories, picking critical junctures in history, establishing different founding movements and golden ages, political narratives ascribe certain agencies, or historical missions, to political actors and justify certain types of political action and policies.

The relationship between political narratives and democratic backsliding is thus essential, even though existing studies have not sufficiently addressed this link. In this book, so far, I have tried to show how political narratives are used in order to justify power grabs for the executive at the expense of other state institutions, particularly the judiciary. I have also demonstrated how narratives are used in order to suppress dissent and to eliminate pluralism through economic narratives, for example, that claim that those opposing the government are mostly willingly (and sometimes out of ignorance) harming the economic well-being of the country and stalling development. As I will show in this chapter, such anti-democratic narratives are deployed particularly well by right-wing authoritarian leaders in their efforts to garner support for their exclusionary and repressive politics. A recent line of research started to delve into the issue of whether we could actually counter authoritarian demagogues and exclusionary populists through narratives (see, for example, Smith 2020). This question gains particular importance as political science research starts to focus more on democratic resilience and the defeat of populist leaders through elections.

In what follows, I will first discuss how narratives are used in efforts to push for non-democratic and discriminatory politics and policies with illustrations, particularly from the US and from Europe. I will then turn to the debates regarding how to best tackle authoritarian politicians who are trying to chip away pluralistic and liberal democratic regimes by paying special attention to the role narratives play in these struggles between democracy and authoritarianism, inclusion and exclusion, and pluralism and homogeneity.

Authoritarian Political Narratives

In our discussion of the Gezi protests in Chapter 5, we have focused on counter-narratives in relation to their democratising and emancipatory potential. The existing literature on counter-narratives also mostly deals with such narratives in relation to resistance and emancipation (albeit mostly at the individual level) but as this chapter will show, counter-narratives can also be deployed for more negative ends. Resentments and anxieties of citizens emanating from various reasons ranging from the feeling of not being represented under the current political system, feeling to be the losers of the system economically or feeling that their culture as they understand it is under threat, are exploited in the hands of politicians, particularly right-wing populist leaders. The far-right alternative to liberal democracy tells populist stories, stories of scapegoating, xenophobic and racist stories, stories of nostalgia, of a golden age that has passed, and narrates the current state of their country and/or the world as a story of decline and doom, which can only be overturned by a particular form of political action, political leader and form of allegiance. In the contemporary world, conspiracy theories constitute the heart of such narratives. Davey and Ebner (2019, 6) define conspiracy theory as follows:

> a theory which seeks to explain a phenomenon by invoking a sinister plot orchestrated by powerful actors. These conspiracies are painted as secret or esoteric, with adherents to a theory seeing themselves as the initiated few who have access to hidden knowledge. Adherents to conspiracy theories usually see themselves as in direct opposition to the powers who are orchestrating the ploy.

The most popular of the far-right populist narrative rendition can be found in the so-called 'Replacement Theory', which like 'conspiracy theory', the original conceptual family to which 'Replacement Theory' belongs, is not really a theory since it does not rely on scientific data or certain testable hypothesis. Rather, it consists of a basic, simple storyline, claiming to unearth the plot behind what is happening, particularly the West, in the contemporary world. I agree with Goetz (2021, 63) who argues that it makes more sense to use the terms 'conspiracy myth' or 'conspiracy narrative' instead of 'conspiracy theory' since the views expressed in these so-called theories rely on assumptions, do not take counterarguments or empirical proof into account, and are 'by no means rational or (scientifically) verifiable theories'. Before focusing on the details of the Replacement conspiracy theory, its journey to the mainstream political discourse and its political implications, providing the historical background and the political context of Replacement Theory will be beneficial.

Pizzagate and QAnon

Cosentino (2020) examines the circulation of conspiracy theories, particularly those of Pizzagate and QAnon, which evolved from concoctions of Internet subcultures of white ethnonationalists over online platforms such as 4chan, 8chan and Reddit to global topics of public conversation and political mobilisation. She then turns to the far-right anti-immigration conspiracy theory, The Great Replacement, to explore the 'the interlocking themes of White identity politics, trolling and the "weaponization" of Internet entertainment'.

Cosentino (2020, 60) argues that the 2016 Pizzagate conspiracy theory provided a blueprint for 'fictional political narratives' which grew out of the contributions of multiple authors in different regions of the world. The Pizzagate conspiracy theory emerged during the 2016 US presidential race and alleged that a pizzeria in Washington, D.C., called Comet Ping Pong, served as the operational base of a high-profile ring of pedophiles and Satanists involving top-level Democrats, including the then presidential candidate Hillary Clinton and her former campaign manager John Podesta (Cosentino 2020, 60–1). Despite the fact that the Washington Police Department investigation had shown that there was no basis for this conspiracy theory, it grew over the Internet via online discussion forms, anonymous imageboarders and the like (Cosentino 2020, 61). As cited by Cosentino (2020, 61), according to Craig Silverman, who was among 'the first journalists to investigate the association between social media and disinformation', Pizzagate 'shows how Trump supporters, members of 4chan and Reddit, and right-wing blogs in the United States and in other countries combined to create and spread viral misinformation during the election season' (Silverman 2016).

When WikiLeaks started making the emails of John Podesta, whose mail servers were hacked by Russian hackers called Fancy Bear and Cozy Bear, available online, the discussion groups that were virtual meeting places for Trump supporters on 4chan and on Reddit were filled by posts from these leaks. Trump supporters searched through the hacked messages and suggested that the emails contained coded messages alluding to pedophiliac practices, the term 'pizza' being used in place of 'underage girls' (Cosentino 2020, 63). With this allegation, the common narrative labelled 'Pizzagate' started. This narrative was later picked up by right-wing partisan groups on Facebook and then by professional conspiracy theorists like the Britain David Icke and the American Alex Jones. Cosentino (2020, 63–5) argues that while a lot of grassroot participation went into the popularisation of Pizzagate 'by means of a collaborative storytelling via social media, imageboards, discussion forums and other alternative on-line information outlets', the role of such social media conspirators was key. Stories such as the Pizzagate worked well for the far-right populist movements such as the American ethnonationalist far-right, which sought for narratives that could mobilise their base against establishment politicians and 'the so-called mainstream liberal media' (Confessore and Wakabayashi, 2017).

In October 2017, Pizzagate morphed into an even more elaborate conspiracy theory named QAnon, again via 4chan. QAnon shared the same narrative core as Pizzagate: 'the existence of a secret global child sex ring run by liberal political and financial elites', this time also claimed to involve the 'deep state entities' (Cosentino 2020, 71). The conspiracy theory, initiated by a 4chan user called Q Clearance Patriot (or simply Q, referring to the highest security clearance available in the US Department of Energy) grew from similar outlets as Pizzagate and revolved around a common theme: 'the role of Donald Trump as savior of regular American citizens against the scheming of political elites and State apparatuses' (Cosentino 2020, 72). As a result of this, the QAnons became even more closely associated with the broader community of Trump supporters. This association also became more noticeable with QAnon t-shirts and signs visible at Trump events (Cosentino 2020, 72).

While both Pizzagate and QAnon migrated from on-line to real life with media coverage and support of public figures and while both led to violent actions (Pizzagate with the armed attack on Comet Ping Pong and QAnon with violent crimes including the murder of a mafia boss; Cosentino 2020, 72–3), it was the conspiracy theory named 'The Great Replacement' that made the most impact both in terms of its infiltration of daily political discourse and the violent events it contributed to. Relatedly, it was the narrative that made the supposed victimisation of white people most explicit and defined the enemies of white people in most concrete terms thereby channelling the anxieties and anger of the population towards certain groups of people, primarily Muslims, African Americans or people of Latin American origin, depending on the political context. It is to the details of this narrative and its political implications that we now turn.

The Replacement Theory

The Replacement Theory has spread to different parts of the world, becoming especially popular among the Identitarian movements in Europe and the so-called 'alt-right' in the US (Bullens 2021). The simplest storyline behind the Great Replacement Theory can be summarised as follows: ethnically homogenous Western populations are being replaced by non-Western populations as part of an orchestrated plan of political and economic elites. Among the European circles, the story is focused on white European populations, which according to the proponents of the story, 'are being deliberately replaced at an ethnic and cultural level through migration and the growth of minority communities' (Davey and Ebner 2019, 7). Some of those who give detailed accounts on this issue rely on the narrative use of demographic projections to point to population changes in the West in favour of certain ethnic and religious groups, primarily Muslims, which are presented as threatening and culturally incompatible with the West (Davey and Ebner 2019, 7). The Replacement Theory is called the '*Umvolkung*' or '*Der Grosse Austauch*' in Germany (Önnerfors 2021, 76). In Swedish it is known as '*folkutbyte*' (ethnic replacement; Ekman 2022, 4) In the US context, the story focuses on white Americans and claims that 'Western elites, sometimes manipulated by Jews, want to "replace" and disempower white Americans' (Confessore and Yourish 2022).

The origins of the Great Replacement Theory date back in history. In 1900, the French nationalist Maurice Barrès had already spoken about a new population that would take over and ruin the homeland. At that time, he wrote an article for the daily newspaper *Le Journal* stating: 'The name of France might well survive; the special character of our country would, however, be destroyed, and the people settled in our name and on our territory would be heading towards destinies contradictory to the destinies and needs of our land and our dead' (cited in Bullens 2021). At that time, anti-Semitism was mainstream and Barrès talked about racial purity, which also explains why the theory became so popular among the Nazis, among others (Mondon, cited in Bullens 2021). After the Second World War, the French far right replaced the explicitly biologically racist overtones of this story with a focus on culture and ethnicity.

While versions of the Replacement Theory could be found in different right-wing circles for over a century, it was the French philosopher and writer Renaud Camus who re-popularised it in his 2011 book called *Le Grand Remplacement* (The Great Replacement) (Cosentino 2020, 74). The term itself was coined by Renaud Camus in that book. Upon presenting his ideas at a meeting titled 'Assises de la Remigration' (Annual Meeting on Remigration) in Paris in 2014, he became one of the most influential ideologues of the European Nouvelle Droite (New Right) and its youth wing, the Identitarian movement, which advocates an ethnically and culturally homogenous Europe and is one of Europe's fastest growing far-right movements with offshoots in countries such as Austria, Germany, Italy, Denmark, Norway, the UK and Ireland (Davey and Ebner 2019, 8). Among those inspired by Camus in France, one can count Eric Zemmour, the far right 2022 presidential candidate who propagated the Replacement Theory in his own books *Le Suicide Français* (The French Suicide) and *Destin Français* (French Destiny) (Bullens 2021).

Camus claims that due to lower birth rates, French natives are slowly being replaced by Muslim immigrants, who have higher birth rates (Bergmann 2021, cited in Ekman 2022, 4). For Camus, immigrants, particularly Muslim immigrants, are 'remplacants'. They are alien elements in French society and culture even if they claim to belong to France since, for Camus, they do not possess the 'cultural essence' that would make them French (Ekman 2022, 4). To the contrary, Camus claims, if Muslims can be French, then, 'to be French has become meaningless, and France has been reduced to a territory' (Bracke and Hernandez-Aguilar 2020, 686, cited in Ekman 2022, 4). While Camus mostly focuses on France in his book, he also argues that mass migration is eroding European civilisation from within by replacing European natives with migrants, particularly Muslims (Önnerfors 2021, cited in Ekman 2022, 4).

What Camus often refers to as 'genocide by substitution' corresponds to the view that 'an elitist group is colluding against white French and European people to eventually replace them with non-Europeans from Africa and the Middle East, the majority of whom are Muslim' (Bullens 2021). Camus claims that technocracies in France and in Europe more generally and a transnational elite that Camus calls the 'Davos-cracy' (after the Davos Conference) are responsible for engineering a plan that aims at replacing White Europeans with immigrants, particularly with those from Muslim countries (Wilson 2019, cited in Cosentino 2020, 75). This plan serves the interest of the elites consisting of liberal politicians and business executives, he argues, as it enables them to turn workers into replaceable units without connections to homeland or cultural heritage (Cosentino 2020, 75).

As it is seen, like other accounts of the Replacement Theory, the process narrated under Camus' version is not told as a natural occurrence but rather as an intentional and orchestrated process, with elites being the mastermind in this process, at the expense of the people. As Cosentino (2020, 60) argues, 'the "Great Replacement" conspiracy theory is discussed as a narrative of victimization of people of White ethnicity, serving as an ideological framework for a growing wave of violent actions by White nationalists worldwide'.

The Great Replacement Theory is strongly affiliated with other stories popular among white supremacist, ethno nationalist and nativist circles, including the stories of 'White Genocide' and 'Eurabia' (Davey and Ebner 2019, 7). Ideas associated with White Genocide have been thriving among neo-Nazi circles since the 1980s (Ekman 2022, 5; see also Askanius 2021). The term 'White Genocide' was popularised by white supremacist David Lane in his 1995 *White Genocide Manifesto* in the US, who claimed that white populations are being replaced through immigration, miscegenation, forced assimilation with non-white immigrants, abortion and violence against white people (Davey and Ebner 2019, 7; Cosentino 2020, 75). Proponents of White Genocide blame Jewish elites for masterminding the plot (Cosentino 2020, 75), who, they argue, want to 'weaken and dominate the White population' (Allington and Joshi 2020, cited in Ekman 2022, 5). Instead of the term White Genocide, which is common among the extreme right in the US, in German-speaking countries, due to historical reasons, references to race and genocide are avoided and words such as *Volkstod* (the death of the people) or *Umvolkung* ('ethnicity inversion') are used instead (Botsch and Kopke 2018, cited in Goetz 2021, 63). These terms have more recently been replaced by the term 'Great Replacement', that is used as a synonym with the other terms (Goetz 2021, 66). While White Genocide relies mostly on explicit anti-Semitism and the Great Replacement Theory focuses on more cultural narratives and is openly Islamophobic (Davey and Ebner 2019, 7; Cosentino 2020, 75), there is a discernable 'historical lineage between older anti-Semitic fantasies of "white genocide", and the more refined contemporary "replacement" conspiracy theory' as evident in the use of empty signifiers such as 'the global elites' in place of the Jews (Ekman 2022, 5).

The concept of 'Eurabia' (heavily referenced by the Norwegian terrorist Anders Breivik, along with the Replacement Theory) was introduced by Bat Ye'or (aka Gisèle Littman) in the early 2000s and refers to the claim that Western countries are slowly being brought under Islamic rule (Davey and Ebner 2019, 7). As Ekman (2022, 5) argues, 'the idea of a foreign colonization by, or a shadow government of, Muslims in Europe are key elements of the Eurabia conspiracy formulated by Bat Ye'or' (see also Bangstad 2019; Carr 2006). According to the story, this 'silent Muslim take-over is facilitated by liberal and/or left-wing politicians, who in various ways enable the replacement by secret agreements with Muslim organizations and/or nations and actors' (Ekman 2022, 5). As it is seen, this story offers its audience internal enemies as well as external enemies. The internal allies of the Muslim colonisers are said to benefit from this takeover (Ekman 2022, 5), as was also argued by Camus.

The common themes of the Great Replacement Theory as well as White Genocide and Eurabia, which are stories that have 'antecedents in right-wing politics during the decolonization era in Europe and in post-Civil War America', have recently become central tenets of the global white supremacist discourse, the motivating factors behind terrorist attacks and cornerstones to the rhetoric of right-wing political parties and populist movements in the West (Cosentino 2020, 75). As Miller-Idriss (2020, 9) argues, 'In its most extreme iterations, far-right extremists rely on three overlapping dystopian fantasy theories: the "great replacement" (used globally), white genocide (used predominantly in the United States), and "Eurabia" (used primarily in

Europe).' It is to the public circulation of such narratives through politicians and public figures that we now turn.

Exclusionary Narratives in Action: The Public Life of the Great Replacement Theory

Conspiracy theories, including the Replacement Theory, are useful tools for populist politicians. Conspiracy theories assume that there is deliberate and evil action behind certain events, which suggests that there are conspirators on the one side and victims on the other. Usefully for the populists, the conspirators are associated with a small but powerful group of elites and victims are associated with 'the people' (Barkun 2013; Butter 2020; Ekman 2022). The storyline proposed by the Replacement Theory victimises the in-group and produces an 'us versus them' distinction based on that. In this case, a common, victimised 'us' consisting of white people, or a particular sub-category of them (the French, the Europeans), are juxtaposed against 'them', meaning the traitorous politicians, powerful elites and immigrants (Ekman 2022, 5). Hence, it is not surprising that many observers of contemporary politics have noted the role elements of the Replacement narrative play in the politics of right-wing populists such as in the case of Trump along with other right-wing populists, particularly in Europe (Berger 2018; Cosentino 2020). Due to such politicians, 'Conspiracy theories are not anymore marginal, niche discourses relegated to an inferior epistemic status, but have gained legitimacy as alternative explanations for social and political problems' (Cosentino 2020, 84).

As Confessore and Yourish (2022) note, Replacement Theory, 'once confined to the digital fever swamps of Reddit message boards and semi-obscure white nationalist sites, has gone mainstream'. The authors particularly stress that the fear that white Americans may lose their majority has been forcefully argued in the conservative media and politics, including congressional hearings and Republican campaign advertisements and involving right-wing candidates and media personalities. They cite an Associated Press poll (P-NORC Center for Public Affairs Research 2022) that finds that one in three American adults believe that there is an effort 'to replace native-born Americans with immigrants for electoral gains'. The same poll also found that 'people who mostly watched right-wing media outlets like Fox News, One America News

Network and Newsmax were more likely to believe in Replacement Theory than those who watched CNN or MSNBC'.

Focusing on European politicians, Davey and Ebner (2019, 16) found that the Great Replacement Theory has penetrated the far-right circles of politicians and political commentators who made both 'explicit and implicit references to the idea of an orchestrated "invasion of the Occident"'. For example, Davey and Ebner (2019) discuss how the former Austrian Vice Chancellor H. C. Strache of the FPÖ posted on Facebook in 2016 and 2017 that 'the Great Replacement had already taken place under the governments of the SPÖ/ÖVP/Greens' and that in an interview with the newspaper *Kronen Zeitung* in April 2019 he pledged to 'continue the battle against the Great Replacement'. Similarly, Davey and Ebner (2019) discuss the 2018 interview of the leading Alternative for Germany (AfD) politician Björn Höcke's mentioning of the conspiracy theory and warning of the 'impeding death of the people through Great Replacement'. In the case of Belgium, Davey and Ebner (2019) show that Dries Van Langenhove, frontrunner of the Belgian far-right populist party Vlaams Belang in the 2019 European Parliament elections, regularly posted about 'the replacement' on social media. In France, Davey and Ebner (2019) refer to the 2016 tweet of Marion Maréchal-Le Pen, niece of Marine Le Pen and former National Assembly member in southern France: '#GreatReplacement: it's a truth in a number of territories in France'. Davey and Ebner (2019, 18) also document cases illustrating how politicians across North America and Europe use 'language which mirrors that of proponents of the Great Replacement theory and related concepts'. For the years 2018 and 2019, they find the following, high profile, examples: Hungarian Prime Minister Viktor Orban described refugees as 'Muslim invaders' and blamed Jewish philanthropic investor Soros for orchestrating the migration crisis; the Italian Deputy Prime Minister Matteo Salvini claimed to have halted the 'migrant invasion'; the president of the Spanish far-right Vox party in Andalucía, Francisco Serrano, tweeted that refuges and Islamic radicals were planning the invasion of Europe for years; an AfD Berlin campaign poster for the 2019 European Parliament elections read, 'Learning from Europe's history. . . so that Europe will not become Eurabia'; US President Trump referred to migrants as 'invaders' on several occasions and has previously retweeted Twitter accounts which promote the White Genocide theory.

Among the politicians and movements that deploy the replacement narrative for right-wing populist ends, Obaidi *et al.* (2021, 2–3) count co-leader of the far-right AfD Alexander Gauland, the former leader of the Danish People's Party Pia Kjærsgaard, the Prime Minister of Hungary Viktor Orbán, the Italian Interior Minister Matteo Salvini, the leader of the far-right movement Rassemblement National (formerly Front National) Marine Le Pen, German anti-Muslim organisation PEGIDA, and the European white-nativist movement Generation Identity. These actors deploy the Great Replacement Theory despite the fact that scholars dismissed the demographic projections that form the basis of the Great Replacement Theory as erroneous and non-scientific (see Alba 2018; Alba, Rumbaut and Marotz 2005 cited in Obaidi *et al.* 2021, 3).

In what follows, we will dive deeper into prominent examples from Europe and from the US that are particularly notorious for giving credence to and perpetuating the narrative of the Great Replacement. We will particularly focus on Trump and the Republican Party in the US and the far-right movements in German-speaking countries as in the illustrations.

The Great Replacement Theory in German-speaking Countries

Based on their textual analysis of ten relevant and dominant social-media currents and actors from the spectrum of conspiracy theorists, right-wing extremists and right-wing populists in Germany, including the sites of the AfD's 'Lügenpresse' (The Lying Press) and PI-News ('Politically Incorrect') pages, along with the Identitaren Bewegung and PEGIDA sites, Baldauf *et al.* (2017, 9) find that the narratives present on the websites can be clustered under seven of what they call 'framing narratives'. These framing narratives are listed as the downfall of the German people, external threats, internal threats, the manipulative establishment, global conspiracy, resistance and solutions, and the repression of resistance. The authors argue that jointly, these framing narratives 'create a coherent pattern and represent elements of a meta-narrative that forms the overarching center of the far-right and populist-right explanatory world'.

Baldauf *et al.* (2017, 10) detect that at the heart of these framing narratives lies the dystopian scenario that forms the backdrop against which the framing narratives are given their context: 'there is a conspiracy against the Germans and the aim of this conspiracy is their destruction'. In this conspiracy narrative, where the main perpetuators are 'a global elite that lords over the press and politics, using them as instruments for the eradication of the Germans', the means of destruction are not open war but rather means such as extermination via mass immigration and Islamisation, re-education and the undermining of the resistance. The authors argue that this scenario arouses anxieties and encourages a compulsion to take action (Baldauf *et al.* 2017, 10).

Baldauf *et al.* (2017, 17) find that the story is seldom told with that clarity and in a fixed manner. Rather, they detect twenty-seven narrations that are based on the framing narratives yet tell these narratives in different fashions. These include, for instance, 'the narrative of the coming decline of the German people' in which the conception of 'genocide' through 'foreign infiltration' or the 'great replacement' is widespread, which includes both external enemies, as well as internal ones, particularly the elites in charge.

These narratives provide crucial political leverage for far-right actors in German-speaking countries as well as elsewhere and they have important political implications. The Great Replacement narrative serves crucial functions for far-right movements such as the Identitarian movement. As Goetz (2021, 70–1) argues, their Great Replacement campaign initiated in 2014 helped the group gain broader social attention and growing recognition. Goetz (2021, 70–1) contends that by continuously repeating the Great Replacement with its framing narrative along with a number of spectacular actions that were covered in daily newspapers, the Identitarians were able to motivate other right-wing and right-wing extremist actors and politicians to join them, which helped further popularise the term and the narrative. As Baldauf *et al.* (2017, 18) argue, 'without the transformation into a concise narrative, the idea that secret forces are working to eradicate the white population of Europe would certainly be much easier to recognize as a delusional conspiracy theory, which would remove the basis for discussing it'.

The usefulness of the replacement narrative is also acknowledged by figures such as Martin Sellner, long-time leader of the Austrian Identitarians, who, in an interview, stated that the term had the ability to describe 'in a communicable and yet vivid way what is really behind Islamization, infiltration, foreign violence etc.' and that it enabled them to 'unite our camp by providing a clear image of the enemy' (Wegner 2015, cited in Goetz 2021, 66).

In addition to being useful in making the far right more acceptable and more resonant to the broader public, the Replacement narrative also manages to compel its proponents toward greater internal unity. As Baldauf *et al.* (2017, 17) note, the right-wing populists, in the face of the alleged threat of the 'great replacement', call for a 'a homogeneous body politic that can stand together in the struggle against this imagined threat'. While creating an internally unified front, the Replacement narrative at the same time fortifies the borders of the 'other', binding together a set of enemies into an amalgam of complete 'other' through the threads of the story. Taking the far-right group Identitarian (founded in German-speaking countries in 2012 following the example of the French *Génération identitaire*) as a case and focusing particularly on their 2014 campaign called '*Stoppt den Großen Austausch*' ('Stop the Great Replacement') which was initiated by their Austrian chapter (IBÖ), Goetz (2021) demonstrates the multi-faceted implications of the Great Replacement narrative. As Goetz (2021, 61) observes, the far right tries to merge different enemies (Islam, feminism, LGBTQ+, the EU, the Left, etc.) 'within the framework narrative of the "exchange of populations"' (see also Davey and Ebner 2019). The threat scenario narrated by the Identitarians, which alleges that people are being threatened from within and without through lower birth rates and 'foreign infiltration' manages to declare both feminism and Islamisation as the enemies of the people simultaneously, implying a common strategic approach between the two (Goetz 2021).

In addition, the Great Replacement narrative also assigns the members of the community certain (gendered) missions. Right-wing extremist policy proposals that rely on Replacement Theory or White Genocide often refer to agendas of population policy, which involve a reproduction policy (Goetz 2021, 61). These policy proposals are strongly linked with assigned gender roles and relations: 'While men are supposed to avert the "exchange of populations" by means of valiant combativeness, women are supposed to do their part by having more children' (Goetz 2021, 65). In the doomsday scenarios created by groups such as the Identitarians for their 'own people', group members are presented as the last generation that can prevent the 'great replacement' and as responsible for saving the Occident from its demise through swift and decisive action (Goetz 2021, 66, 68).

What men can do under this scenario is to regain their valiant combativeness allegedly mostly destroyed by the 1968 generation (due to anti-authoritarian upbringing, liberalism, feminism, homosexuality, etc.) and to undertake 'natural masculine tasks' such as 'protecting the fatherland, the people and the women' from the invoked threats (Goetz 2021, 68). On the other hand, the Identitarian movement attributes women the mission to prevent 'the great replacement' by having children, thereby mainly reducing their roles to motherhood (Goetz 2021, 67). Women are also blamed for enabling the great replacement since they vote significantly more for liberal or left-wing parties than men (Goetz 2021, 67, 70). The third role attributed to women in these narratives is the role of the victim, particularly threatened by the sexualised violence of men defined as foreign (Goetz 2021, 68–9).

Within the context of the Replacement Theory, the ageing of the population is also interpreted as the 'absence of young, virile men, which is said to contribute to the weakening of the people by undermining their defensive potential and their ability to compete in economic and more general terms' (Goetz 2021, 61).

Goetz (2021, 68) notes that, in line with the expectations, well-known Identitarian activist women such as Melanie Schmitz, Ingrid Weiß or Alina Wychera became mothers themselves and celebrated this on social media as a great achievement in line with their mission. Goetz illustrates the pro-natalist and familist (and I would add, heteronormative) approach of the German Identitarians with the following statement of the organisation (Identitäre Bewegung Deutschland 2017, cited in Goetz 2021, 68):

> The most wonderful of all gifts is new-born life, which is the blessed offspring of the love between man and woman, which makes a family and binds it at its innermost core . . . This gives us the opportunity to see ourselves as a unique moment and as part of a continuous, communal narration and experience, opening us up for a deeply-felt connection with those who have preceded us, making us one with our ancestors.

The Replacement narrative also has implications for abortion rights debates as the use of the far-right slogan '*Lebensschutz ist Heimatschutz!*' ('Pro-life is pro-homeland!') by the Identitarians also illustrates (Goetz 2021, 66).

The Great Replacement Theory in the US

In the US case, former president Trump, some parts of the Republican Party close to Trump, and political commentators, again, closely associated with Trump and with the more exclusionary part of the Republican Party, are among the key proponents of the Replacement narrative.

Throughout his political career, Trump repeatedly presented the story of immigration in the US as one of invasion in which the American people were put under threat. He tweeted that Americans should be angry with 'the millions of illegals taking over America'. His campaign ads repeatedly attributed Trump the mission to 'stop the invasions' (Baker and Shear 2019). Trump recurrently warned Americans about being under attack by immigrants who were heading for the border. As he once put it, 'You look at what is marching up, that is an invasion! That is an invasion!' (Baker and Shear 2019; see also Cineas 2022).

Pape, a leading scholar on the intersection of warfare and politics and director of the University of Chicago Project on Security and Threats, in his interview with Gellman (2021), draws worrying similarities between Milosevic and Trump arguing that Milosevic inspired bloodshed by appealing to Serbia's perceived loss of dominance against upstart minorities in his 1989 speech, for example, that claimed 'Muslims in Kosovo and generally throughout the former Yugoslavia are essentially waging genocide on the Serbs'. According to Pape, Milosevic did not use the word 'replaced' but that would be the contemporary version of what he said (Gellman 2021).

Trump's language is echoed by his supporters such as the Arizona senator Wendy Rogers who tweeted that the US was being replaced and invaded by illegal immigrants (Confessore and Yourish 2022). Relatedly, Republican senator Ron Johnson claimed that Democrats deliberately encouraged immigration in order to ensure electoral victory and support (Ekman 2022, 6).

Tucker Carlson, the most popular personality on Fox News is known for repeatedly expressing the idea that 'white Anglo-Saxons' are being replaced by immigrant populations (Åsard 2021, cited in Ekman 2022, 6) and for telling stories associated with the Great Replacement as evident in the following quote:

> I know that the left and all the gatekeepers on Twitter become literally hysterical if you use the term 'replacement', if you suggest the Democratic Party is trying to replace the current electorate, the voters now casting ballots, with

new people, more obedient voters from the Third World. But they become hysterical because that's what's happening, actually, let's just say it. That's true. (cited in Bauder 2022)

The effect of narratives can be seen very visibly in the case of the Replacement Theory. Policy-wise, the way one draws a storyline and the way one defines the actors in the story have significant implication for the way one deals with an issue. This is very explicit in the case of the immigration discourse and policy. As evident in the case of Trump, once you see immigrants as 'invaders' then it is justified to build a wall, to treat immigrants in inhumane ways, and to feel the obligation to combat immigrants to protect your own people. Naturally, when Trump was arguing for the border wall between Mexico and the US, he employed the term 'invaders' in his inflammatory rhetoric about immigrants (Confessore and Yourish 2022). One campaign ad by Trump read:

We have an INVASION! So we are BUILDING THE WALL to STOP IT. Dems will sue us. But we want a SAFE COUNTRY!

It's CRITICAL that we STOP THE INVASION. Nancy Pelosi and Democrats have not negotiated in good faith to fund a wall at our Southern Border, proving that OBSTRUCTION is far more important to them than YOUR SAFETY . . . (cited in Baker and Shear 2019)

These examples are not limited to Trump alone. In his attempt to sponsor anti-immigration policies not only for Hungary but also for the entire EU, Hungarian Prime Minister Orban relied on the replacement narrative. He framed immigration as an existential threat. He argued that 'if Europe is not going to be populated by Europeans in the future and we take this as given, then we are speaking about an exchange of populations, to replace the population of Europeans with others' and claimed that '[t]here are political forces in Europe who want a replacement of population for ideological or other reasons' (Walker 2019, cited in Ekman 2022, 5). As Polletta and Callahan (2017) argue, one of the advantages of narratives is that once a story is told and made widespread, you do not even have to tell the story in its complete form every time. These stories can be 'referred to often by way of their protagonist' as is the case with references to the 'welfare queen' and 'anchor babies', among others. In our case, simple references to 'invaders' can fulfil the purpose of the story without having to tell the entire story.

As the next section shows, the Replacement narrative not only provides justification for anti-immigration policies but also gives an ideological framework that provides justification through its narrative for violent actions (Bélanger *et al.* 2019, cited in Obaidi *et al.* 2021).

Replacement Theory and Political Violence

In two correlational studies and one experiment based on the Scandinavian cases of Denmark and Norway, Obaidi *et al.* (2021) provide evidence that elements of Replacement Theory are associated with the persecution of Muslims, violent intentions and Islamophobia, and they show that such associations are mediated through symbolic threats. Facts on the ground support this argument in a very sad and shocking manner. The Replacement Theory fuelled violent and hostile events such as the 2017 right-wing rally in Charlottesville, Virginia, that erupted into violence (Confessore and Yourish 2022). Even more extreme, in 2018, a white man with a history of antisemitic Internet posts killed eleven worshippers in a Pittsburgh synagogue, blaming Jews for allowing immigrant 'invaders' in the US (Confessore and Yourish 2022). An Australian far-right terrorist and white supremacist circulated a seventy-four-page manifesto via Twitter and on 8chan titled 'The Great Replacement', before killing fifty-one people in two separate attacks on mosques in Christchurch, New Zealand on 15 March 2019 (Cosentino 2020, 74). The manifesto included statements like: 'We are experiencing an invasion on a level never seen before in history. Millions of people pouring across our borders, legally. Invited by the state and corporate entities to replace the White people' (Cosentino 2020, 75). The terrorist accused liberal politicians of 'deliberately engineering the extinction or replacement of White Westerners through mass immigration of non-Whites' (Obaidi *et al.* 2021, 2).

The same year, another white man killed twenty-three people in an attack at an El Paso shop in the US. The shooter was angry about the 'the Hispanic invasion of Texas' and was seeking to kill Mexicans, according to what he later told the police (Confessore and Yourish 2022). The El Paso shooter also posted a manifesto on 8chan and he, too, referenced the Great Replacement conspiracy theory (Cosentino 2020, 79) arguing that he was 'simply defending my country from cultural and ethnic replacement brought on by an invasion' (Obaidi *et al.* 2021, 16). Most recently, in May 2022 in Buffalo, a white man again, killed ten people at a supermarket in a predominantly African American neighbourhood. In a 180-page-long text, posted online before the attack, he claimed that the shoppers he attacked came from a culture that sought to 'ethnically replace my own people'. As Confessore and Yourish (2022) put it, 'reflecting the most extreme versions of replacement theory, the suspect deemed Black people, like immigrants, as "replacers": people who "invade our lands, live on our soil, live on government support and attack and replace our people"'. The Anti-Defamation League, in a detailed analysis for the *New York Times*, found that the perpetuator plagiarised almost two-thirds of his text from the manifesto of the 2019 terrorist responsible for the Christchurch attacks (Confessore and Yourish 2022).

The events related to the Replacement narrative can unfortunately be multiplied. As Davey and Ebner (2019, 5) argue,

> The Great Replacement theory is able to inspire calls for extreme action from its adherents, ranging from non-violent ethnic cleansing through 'remigration' to genocide. This is in part because the theory is able to inspire a sense of urgency by calling on crisis narratives.

As Cosentino (2020, 79) argues, the recent sequence of violent actions by the white ethnonationalists present a pattern 'with imageboards and other fringe on-line venues serving as platform of radicalization, ideological support and inspiration that travel across borders, and memes and conspiracy theories serving as a common language and discourse' (see also Davey and Ebner 2019). This way, they go beyond being solely American or European political narratives and turn into a 'call to arms to protect what is seen as the white race on a transnational level' (Schwartzburg 2019, cited in Cosentino 2020, 79).

As we discussed above, it is not only the development of the Replacement Theory over the Internet that is responsible for its propagation. Rather, politicians, social media figures, political commentators and so on are taking part in perpetuating the narrative and spreading it to a wider audience at the same time giving credibility to it. These are the ones responsible for mainstreaming the Great Replacement Theory 'by making explicit and implicit references to the conspiracy theory in their speeches, social media posts and policies' (Davey and Ebner 2019, 5).

The Replacement Theory also relies on narratives that are economic, historical and patriarchal. Aside from the valorisation of the economic repercussion of 'foreign invasions', the story refers to historical battles and struggles with the non-Western world in presenting the current struggles as a continuation of the past while at the same time demonstrating the 'evil nature' of the 'other'. Examples discussed in Chapter 4 with regard to the Austrian and Hungarian cases illustrated the use of historical narratives well. These narratives, such as the ones about the Sieges of Vienna by the Ottomans, present a fertile ground for the Replacement Theory. Thus, it should not come as a surprise that violent acts in the name of preventing the 'replacement of the White people' present selective elements of the past. For example, the Christchurch terrorist seems to be obsessed with the religious conflicts between Islam and Christianity in Europe, particularly in the Balkans. His soundtrack during his self-recorded drive to the Christchurch mosques included a nationalist Serbian song from the 1992–5 Bosnian war glorifying Serbian fighters and the genocidal former Bosnian Serb political leader Radovan Karadzic. What is more, he named the rifles he used after 'legendary Serbs and Montenegrins who fought against the 500-year-rule of the Muslim Ottomans in the Balkans, written in the Cyrillic alphabet used by the two Orthodox Christian nations' (Gec 2019).

The role political narratives such as the Great Replacement Theory play in the rise of authoritarian, exclusionary and homogenising political figures, parties and movements, as well as their role in authoritarian, inhumane measures taken and violent political acts committed, make the question of countering such narratives more urgent than ever. The next section focuses on discussions related to such narratives that can counter authoritarian, restrictive and homogenising politics.

Countering Authoritarian Political Narratives

Cosentino (2020, 84) argues that conspiracy theories are symptoms of a power crisis, which he defines as 'the crisis of political power and of its representative institutions, from the media to cultural-scientific institutions'. He believes that it is this crisis that leads 'marginal, unorthodox political narratives to breach into the public conversation'. Cosentino (2020, 85) maintains that the conspiracy theories that share the theme of a globalist elite of liberal politicians acting secretly to undermine the people of white ethnicity could be seen as a popular narrative that 'disenfranchised White Westerners tell themselves to process their cultural and political crisis and exorcise their fear of an irreversible decline'. Others have, in different ways, attributed the rise of far-right parties to some crises in the political system of liberal democracies. Depending on how the crisis was defined, the policies and politics proposed varied. While some argued that the crisis of liberal democracy stems from economic grievances, others focused on cultural ones, or both combined.

How authoritarian, discriminatory and exclusionary politicians, particularly right-wing populists, can be countered is the subject of heated debate, particularly amongst the Left and the liberals. While some argue that focusing on economic issues is the answer, others point out that issues of recognition also need to be addressed. While many are not explicit about the role political narratives can play, a small part of the literature focuses precisely on the role of narratives in countering authoritarian, exclusionary narratives as will be discussed in further detail below. In what follows, we will first discuss the debates regarding countering populism. We will then turn to the role of political narratives in the struggle against populism.

Countering Populists

One important centre of gravity for strategies to oppose populism, particularly right-wing populism, which is haunting many parts of the world, including Europe and the US, consists of the role social democracy can play in this process. The reasons for this are manifold. Populism stands as an alternative path to the success of the Left for some, and it also appears to be social democracy's main electoral rival. At the same time, social democratic leaders are not immune to the lures of populism either and within social democratic parties, the threat of populism is also always present. While some populist traits (such as charismatic leadership or the claim to represent the disadvantaged) can exist in every political movement, it is when these traits mix with the distinguishing characteristics of populism, particularly its presentation of the leader as the embodiment of the will of the people, its Manichean outlook to politics and its disdain for political institutions, that leaders become populist and carry the potential to be inimical to democracy in general and social democracy in particular.

There are some distinguishing factors of social democracy that set it apart from populism. Social democracy is an advocate of redistribution and social protection from market insecurities. It tries to do this without overthrowing the capitalist system altogether. It accepts liberal democracy's respect for individual rights and liberties as well as its commitment to competitive elections but it is at the same time concerned with reducing social and economic inequality, and providing social rights to citizens via state authority (Roberts 2008). It is the emphasis put on pluralism and democracy that distinguishes social democracy from populism (Roberts 2008), whose constitutive elements are as discussed earlier, a Manichean anti-establishment discourse and a mass support base combined with a leader who is seen as the embodiment of 'the will of the people' and who builds vertical ties that by-pass institutions.[1]

While for some scholars and thinkers inequalities and lack of representation in contemporary democratic politics can only be resolved with left populism that enables hitherto excluded groups to mobilise against inequality, injustice and lack of proper representation (Laclau 2005; Mouffe 2018), many opponents of this idea have shown that the risks of populism are too high to make it a viable option. Populism targets democratic institutions and attacks pluralism as 'the people and the nation speak with one voice, that of a small clique of politicians and ultimately the voice of the leader' (de la Torre 2019, 68; see also Müller 2016). Populist leaders claim to have unmediated ties to 'the people' and therefore often disregard institutions once they are in power, either by dissolving them altogether or turning them into auxiliaries for their power (Weyland 1996). Arato (2013, 167) exposes the risks of Laclau's populism by pointing at the authoritarian implications of the characteristics attributed to populist leaders and Cohen (2019, 398) stresses the elective affinity between populism and competitive authoritarianism as populism is not conducive to a plural civil or political society and instead leads to the expansion of personal power, the delegitimisation of the opposition, and the destruction of democracy.

Debates have been heightened as left populism has risen, particularly in the south European context, as evident in the cases ranging from Podemos to Syriza. Kioupkiolis (2016, 111) for example, notes how in the case of Podemos populism reinforced vertical tendencies in the movement whose prominent figures transformed from 'nodal points of popular unity' to 'leaders who direct their parties in an authoritative style'. What started as a horizontal grassroots movement in early 2014 turned into a plebiscitary relationship between the leader and his followers, shifting 'the notion of the "people" . . . from an open and participative multitude of active citizenry to a passive and homogeneous mass led by an elite'.[2]

Social Democracy and Issues of Redistribution and Recognition

The loss of social democracy's traditional power basis (the large working classes of the industrial age) as a result of capitalist restructuring as well as the challenges of rising new social movements and identity-based activism in the post-Cold War world led to a changing landscape in the Left (Eley 2002; Therborn 2018). Political theorists such as Iris Marion Young (1990) have simultaneously criticised the reduction of social justice to social distribution and argued for the accommodation of group difference, while scholars of party politics such as Kitschelt (1994, 285) have pointed out that social democratic parties need to transform themselves to accommodate 'libertarian concerns with individual self-realization and communitarian participation' in light of recent changes.

In response, while scholars such as Hobsbawm (1996) have argued that the Left should move away from identity politics and stick to economic issues, Fraser (1999) has called for a comprehensive framework that can integrate redistribution and recognition in order to fight injustice on both fronts.[3]

Those who call for a renewed interest in issues of redistribution are primarily concerned with the fact that identity politics leads to the abandonment of broader systematic problems such as rising income inequality that perpetuate societal inequalities. Reed and Chowkwanyun (2012, 169) believe that if we see discrimination as the only real injustice, then we are in fact playing into the hands of the capitalist system, as there is no basis left to talk about economic inequality and the remedy thereof. Similarly, Fraser (2000, 108) argues that the move from redistribution to recognition is happening at a time of increasing economic inequality and that 'questions of recognition are serving less to supplement, complicate and enrich redistributive struggles than to marginalize, eclipse and displace them'. The key political question as formulated by Fraser (1998, 10) thus becomes: 'How can one develop a coherent programmatic perspective that integrates redistribution and recognition' so as to bring about justice for all?

Another set of critiques (mostly focusing on the European experience) concerns the acceptance of the neoliberal economy by social democratic parties. Berman and Snegovaya (2019), for example, argue that the underlying reason that accounts for the global decline of the Left is its shift to the centre on economic issues and its acceptance of neoliberal reforms, which prevented the Left from becoming the voice of the grievances of the people against the neoliberal reforms and the 2008 financial crisis, and played into the hands of far-right and populist parties, which stressed cultural and social issues, instead of economic ones.

Scholars have stressed the need for social democracy to appeal to the socially disadvantaged groups with social protection and redistributive policies if they want to recover politically (Dostal 2017, 239; Berman 2020). Berman and Snegovaya (2019) argue that, if the Left is to succeed, it needs to offer a clear alternative by differentiating itself economically from the Right, and by decreasing the salience of social and cultural issues, and identities, on which right-wing populist parties thrive (Berman and Kundnani 2021, 34; also see Cuperus 2018). The multicultural Left is not an alternative for Berman (2016, 75), as she finds that the emphasis on 'politics of recognition' as opposed to the 'politics of redistribution' has diverted attention away from economic issues and has fragmented the Left thereby making it hard to build broad coalitions and win elections.

As Manwaring and Holloway (2021, 16) note, 'there is an ongoing tension between social democrats' "old" class politics, and balancing or supplanting these with the "new" identity politics' since social democratic parties 'appear uncertain as to how (and whether) to emphasize issues of underprivileged and minority groups amid the popularity of far-right parties (or centre-right parties acceding to far-right policy positions)' as they are rediscovering ways to restrain unfettered capitalism.

Given the threats of populism, the question of how the Left can best address the inequalities, injustices and lack of representation in the system becomes one of how to both create a broad appeal within society and mobilise groups around more egalitarian causes while at the same time keeping politics as the realm of plurality, and not succumbing to the Manichean and anti-institutionalist impulses of populism.

It is true that social democracy can play a pivotal role in democratisation. In the Turkish case, as well as in other increasingly authoritarian settings, social democracy, with its emphasis on institutions and justice, can occupy a central role in democratisation and can play a counterbalancing role against the threat of populism and competitive authoritarianism. Under these conditions, social democracy has the potential to mobilise voters not just on issues of redistribution and recognition but also those of democracy, institutionalism and pluralism, characteristics, which by its very ideological disposition, social democracy can rightfully claim (Eley 2002; Frega 2021). The democratic potential of social democracy, with its emphasis on institutions, organisation, inclusion and justice can serve as an important source of mobilisation and anchoring without succumbing to the monism and authoritarianism inherent in populism. The necessities of democracy and justice, both central pillars of social democracy, point to the need to have economic inequality at the centre of politics but also reveal that issues of identity and the recognition of identity-based injustices are not to be disregarded.

As the discussion in this section has shown, while social democracy offers various answers to the reasons behind the rise of right-wing populism and proposes certain solutions to counter it, there is not a systematic focus in the relevant literature on what role political narratives can play in this process. The next section will demonstrate that political narratives are crucial in not only countering populist claims but also in proposing alternative, more inclusive, democratic and pluralistic policies. These findings will show that social democratic projects also need to be able to find ways to narrate issues of social justice, equality, pluralism and democracy if such projects are to succeed.

Toward Narratives of Inclusion and Democracy in Politics

The historian Hayden White was among the forerunners in understanding the role narratives play for human beings. White (1980) argued that annals and chronicle forms of historical representation are not failed anticipations of 'the fully realized historical discourse that the modern history form is supposed to embody'. In other words, they are not less worthy forms in the discipline of History. Instead, they are alternatives to modern history writing, which comes in narrative form. White claimed that it is the modern historiographical community that has distinguished between annals, chronicle, and other forms of historical representation on the basis of their attainment of narrative fullness or failure to attain it. It is White's contention that historical narratives are not scientifically superior to annals and chronicles but historical narratives are dominant because the narrative form 'speaks to us, summons us from afar (this "afar" is the land of forms), and displays to us a formal coherency that we ourselves lack'. White adds that 'The historical narrative, as against the chronicle, reveals to us a world that is putatively "finished", done with, over, and yet not dissolved, not falling apart. In this world, reality wears the mask of a meaning, the completeness and fullness of which we can only imagine, never experience.' White, thus saw historical narratives' predominance in the history discipline as a result of humans' needs, motivations and desires rather than scientific superiority or a more realistic representation of the past.

Since then, other scholars, in different disciplines have noted the central role narratives play for human beings in making sense of the world and in giving meaning and direction to their lives. As Wibben (2010, 43) argues, in addition to being *homo significans* (meaning 'makers') for whom the world is only accessible through interpretations, human beings are also *homo fabulans* 'because we interpret and tell stories about our experiences, about who we are or want to be, and what we believe'. As she also adds, narratives are profoundly political because they both enable and limit our representation and these representations shape our world and what we believe is possible in it.

Ewick and Silbey (2003) claim that a chief means for extending the social consequences of resistance is through the transformation of an act of resistance into a story of resistance. because the act of storytelling extends temporally and socially what might otherwise be an individual, discrete and ephemeral transaction. In their analysis of narratives of resistance to law and legal authority, the authors find that by narratively taking a stance against the law, respondents not only reveal their understandings of power and identity, they also actively construct legality and subjectivity. The stories told by those resisting the law and legal authority include the selective appropriation of events, a particular event order, the positioning of character in relation to a situation of relative powerlessness, and a sense of closure that provides a moral evaluation. Through their stories, the respondents enact and communicate conceptions of self that insists on human agency and dignity.

Hayward (2010) argues that one way through which state actors teach citizens about collective identities is through teaching them to weave into their personal stories of 'who I am' shared or public narratives of 'who we are'. Using the example of racial identities in the twentieth-century United States, Hayward argues that when states institutionalise and objectify identity narratives, they lend them a resilience they would not otherwise enjoy. The solution against 'bad' stories (in the case she analyses these are racist stories) is not just to 'tell better stories', but also to intervene in the institutions in which bad stories are built.

Studies of past cases can be helpful in understanding the role that political narratives can play in power struggles to the advantage of those who tell such stories. Steinmetz (1992), in his analysis of the role of social narratives in working-class formation, argues that more successful cases of working-class formation involve the elaboration of coherent narratives about individual and collective history, stories that are coordinated with one another and that are organised around the category of social class.

Davis (2005), in his analysis of the Iraqi political elites, shows the role historical memory has played in their struggle to make their vision of Iraq hegemonic and thereby hold power. In a Gramscian fashion, Davis focuses on the competition between what he calls the 'Iraqist' and 'Pan-Arabist' hegemony aspiring groups in Iraq. Davis argues that as the pan-Arabists' success in the hegemonic struggle between the Iraqist and pan-Arabist visions in Iraq shows, those who can make better use of historical memory have more advantage in the struggle for hegemony. Though not directly engaging with narratives, Davis argues that political elites need to make their 'projects' about society appear 'commonsensical and natural' and as genuinely representing the populace's interest if they want to succeed. Historical memory is a very strong weapon in this hegemonic struggle precisely because of its ability to appear 'commonsensical and natural' and due to its covert and indirect nature.

In his analyses of why the Iraqists – who relied on a culturally inclusionary and ethnically diverse definition of an Iraqi nation – lost the battle against pan-Arabism, Davis argues that the strategies and priorities of the two camps were different and resonated differently with the Iraqi community. While the Iraqists focused solely on issues of social justice and being inspired by Western ideas, they did not put enough emphasis on Arab or rather, local elements, particularly the historical heritage of the country. The approach of the Iraqists was also fairly isolated and remained at the elite level. Iraqist groups talked to each other rather than to the public, thereby failing to fight an effective 'war of position'. The pan-Arabists Ba'athists on the other hand, relied on a continuation of the past and the 'glorious days' of the Iraqis. Davis claims that appeals to social issues such as social justice and class inequality are not enough and that the emotional needs of political communities, such as a sense of unity and self-confidence, have to be addressed too. While Davis does not connect his discussion to the role of narratives directly, given the fact that historical memory is disseminated through narratives, the crucial role of narratives for more democratic and inclusionary visions of peoplehood against the more authoritarian and exclusionary ones becomes visible.

Polletta (2009, viii), in her analysis of Bush's success in the 2004 elections contrary to the expectations of the Democrats, states that Republicans were successful because they 'gave voters villains and heroes; new characters in age-old dramas of threat, vengeance, and salvation', whereas Democrats 'ticked off a dry list of familiar issues'. Polletta and Callahan (2017) make similar observations regarding Trump's victory in 2016, arguing that storytelling's capacity to build collective identity makes it an enduring feature of politics. Going further into the mechanisms of the political narratives, they argue that the success of Trump did not win the election by telling a single story that 'knitted together Americans' fears, hopes, and anxieties in a compelling way'. Instead, his stories, arguments, slogans and claims 'drew on and reinforced already existing stories of cultural loss that . . . owed as much to what people heard about on TV and radio, remembered from childhood, and perceived their group as having experienced as it owed to what they directly experienced themselves'. Polletta and Callahan (2017) stress the importance of the contemporary media landscape which they argue made the features of storytelling even more important in the 2016 election. In addition to Trump, conservative media commentators within the growing 'industry of conservative commentary' increased the density of the stories by styling a personal relationship with their audiences 'in which allusive stories reinforced the bond between speaker and audience'. The audience was also able to share, like and comment on outrage stories due to the growth of user-shared digital 'news' stories, which reinforced the bonds of political partisanship through narratives.

The scholar who most systematically deals with the role narratives can play in countering what he calls pathological populism is Rogers Smith. His earlier works on stories of peoplehood show the role of narratives in building senses of peoplehood (Smith 2003; 2015). One of his most recent works, *This is not who we are! Populism and Peoplehood*, directly deals with good stories that can defeat exclusionary and authoritarian stories. Smith (2020) argues that nationalist populists so far have done a better job than liberals in providing their followers stories of peoplehood that support their worldview. These stories are 'ethnically defined, threatened by enemies, and blameless for its troubles, which come from its victimization by malign elites and foreigners'. It is his argument that liberals need to offer their own alternative stories that support inclusive values. These more positive, more egalitarian and inclusive stories of national peoplehood should counter authoritarian populisms and they should engage with the anxieties and resentments articulated by the populists (Smith 2020, 6, 9).

Against those who solely focus on material interest in politics, Smith (2020, 6) argues that such conceptions of interests, as well as desirable forms of power and force 'inevitably gain content from larger stories of our identities, even if some are more explicit and elaborate than others'. In parallel with our discussion on social democracy, Smith (2020, 53) argues that 'good policies must be part of all effective responses to pathological populisms. But policies are less persuasive – they can seem like arbitrary laundry lists – when they do not gain meaning and legitimacy from a broader narrative of national identity and purpose'. While he argues that good stories will have specific details regarding a 'wide range of policies, laws, and institutions that can respond to the most deeply felt needs and aspirations of community members', they also need to 'provide understandings of why those policies, laws, and institutions are appropriate for that people and their hopes and needs, why those measures can be expected to work, and why they can be deemed morally right' (Smith 2020, 10).

Citing Yuval Harari's bestseller book *Sapiens* (2015) in which the author argues for the importance of narratives in enabling large-scale cooperation through humanity's history, Smith (2020, 20–1) focuses specifically on how narratives appealing to the national identity of people will enable politicians to bring about more support for inclusionary and pluralistic policies. He argues that political leaders need to 'elaborate not just narratives of human values, goals, and strategies for realizing them, but stories of political peoplehood, defining what they hope their audiences will accept as the best account of the identities of their particular political societies'. Smith (2020, 9) argues that good stories must 'give voice to people's existing senses of aspects of themselves that they most value' while at the same time expressing respect and generosity toward others. Since, he argues, 'the most dominant, familiar stories of political peoplehood for most of the world's inhabitants are narratives of nation-states', it is precisely such stories that will resonate most with most of the people. While nationalist populists tell such nationalist stories in ways that assign blame to factors such as forces of economic globalisation, to racial, ethnic, and religious minorities and immigrants, we need to find ways of countering them with stories that appeal to the sense of national identity of the people (Smith 2020, 49–50).

Smith (2020, 51) argues that good stories need to be resonant, respectful and reticulated (namely, patterned networks that are open to many contents):

> Political stories must take people where they are, drawing on existing senses of identity and values and speaking to felt needs and grievances. But they must also incorporate respect for all persons, and a spirit of accommodation expressed in support for pluralism and policies that accord people different, reticulated treatment according to their different circumstances and aspirations.

Smith believes that with such narratives of political identity, it will be possible for us to say to proponents of cruelty 'that is not who we are!' – or, at least, 'that is not who we want to be or who we are trying to be' (Smith 2020, 61). Within the American context, Smith (2020, 8) argues, for instance, that Trump's 'America First' visions of national peoplehood can be countered by 'more egalitarian, inclusive stories that draw on American traditions of democracy; the Constitution's quest for a more perfect union; and the project, set forth in the Declaration of Independence, of creating forms of government that can secure basic rights for all'.

Talking specifically about the countering of the Replacement narrative, Baldauf *et al.* (2017) first make a clear case that far-right movements are strengthened by the replacement narrative, as discussed above, and then they propose that the telling of 'democracy narratives' is the only way to counter such 'toxic narratives'. Based on the findings of their research, Baldauf *et al.* (2017, 18) conclude that the source of effectiveness of the alternative right-wing media landscape lies in 'well-told, carefully placed and widely multiplied narratives'. These narratives are offered in different variants and guises and are adapted to new circumstances. The authors argue that such narratives used within the alternative right-wing scene help 'emotionally anchor, confirm and reinforce certain world views', while at the same time they also aid their proponents in argumentation 'conveyed to the comment boxes of the media landscape throughout Germany, from the Tagesschau to the Süddeutsche Zeitung' thereby enabling the dissemination of far-right ideology far beyond their own circles. It is here where Baldauf *et al.* (2017, 19) see the disadvantage of democracy as democracy adheres to fair debates and allows the publication and discussion of even controversial contents. Under these conditions, 'the alarmist narratives propagated by the alternative-right media landscape function like a background noise to which it is difficult to respond'. The authors maintain that this fact makes it even more crucial to translate 'democracy's strengths and values into powerful narratives'. Baldauf *et al.* (2017, 21) summarise their proposed strategy as follows:

> Our response to hate and aggressive agitation must be our own narratives: strong stories and images that – grounded in the reality of our own lives – champion values-oriented interactions and support human rights and an open society. In short, the alternative-right narratives must be answered from a social perspective, with creative political imagery.

It is Baldauf *et al.*'s (2017, 21) contention that works on narratives and counter-narratives are becoming increasingly important for the substantive engagement with ideologies that sponsor inequality and with conspiracy narratives.

The discussion presented above brings us to the next issue, which is the space provided and strategies available for those who want to counter far-right populists, especially if they are in power. Scholars have already pointed at the asymmetry of resources available for different actors in terms of storytelling. Polletta and Chen (2012, 119), for example, have pointed out that political entrepreneurs with their financial resources and wide political connections are better at securing a favourable hearing for their stories than others. The situation is of course more difficult in authoritarian or competitive authoritarian settings in which the story of the opposition has difficulty being heard. As Polletta and Lee (2006) argue, disadvantaged groups are at a disadvantage when they want to tell a story to challenge the status quo because the veracity, authority or generalisability of their stories are especially vulnerable to scepticism while the use of narratives by advantaged groups may be even less likely to be heard as telling stories. It is thus important to acknowledge the difficulties compounded in hybrid or fully authoritarian political settings in which the opposition gets either limited or no platform to tell their stories and/ or in which the stories of the opposition are either hijacked or distorted by the incumbents.

Nevertheless, there are cases in which even under very difficult situations, political and public figures can manage to tell alternative stories to the authoritarian, exclusionary and polarizing ones of the incumbents. A case in point is the current mayor of Istanbul, who, against all impediments and a cancelled election, was able to tell a non-polarising, inclusive story to the Istanbul electorate and to Turkey at large (Wuthrich and Ingleby 2020) that won him the 2019 local elections. The crucial task before politicians, political scientists, public intellectuals and political philosophers who have more inclusive, pluralistic and democratic visions for the future is to give more thought to how authoritarian and exclusionary narratives and their corresponding political projects can be countered with help from the political narratives that are told about each political community at hand as well as humanity at large.

Notes

1. On defining features of populism, see Barr 2009; Filc 2010; Gidron and Bonikowski 2013; Mudde 2004; Mudde and Rovira Kaltwasser 2018; and Weyland 1996.
2. On Podemos and populism and authoritarianism, see also Booth and Baert 2018. On left populism and competitive authoritarianism, see Weyland 2018.
3. For a critique and rejoinder of Fraser's discussion of recognition and redistribution, see *European Journal of Political Theory*, 2007, 6 (3). On the discussion of the Left and identity politics, see also special issue of *Historical Materialism*, 2018, 26 (2).

7

CONCLUSION: NARRATIVES OF MEMORY, PATRIARCHY AND ECONOMY IN TURKEY AND BEYOND

This book has tried to provide a multifaceted look toward the role political narratives play in politics. In Chapter 1, I provided the theoretical and methodological framework of the book and introduced the main topics. In Chapter 2, I focused on how the competing visions of nationhood of Kemalists and Islamists are played out in the Ulus District of Ankara by providing alternative historical narratives of the nation. In Chapter 3, I discussed how economic development narratives are deployed by the AKP to suppress main elements of liberal democracy such as pluralism, and checks and balances. Chapter 4 adopted a comparative perspective and traced the place of narratives of economic development, patriarchy and history in the toolkit of populist leaders, illustrated through the cases of Austria, Hungary and Turkey. Chapter 5 focused on counter-narratives. Through the Gezi case, it analysed how counter-narratives are used to subvert the core patriarchal narratives of authoritarian governments in order to expose and challenge the core assumptions of hierarchical and arbitrary rule. Chapter 6 turned its attention to global discussions and focused on the implications of political narratives for policies and political actions. It first discussed how conspiracy theories, particularly the Replacement Theory (which is in fact a narrative), function in the political realm by ways such as bringing far-right ideas into the mainstream, encouraging bottom-up participation in exclusionary visions of nationhood, and by creating unified camps of 'us' and 'them'. After showing the prevalence of and the deployment of the Replacement narrative by right-wing populists, I turned to the discussion of the potential for countering right-wing populists and their exclusionary, authoritarian and monist stories with inclusive, democratic and pluralist ones.

The different topics covered in the chapters of this book gave me the opportunity to provide a lively and panoramic picture of the political landscape of Turkey. They also enabled me to delve deeply into the functions that political narratives serve in politics and society. As I tried to show, narratives provide us a dynamic lens in situating and analysing political events and phenomena. Narratives play both individual and collective roles due to their essential role in co-constituting personal and communal (mostly national) identity. The interchangeable use of personal stories with collective ones, the use of 'we' to refer to different scales of groups, and the construction of a linear time with selections from the past to the present are all vital steps in the merging of individual and collective identities through stories. The historical continuity drawn between separate events in time, which is arbitrary and even stretches throughout centuries sometimes, not only creates certain visions of peoplehood, but also provides justification for political causes. Through these stories, the distinctions between 'us' and 'them' are fortified. As past characters (heroes, victims . . .) are replaced with new ones, seamlessly, like in a relay, a broader mission is defined for the present with new actors taking over past struggles.

The fact that stories provide a bigger 'lesson', a normative message that leads to a sense of urgency and moral justification for action is not only true for historical narratives but all political narratives, as seen in the narratives covered in this book. Cultural and global tropes are carried through stories, which serve as legitimisation tools as evident in the case of gendered hierarchies that serve authoritarian and patrimonial rule, and development narratives that pressure for a vaguely defined economic prosperity and pit this development against democracy. The same is true for conspiracy theories, which, based on alleged internal and external threats, call for urgent action that materialises itself in authoritarian measures or violent political action, among other things. Yet at the same time, stories can also serve subversion rather than legitimisation as the Gezi case has also shown, albeit that it is more difficult for bottom-up narratives to reach the same platforms as those offered from the top. Finally, narratives appear to be crucial in countering the authoritarian, exclusionary narratives offered by political leaders, if such leaders are to be defeated. While policy proposals and appeals to legality and data are important, it appears to be crucial that democratic, inclusive and pluralistic politicians and public figures find ways to tell good stories about the issues that appeal to the senses of identity and virtue of the people. In the remainder of this chapter, I discuss some of the implications of the findings of the book and possible directions for further research.

Narratives and the Prospects of Coming to Terms with the Past

Let us start with the discussion of historical narratives, which, as multiple chapters of the book have shown, play a crucial role for the promotion of different senses of nationhood, the furthering of populist causes, and relatedly, the perpetuation of conflict, and polarisation. As we have discussed in the previous chapter, the political implications of historical narratives are directly linked with the content and form these narratives take. As Polletta (2009, viii) argues, 'the possibility remains that the same events told differently would have yielded a different normative point'. In light of this, it makes sense to ask the question of the relationship between historical narratives and the prospects for a more democratic, just and pluralistic society. The more deeply we delve into this issue, however, the more we will see that it is hard to find clear-cut answers without considering the complexities of the situations at hand.

First of all, as we discussed in Chapter 2, there is always the danger that what might ostensibly look like an attempt of 'coming to terms with the past' may in fact be the instrumentalisation of the past for populist political causes, as the case of Ulucanlar has also shown us. 'Coming to terms with the past', or related concepts such as 'transitional justice' need to be understood not only in their initial conceptualisation, particularly the postwar European era, but also in the contemporary contexts in which they are employed. While the original idea of 'coming to terms with the past' is of course commendable and worked particularly well in some cases, such as Germany, and while there is no reason why it could not be replicated in non-European settings, it is important to understand how the positive connotations associated with 'coming to terms with the past' and its association with human rights and democracy are manipulated by those who want to exploit the moral high ground occupied by the concept. This, as discussed in Chapter 2, can lead to attempts at executive aggrandisement been covered up with what may seem as 'coming to terms with the past' on the façade.

In the Turkish case, we saw repeatedly during multiple constitutional referenda in the AKP era how the traumas of military interventions were used in the quest for extended power, the silencing of pluralism and for the creation of a unilinear trajectory straitjacketing the country's future, which were all epitomised in the museumification process of Ulucanlar (Ugur-Cinar and Altınok, 2021). There is a sense of irony then in the way 'coming to terms with the past' is utilised by populists: a concept developed to bolster constitutionalism and democracy is used to erode both. Instead of serving the creation of a more conscientious and pluralistic society that takes ethical responsibility for the consequences of its actions, which was one of the primary goals of the original effort of coming to terms with the past, in the hands of populists it becomes a slogan used to silence opposition and expand executive power with the moral high ground obtained by discursively employing this very phenomenon.

As we see, populism exploits past traumas and propagates animosity and revanchism within society and thereby deepens existing cleavages and increases polarisation. In addition to valorising the us versus them distinction, deepening cleavages and providing justifications for the seizure of more power, the way the past is dealt with in cases such as Turkey under AKP rule are also problematic for other reasons. Attributing all wrongdoings to the time before the populist came to power negates the very purposes of coming to terms with the past, which then becomes a buzzword, kitsch. Time becomes compartmentalised as it is divided clearly from the time the populist comes to power and all wrongdoings are treated as things that belong to the era before the populist was in power. Once the populists introduce their policies, the themes that appear in the past wrongdoings are relegated and confined to the past. They are deemed as dealt with and done. This is extremely evident in the contrast of Turkey's backsliding on civil liberties, the rule of law, and its human rights record on the one hand, and the AKP's claim at Ulucanlar that the AKP has remedied past wrongdoings in relation to democracy and human rights.

My criticism of this embargo on further reflection in the present and of this hijacking of the story of past wrongdoings and giving it an ending echoes

Traverso's (2019) critique of the instrumentalisation of commemorations (such as 9/11 or World War II) in order to justify present political actions and in order to vindicate the status quo of the powerful. In response, Traverso reminds us of the Frankfurt School's messages, particularly regarding the fact that past wrongdoings are not alien to our contemporary world but can instead only be understood as embedded in it.

Relatedly, the alternative provided to the homogenising secular nationalistic projects should not be uncritically celebrated as the request for pluralism or the flourishing of the 'good old days' of cohabitation. As the Ulus case in Chapter 2 and the discussion on populism and cleavages in Chapter 4 made apparent, most of the time, in the hands of populist leaders, the past is a tool for the imposition of another alternative monist identity. As the SOKÜM and Ulucanlar cases in Chapter 2 illustrated, for example, the ties to the Ottoman past or to the early years of the Republic were not narrated so as to tell the past 'as it actually was' but rather to impose a unity and monism on the past that made it useful for present political projects. In the SOKÜM case, we see that narratives are utilised in merging the past 'us' with the present 'us' and for merging the personal narrative with the collective narrative. Details that do not fit the story, such as the multi-ethnic history of the Ottoman era or the role of right-wing parties in the executions at Ulucanlar, are conveniently left to oblivion.

As Roediger and Wertsch (2008, 14) find, a great deal more remains to be explored when it comes to the power of the 'lessons of history' to shape political thought and decisions. Studies so far have shown how past traumas and victimhood can fuel current political conflicts. Oren, Nets-Zehngut and Bar-Tal (2015, 220) demonstrate, for example, how in Israel conflict-supporting narratives, which are stubborn barriers to peacemaking, rely on sources such as testimonies, documents, journalists and scholars that support the narratives' themes while ignoring or minimising those that contradict the conflict themes. In these conflict-supporting narratives Oren, Nets-Zehngut and Bar-Tal (2015, 221) argue, especially those events in the conflict that 'concern justness of goals, positive self-presentation, self-presentation as the victim in the conflict, and delegitimization of the rival', are magnified, serving the continuation of the intractable conflict. A similar case can be made in Russia's most recent aggression toward Ukraine, in which narratives of the

Second World War, and the spectre of the Nazi past are used as justifications on the part of Russia, especially in the speeches of Putin (see for instance, Teisman 2022).

Given how susceptible the past is to the instrumentalisation of populists, trying to find answers to the following question becomes vital: How can we do justice to past wrongdoings without perpetuating a culture of vengeance and parochialism, without instrumentalising selected traumas and victimhood for political ends and without playing into the hands of populists? That is the ultimate question, which deserves further attention academically and politically.

Narratives and Ethics

The next issue in relation to the role of historical narratives in particular and political narratives in general deals with the characteristics of the narrative form itself. It is particularly interested in the emancipatory, remedial potential of narratives and the limits of such potential. Henceforth, the existing literature has mostly paid attention to the positive role narratives can play in this regard given their relations to our senses of justice and ethics.

In addition to giving cognitive order to people's comprehension of time and events, the role of narratives as ethical tools is made evident by scholars and philosophers such as Alasdair MacIntyre (2007 [1981]) and Charles Taylor (1989), who argue that narratives are essential for a sense of good life, full personhood and moral integrity, and that they serve an integral task in transferring such notions across generations. According to MacIntyre, human beings are storytelling animals. MacIntyre argues that narrative gives clarity to one's moral vision. It is through stories that we make sense of our morality. Humans understand what a good, or virtuous, life is through narratives about their lives. MacIntyre's narratives are connected to what he calls living traditions. He defines a living tradition as 'a historically extended, socially embodied argument, and an argument precisely in part about the goods which constitute that tradition'. In this sense, these traditions are embedded in narratives and are transferred to new generations in the form of storytelling. Charles Taylor's *Sources of the Self* (1989) also claims that we understand our lives in narrative form. In Taylor's words: 'in order to have a sense of who we are, we have to have a notion of how we have become, and of where we are going' and we only reach this notion via narratives. This includes our sense of what is good, which is woven into our understanding of our lives as unfolding stories.

Other scholars have also pointed at the moral implications of narratives. Ewick and Silbey (1995, 200) maintain that the temporal and structural ordering inherent in narratives ensures at the same time 'narrative closure' and 'narrative causality', which is to say they state simultaneously how and why the recounted events occurred (see also Wibben 2010 and Miskimmon, O'Loughlin and Roselle 2013). Polletta (2009, 139–40) similarly maintains that narratives' 'temporally configurative capacity' equips them with the capacity 'to integrate past, present, and future events' and gives them an action-oriented character since a 'story's chronological end is also its end in the sense of moral, purpose or telos, they project a future'.

The link between narratives and morality becomes especially salient in the case of autobiographical narratives. Paul Ricoeur (1980) argues that our sense of temporality is linked to narratives. Narrative plots, with their beginnings and ends, enable us to gain a sense of time that goes beyond chronology. Autobiographies and memoirs become central to the relationship between narratives, time and identity. This is the case to the point where Bruner (1987, 15) claims that 'we become the autobiographical narratives by which we "tell about" our lives'. Autobiographical narratives merge individual with collective identity as the protagonist aspires to present a coherent story that is both general and personal at the same time. As Brockmeier (2000, 51, 55) argues, autobiographical identity construction synthesises cultural and individual orders of time as both become ways of understanding 'one's self in time'. The 'individual life history and history in the broader sense' are merged through the temporal dimension of autobiographical narratives (Brockmeier 2000, 55). It is through autographical narratives that we trace the trajectories of our lives and give them meaning (Freeman and Brockmeier 2001, 79) and communicate to others and to ourselves why our lives are worth living (Kearney 2006, 3). In this regard, autobiographical narratives are not just descriptive but also evaluative (Brockmeier 2000, 60) and prescriptive.

Autobiographical narratives are not objective texts following the natural occurrences of events in one's lifetime. They evaluate the past, both at the individual and collective level, in light of the present. Autographical narratives possess a retrospective teleology in which the 'life story starts in the here and now and reconstructs the past as if it were teleologically directed towards this specific present' (Brockmeier 2000, 55). As Elliot G. Mishler argues (2006, 41), the way turning points in lives are told are particularly striking in this regard as they make it explicit how we reconstruct the meaning of past experiences while remaking ourselves. For Mishler (2006, 41), the evaluation of ourselves through narratives is a continuous and iterated process of 'ongoing, unending . . . revising, and re-revising our life stories and our identities, as we come to understand what happened in terms of ever-widening contexts of what happened later'.

As the literature discussed above reveals, so far scholarship has mostly focused on the potential of the narrative structure to enhance ethics and morality due to its ability to provide coherence, unity and the evaluation of life through a moral lens. I have become increasingly interested in the unintended and undetected consequences of narratives. In a study, coauthored with Gökhan Şensönmez, we look at the memoirs of imprisoned far-right militants (the Ülkücüs) in the post-1980 coup era in Turkey and find that these militants used narratives to make sense of the disruption they faced in the post-coup era and that these narratives provided them an escape from coming to terms with past wrongdoings (Ugur-Cinar and Şensönmez 2022). We find that in their autobiographies, which were later published as books, the militants rely on religious narratives in multiple ways. The far-right militants who fought on the streets against the leftists during the 1970s were left in shock in face of their torturous treatment in the hands of the junta. They were in disbelief for being punished by the state while they were claiming to have fought for the state and for the nation. The shock and disappointment were multiplied as the organisational apparatus became dysfunctional and the leadership was kept detached from the militants. In the case of Ülkücüs, the 1980 coup served as a turning point as the narratives in the memoirs reveal. This turning point served as a basis around which past experiences were re-emplotted from the vantage point of the present with the purpose of weaving a coherent, meaningful and worthy narrative around the self.

In order to deal with this rupture, the militants employed narratives, particularly religious ones, which helped them make sense of their situation and enabled them to regain coherence and meaning in terms of their life and identity. Religious narratives served to give coherence to the Ülkücü identities along with a sense of purpose, worth and moral high ground. By formulating their autobiographical narratives in religious terms, the militants were able to reformulate their lives as ones not of failure and defeat but instead as meaning-ful, given the new Islamic context and mission they situated themselves in. The militants utilised the advantages of narratives, such as their ambiguity, reliance on emplotment in place of factual truths (Polletta 1998; 2011) and selective-ness, by selectively borrowing from the past, leaving out and distorting facts where it was deemed necessary.

At the same time, these very same narratives also enabled the Ülkücüs to deflect their responsibility for the events of the 1970s, including the murder of their political opponents. Through these narratives, they were able to present their life stories as ones in which they were deceived by false, earthly ideologies only to gain consciousness through religion in the aftermath of the coup. The moral superiority and the belief that they were serving larger-than-life, eternal goals in the service of God, which was inbuilt in the religious narratives, also helped further justify their actions in the 1970s and beyond. As they were now formulating their struggle as one between good and evil in religious terms, the ends justified the means even more so than in the case of nationalism. Along with supporting narratives of victimhood and structural reasons that went beyond personal agency, these stories never led to a proper coming to terms with the past and accountability. As evident in such narratives, which were told either in passive voice or with terms such as 'someone, one, one's, some groups' the narrators were able to keep themselves clear of responsibility and blame.

The findings of the militant autobiographies shed further light on the role that autobiographical narratives play in the construction of identity and a sense of a good life. At the same time, they open a new path of inquiry that takes at its focal point the relationship between autobiographical narratives, collective memory and the potential to come to terms with the past. Fur-ther studies could investigate stories among other participants of civil wars and perpetrators of personal or collective crimes to compare narrative pat-terns. Another fruitful future line of work could also investigate stories of the Left and see if other, secular, stories serve similar purposes as the religious narratives examined in this study. As there is still a lot to be explored with regard to the link between lessons derived from the past and their political implications (Kansteiner 2002; Wertsch and Roediger 2008), narratives can help us make a lot of headway in this regard.

Narratives and Regimes

As discussed earlier, the relationship between regimes and narratives opens a fruitful path for further research. In this section, I want to diversify my discussion of this relationship, focusing on the affinity between different types of narratives and regimes. In terms of regime types discussion, one suggestion for further research that I could make would be to think about what type of stories (both in terms of form and content) have elective affinities with what type of regimes, be they largely political or mostly economic. The first discussion I will open here will be with regard to the relationship between capitalism and, particularly, neoliberalism as a global and domestic regime on the one hand, and the narratives supporting the regime on the other. While neoliberalism prides itself on being based on market realities and draws mostly on technicalities in laying out its advantages, it is through narratives that it retains its dominance. In addition to these technicalities, neoliberalism is also presenting a storyline in which people and countries are expected to prosper under minimal state intervention and the free functioning of market forces. In Somers' (1994, 619) terms, neoliberalism serves as a meta-narrative or master narrative that subsumes a network of narratives that praise buzzwords such as 'self-help', 'resilience', 'entrepreneurship', 'efficiency', 'performance', 'growth', 'discipline', 'deregulation', 'stakeholder' and 'trickling down'. It also provides a discernable storyline in which human beings are depicted as certain types of actors.

As Polanyi (1957 [1944]) notices early on, even before the rise of neoliberalism, most of these assumptions are myths rather than reality but nevertheless these stories, as evident in the 'American dream', have concrete implications for political and economic choices both at the individual and the collective level. Most of the time, the story of neoliberalism does not even have to be told in an uninterrupted fashion. As Polletta and Callahan (2017) observe, simply referring to labels such as 'welfare queen' would call up 'a story, or stories, of women on welfare taking advantage of the system to live in the lap of luxury'. This has of course immense implications with regard to how we understand welfare, human nature and our duties toward fellow human beings or citizens. As shown in Chapter 3, the economically deterministic nature of neoliberalism, with its fixation on development and growth, is used in suppressing democracy and, therefore, it is long overdue to reassess the main premises of the neoliberal storyline. Countering the injustices of neoliberalism would require us to tell alternative stories of development, freedom and justice, which would provide alternative accounts to how the economy and society work, what the priorities of life should be, and what it means to live a full and meaningful life. Future research focusing on such issues can zoom into the narratives of politicians or technocrats, yet it can also look into the language of 'influencers' for example, to see how neoliberal narratives are perpetuated and/or countered.

The relationship between regimes and narratives is also very prominent in the patriarchal narratives and the subsequent political regimes in which they are deployed. In my earlier research (Ugur-Cinar 2017), I pointed at the need to restore the original link between patriarchy and patrimonialism in our understanding of current day neopatrimonial rules. This, I argued, is an important point often left out in the neopatrimonialism literature, which mostly approaches neopatrimonialism as a material and interest-based exchange. I believe that there is still a lot to be gained from the collaborations of the research agendas on political regimes and those of gender studies in order to understand the impact of narratives on regime trajectories. A fruitful research question would thus be, 'What type of political regimes go with what type of gender regimes, and how do these two types of regimes reinforce each other through narratives?' It would be interesting to carry research further with such questions either in single country settings or through a comparative research design. For instance, the populist regimes of Eastern Europe are very keen to make patriarchal stories, particularly stories with regard to the protection of family, a key element of their campaigns. While in some cases these stories include control over women's bodies, in others they are restricted to attacking LGBTQ+ rights. Yet in some other European cases, the far right is also seeking for allies among the LGBTQ+ community against the perceived threat of ethnic minorities and immigrants. The preexisting political conditions and institutional settings can play important roles in what kind of narratives are propagated by politicians in different regime settings, which is an important future research area to be pursued.

In closing, I hope that this book serves as an inspiration both for those who want to understand the role of narratives in politics, and for those who are motivated to build more inclusive, pluralistic and democratic societies. I am rooting for them, I hope they win.

BIBLIOGRAPHY

Abi-Hassan, Sahar. 2017. 'Populism and Gender.' In *The Oxford Handbook of Populism*, edited by C. R. Kaltwasser, P. Taggart, P. O. Espejo and P. Ostiguy. http://www. oxfordhandbooks.com/view/10.1093/oxfordhb/9780198803560.001.0001/ oxfordhb-9780198803560-e-16.

Abu-Lughod, Lila. 1991. 'Writing Against Culture.' In *Recapturing Anthropology: Working in the Present*, edited by Richard G. Fox. Santa Fe: School of American Research Press.

Abu-Lughod, Lila. 1993. *Writing Women's Worlds: Bedouin Stories*. Berkeley: University of California Press.

Abu-Lughod, Lila. 1997. 'The Interpretation of Culture(s) after Television Author(s).' *Representations* 59 (Summer): 109–34.

Adaman, Fikret, and Murat Arsel. 2012. 'Environment.' In *The Routledge Handbook of Modern Turkey*, edited by Sabri Sayari and Metin Heper. London: Routledge.

Adaman, F., B. Akbulut, M. Arsel and D. Avci. 2014. 'De-growth as Counter-Hegemony? Lessons from Turkey.' In *4th Int. Conf. on Degrowth for Ecological Sustainability and Social Equity, Leipzig*.

Adams, Julia. 2005. *The Familial State: Ruling Families and Merchant Capitalism in Early Modern Europe*. Ithaca: Cornell University Press.

Ahaber. 2018. 'Cumhurbaşkanı Erdoğan'dan önemli açıklamalar.' 6 October 2018. https://www.ahaber.com.tr/gundem/2018/06/10/cumhurbaskani-erdogandan-onemli-aciklamalar.

Ahıska, Meltem. 2019. 'Memory as Encounter: The Saturday Mothers in Turkey.' In *Women Mobilizing Memory*, edited by A. G. Altinay, M. A. Contreras, M. Hirsch, J. Howard, B. Karaca and A. Solomon. New York: Columbia University Press.

Akbulut, B., and F. Adaman. 2013. 'The Unbearable Charm of Modernization: Growth Fetishism and the Making of State in Turkey.' *Perspectives: Political Analysis and Commentary from Turkey* 5 (13): 1–10.

Akdağ, Çilem Tuğba, and Ebru Davulcu. 2016. 'Magazine of Intellectual Community in Building a New Nation, Hayat (1926–1929).' *International e-Journal of Advances in Social Sciences* 2 (5): 432–5.

Akşam. 2013. 'Başkanlık sistemi gelmezse ekonomik kriz gelir.' 6 April 2013. http://www.aksam.com.tr/siyaset/baskanlik-sistemi-gelmezse-ekonomik-kriz-gelir/haber-184204.

Alba, R. 2018. 'What Majority-Minority Society? A Critical Analysis of the Census Bureau's Projections of America's Demographic Future.' *Sociological Research for a Dynamic World* 4: 1–10. https://doi.org/10.1177/2378023118796932.

Alba, R., R. G. Rumbaut and K. Marotz. 2005. 'A Distorted Nation: Perceptions of Racial/Ethnic Group Sizes and Attitudes Toward Immigrants and Other Minorities.' *Social Forces* 84: 901–19. https://www.jstor.org/stable/3598484.

Allington, D., and T. Joshi. 2020. '"What Others Dare Not Say": An Antisemitic Conspiracy Fantasy and Its YouTube Audience.' *Journal of Contemporary Antisemitism* 3 (1): 35–53.

Altinay, Aysegul, María José Contreras, Marianne Hirsch, Jean Howard, Banu Karaca and Alisa Solomon, eds. 2019. *Women Mobilizing Memory*. New York: Columbia University Press.

Anadolu Ajansı. 2016. 'Gezi en büyük tahribatı ekonomiye Verdi.' 27 May 2016. http://aa.com.tr/tr/ekonomi/gezi-en-buyuk-tahribati-ekonomiye-verdi/579541.

Andrews, Molly. 2004. 'Opening to the Original Contributions: Counter-Narratives and the Power to Oppose.' In *Considering Counter-Narratives: Narrating, Resisting, Making Sense*, edited by Michael Bamberg and Molly Andrews, 1–6. Amsterdam: John Benjamins.

Andrews, Molly, Catarina Kinnvall and Kristen Monroe. 2015. 'Narratives of (In) Security: Nationhood, Culture, Religion, and Gender: Introduction to the Special Issue.' *Political Psychology* 36 (April): 141–9.

Appadurai, Arjun. 1988. 'Putting Hierarchy in Its Place.' *Cultural Anthropology* 3 (February): 36–49.

Arato, A. 2013. 'Political Theology and Populism.' *Social Research* 80 (1): 143–72.

Art, David. 2006. *The Politics of Nazi Past in Germany and Austria*. Cambridge: Cambridge University Press.

Åsard, Erik. 2021. 'Han kan bli USA: s nästa president – med hjälp av en rasistisk konspirationsteori' [He could become the next US president – with help from a racist conspiracy theory]. *Dagens Nyheter*, 3 May 2021. https://www.dn.se/kultur/erik-asard-han-kan-bli-usas-nasta-president-med-hjalp-av-en-rasistisk-konspirationsteori/.

Askanius, T. 2021. 'On Frogs, Monkeys, and Execution Memes: Exploring the Humor-Hate Nexus at the Intersection of Neo-Nazi and Alt-Right Movements in Sweden.' *Television and New Media* 22 (2): 147–65.

Aslanidis, Paris. 2016. 'Is Populism an Ideology? A Refutation and a New Perspective.' *Political Studies* 64 (1): 88–104.

Aydın, Suavi. 2010. 'The Use and Abuse of Archaeology and Anthropology in Formulating the Turkish Nationalist Narrative.' In *Nationalism in the Troubled Triangle*, edited by A. Aktar, N. Kızılyürek and U. Özkırımlı, 36–46. New Perspectives on South-East Europe. London: Palgrave Macmillan.

Aysu T. 2015. 'Turning Ulucanlar Prison into Ulucanlar Prison Museum: The Politics of Creating a Memory Place', Masters thesis, İstanbul Bilgi University.

Aytaç, S. E., and E. Elçi. 2018. 'Populism in Turkey.' In *Populism Around the World*, edited by D. Stockemer, 89–108. New York: Springer International.

Aytaç, S. E., and Z. Öniş. 2014. 'Varieties of Populism in a Changing Global Context: The Divergent Paths of Erdoğan and Kirchnerismo.' *Comparative Politics* 47 (1): 41–59.

Aytac, Selim E., and Susan C. Stokes. 2019. *Why Bother? Rethinking Participation in Elections and Protests*. Cambridge Studies in Comparative Politics. Cambridge: Cambridge University Press.

Baker, Peter, and Michael D. Shear. 2019. 'El Paso Shooting Suspect's Manifesto Echoes Trump's Language.' *New York Times*, 4 August 2019. https://www.nytimes.com/2019/08/04/us/politics/trumpmass-shootings.html.

Bakhtin, Mikhail. 1986 [1953]. 'The Problem of Speech Genres.' In *Speech Genres and Other Late Essays*, edited by C. Emerson and M. Holquist, translated by V. W. McGee, 60–102. Austin: University of Texas Press.

Bakhtin, Mikhail. 2013. *Problems of Dostoevsky's Poetics*. Minneapolis: University of Minnesota Press.

Bakiner, Onur. 2018. 'A Key to Turkish Politics? The Center–Periphery Framework Revisited.' *Turkish Studies* 19 (4): 503–22.

Baldauf, Johannes, Miro Dittrich, Melanie Hermann, Britta Kollberg, Robert Lüdecke and Jan Rathje. 2017. 'Toxic Narratives – Monitoring Alternative-Right Actors.' Berlin: Amadeu Antonio Foundation.

Balibar, Etienne. 1990. 'The Nation Form: History and Ideology.' *Review (Fernand Braudel Center)* 13 (3): 329–61.

Balibar, Etienne. 1992. 'The Nation Form: History and Ideology.' In *Race, Nation, Class: Ambiguous Identities*, edited by Etienne Balibar and Immanuel Wallerstein, trans. Chris Turner. London: Verso.

Bamberg, Michael. 2004. 'Considering Counter-Narratives.' In *Considering Counter-Narratives: Narrating, Resisting, Making Sense*, edited by Michael Bamberg and Molly Andrews. Amsterdam: John Benjamins.

Bangstad, S. 2019. 'Bat Ye'or and Eurabia.' In *Key Thinkers of the Radical Right: Behind the New Threat to Liberal Democracy*, edited by M. Sedgwick, 170–84. Oxford: Oxford University Press.

Barkun, M. 2013. *A Culture of Conspiracy*. Berkeley: University of California Press.

Barobirlik. 2017. 'Anayasa Değişikligi Teklifi'nin Karşılaştırmalı ve Açıklamalı Metni.' http://anayasadegisikligi.barobirlik.org.tr/Anayasa_Degisikligi.aspx.

Barr, Robert R. 2009. 'Populists, Outsiders and Anti-Establishment Politics.' *Party Politics* 15 (1): 29–48.

Batuman, Bulent. 2011. 'Ulucanlar Cezaevi Muzesi.' 26 June 2011. http://www.radikal.com.tr/radikal2/ulucanlar-cezaevi-muzesi-1054190/ (accessed 7 July 2020).

Bauder, David. 2022. 'What Is "Great Replacement Theory" and How Does it Fuel Racist Violence?' *PBS*, 16 May 2022. https://www.pbs.org/newshour/politics/what-is-great-replacement-theory-and-how-does-it-fuel-racist-violence.

BBC. 2013. 'FT: "BDDK incelemesi yatırımcıları soğutabilir".' 11 July 2013. http://www.bbc.com/turkce/ekonomi/2013/07/130711_ft_bddk_inceleme.

Béland, Daniel, and Robert H. Cox. 2010. 'Introduction.' In *Ideas and Politics in Social Science Research*, edited by Daniel Béland and Robert H. Cox. New York: Oxford University Press.

Bélanger, J. J., M. Moyano, H. Muhammad, L. Richardson, M. K. Lafrenière, P. McCaffery, K. Framand and N. Nociti. 2019. 'Radicalization Leading to Violence: A Test of the 3N Model.' *Frontiers in Psychiatry* 10: article 42. https://doi.org/10.3389/fpsyt.2019.00042.

Bell, V. 1999. 'Performativity and Belonging: An Introduction. *Theory, Culture and Society* 16 (2): 1–10. https://doi.org/10.1177/02632769922050511.

Benford, Robert D., and Scott A. Hunt. 1992. 'Dramaturgy and Social Movements: The Social Construction and Communication of Power.' *Sociological Inquiry* 62 (1): 36–55.

Benford, Robert D., and David A. Snow. 2000. 'Framing Processes and Social Movements: An Overview and Assessment.' *Annual Review of Sociology* 26 (August): 611–39.

Berger, J. M. 2018. 'Trump is the Glue That Binds the Far Right.' *The Atlantic*. https://www.theatlantic.com/ideas/archive/2018/10/trump-alt-right-twitter/574219/.

Bergmann, Eirikur. 2021. 'The Eurabia Conspiracy Theory.' In *Europe: Continent of Conspiracies: Conspiracy Theories in and about Europe*, 1st edn, edited by Andreas Onnerfors and Andre Krouwel, 36–53. Abingdon: Routledge.

Berman, Sheri. 2010. 'Ideology, History, and Politics.' In *Ideas and Politics in Social Science Research*, edited by Daniel Béland and Robert H. Cox. New York: Oxford University Press.

Berman, Sheri. 2016. 'The Specter Haunting Europe: The Lost Left.' *Journal of Democracy* 27 (4): 69–76.

Berman, Sheri. 2020. 'Europe: Will This Crisis Be Different?' *Dissent Magazine*, Summer 2020.

Berman, Sheri. 2021. 'The Causes of Populism in the West.' *Annual Review of Political Science* 24: 71–88.

Berman, Sheri, and Hans Kundnani. 2021. 'The Cost of Convergence.' *Journal of Democracy* 32 (1): 22–36.

Berman, S., and M. Snegovaya. 2019. 'Populism and the Decline of Social Democracy.' *Journal of Democracy* 30 (3): 5–19.

Bermeo, Nancy. 2016. 'On Democratic Backsliding.' *Journal of Democracy* 27 (1): 5–19.

Bianet. 2013. 'Avrupa Parlamentosu'nun Kararını Tanımıyorum.' 13 June 2013. http://bianet.org/bianet/siyaset/147529-avrupa-parlamentosu-nun-kararini-tanimiyorum.

Bianet. 2014. 'Erdoğan "Fıtrat Sözlerim Çarpıtıldı" Dedi, Aynı Cümleleri Tekrarladı.' 26 November 2014. http://bianet.org/bianet/kadln/160284-erdogan-fitrat-sozlerim-carpitildi-dedi-ayni-cumleleri-tekrarladi.

Bloomberg. 2018. 'Sultan Who Raged at the West Becomes a Hero in Erdogan's Turkey.' 19 March 2018. https://www.bloomberg.com/news/articles/2018-03-19/sultan-who-raged-at-the-west-becomes-a-hero-in-erdogan-s-turkey.

Blyth, Mark M. 1997. 'Any More Bright Ideas? The Ideational Turn of Comparative Political Economy.' *Comparative Politics* 29 (January): 229–50.

Booth, J., and P. Baert. 2018. *The Dark Side of Podemos? Carl Schmitt and Contemporary Progressive Populism*. London: Routledge.

Botsch, G., and C. Kopke. 2018. 'Der Volkstod. Zur Kontinuität einer extrem rechten Paranoia.' In *Antifeminismus in Bewegung: Aktuelle Debatten um Geschlecht und sexuelle Vielfalt*, edited by J. Lang and U. Peters, 63–90). Hamburg: Marta Press.

Bottici, C. 2010. 'Narrative.' in *Encyclopedia of Political Theory*, edited by Mark Bevir, 919–20. New York: Sage.

Bozkurt, U. 2013. 'Neoliberalism with a Human Face: Making Sense of the Justice and Development Party's Neoliberal Populism in Turkey.' *Science & Society* 77 (3): 372–96.

Bozoğlu, G. 2020a. *Museums, Emotion and Memory Culture: The Politics of the Past in Turkey.* London: Routledge.

Bozoğlu, G. 2020b. '"A Great Bliss to Keep the Sensation of the Conquest": The Emotional Politics of the Panaroma 1453 Museum in İstanbul.' In *European Memory in Populism: Representation of Self and Other*, edited by C. De Cesari and A. Kaya, 91–111. London: Routledge.

Bracke, Sarah, and Luis Manuel Hernández Aguilar. 2020. '"They Love Death as We Love Life": The "Muslim Question" and the Biopolitics of Replacement.' *British Journal of Sociology* 71: pp. 680–701.

Braun V., V. Clarke, N. Hayfield and G. Terry. 2019. 'Thematic Analysis.' In *Handbook of Research Methods in Health Social Sciences*, edited by P. Liamputtong, 1–18. Singapore: Springer.

Bridger, Jeffrey C., and David R. Maines. 1998. 'Narrative Structures and the Catholic Church Closings in Detroit.' *Qualitative Sociology* 21 (3): 319–40.

Brockmeier, Jens. 2000. 'Autobiographical Time.' *Narrative Inquiry* 10 (1): 51–73.

Brockmeier, Jens. 2002. 'Remembering and Forgetting: Narrative as Cultural Memory.' *Culture & Psychology* 8 (March): 15–43.

Brockmeier, Jens, and Rom Harre. 1997. 'Narrative: Problems and Promises of an Alternative Paradigm.' *Research on Language and Social Interaction* 30 (June): 263–83.

Bruner, Jerome. 1986. *Actual Minds, Possible Worlds.* Cambridge, MA: Harvard University Press.

Bruner, Jerome. 1987. 'Life as Narrative.' *Social Research* 54 (1), 11–32.

Bruner, Jerome. 1990. *Acts of Meaning.* Cambridge, MA: Harvard University Press.

Bruner, Jerome. 1991. 'The Narrative Construction of Reality.' *Critical Inquiry* 18 (1): 1–21.

Bruner, Jerome. 1996. *The Culture of Education.* Cambridge, MA: Harvard University Press.

Buğra, A., and A. Candaş. 2011. 'Change and Continuity under an Eclectic Social Security Regime: The Case of Turkey.' *Middle Eastern Studies* 47 (3): 515–28.

Buğra, Ayşe, and Osman Savaşkan. 2014. *New Capitalism in Turkey: The Relationship between Politics, Religion and Business.* Cheltenham: Edward Elgar.

Bullens, Lara. 2021. 'How the French Great Replacement Theory Conquered the Far-Right.' France24, 8 November 2021. https://www.france24.com/en/europe/20211108-how-the-french-great-replacement-theory-conquered-the-far-right.

Bunce, Valerie. 2000. 'Comparative Democratization: Big and Bounded Generaliza-
tions.' *Comparative Political Studies* 33: 703–34.

Business HT. 2015. 'Sayek Böke: Türkiye'nin yatırımdaki sorunu faiz değil, ortamla ilg-
ili.' 13 October 2015. http://www.businessht.com.tr/ekonomi/haber/1139609-
chpnin-ekonomik-vaatleri.

Butter, M. 2020. *The Nature of Conspiracy Theories*. Cambridge: Polity.

Cambridge University. 2017. '"Populism" Revealed as 2017 Word of the Year by
Cambridge University Press.' 30 November 2017. https://www.cam.ac.uk/news/
populism-revealed-as-2017-word-of-the-year-by-cambridge-university-press.

Cameron, M. 1998. 'Self-Coups: Peru, Guatamala, and Russia.' *Journal of Democracy*
9 (1): 125–39.

Camus, R. (2011). *Le Grand Remplacement*, 3rd edn. Paris: Reinharc.

Candaş, Aysen, and Ayse Buğra. 2010. 'Solidarity Among Strangers: A Problem of
Coexistence in Turkey.' *Constellations* 17: 293–311.

Çarkoğlu, Ali. 2008. 'Ideology or Economic Pragmatism?: Profiling Turkish Voters in
2007.' *Turkish Studies* 9 (2): 317–44.

Çarkoğlu, A., and M. J. Hinich. 2006. 'A Spatial Analysis of Turkish Party Prefer-
ences.' *Electoral Studies* 25: 369–92.

Carr, M. 2006. 'You Are Now Entering Eurabia.' *Race and Class* 48 (1): 1–22.

Çavuşoğlu, E. 2011. 'İslamcı Neoliberalizmde İnşaat Fetişi ve Mülkiyet Üzerindeki
Simgesel Hale.' *Birikim* 270: 40–51.

Cengiz, Orhan Kemal. 2013. 'Erdogan's "Morality Police" Assume Duty.' 6 November 2013. http://www.al-monitor.com/pulse/originals/2013/11/turkey-morality-
police-erdogan.html#.

Cento Bull, Anna. 2016. 'The Role of Memory in Populist Discourse: The Case of the
Italian Second Republic.' *Patterns of Prejudice* 50 (July): 213–23.

Central Intelligence Agency – The World Factbook. n.d.a. 'Country Comparison:
GDP – per Capita (PPP).' https://www.cia.gov/the-world-factbook/field/real-
gdp-per-capita/country-comparison (accessed 9 December 2021).

Central Intelligence Agency – The World Factbook. n.d.b. 'Net Migration Rates.'
https://www.cia.gov/library/publications/the-world-factbook/rankorder/
2112rank.html (accessed 27 November 2018).

Cinar, Alev. 2005. *Modernity, Islam, and Secularism in Turkey: Bodies, Places, and
Time*. Minneapolis: University of Minnesota Press.

Cinar, Kursat. 2016. 'Local Determinants of an Emerging Electoral Hegemony:
The Case of Justice and Development Party (AKP) in Turkey.' *Democratization*
23 (7): 1216–35.

Cinar, Kursat. 2019. *The Decline of Democracy in Turkey: A Comparative Study of Hegemonic Party Rule*. London: Routledge.

Cinar, K., and M. Ugur Cinar. 2015. 'Building Democracy to Last: The Turkish Experience in Comparative Perspective.' *Mediterranean Politics* 20 (3): 342–63.

Cinar, Kursat, and M. Ugur Cinar. 2018. 'What the City Has to Offer: Urbanization and Women's Empowerment in Turkey.' *Politics & Gender* 14 (June): 235–63.

Cineas, Fabiola. 2022. 'Where "Replacement Theory" Comes From – and Why It Refuses to Go Away.' *Vox*, 17 May 2022. https://www.vox.com/23076952/replacement-theory-white-supremacist-violence.

Clifford, James. 1988. *The Predicament of Culture: Twentieth-Century Ethnography, Literature, and Art*. Cambridge, MA: Harvard University Press.

CNN Turk. 2014a. 'Erdoğan Gezi Parkı Çağrısı İçin Çok Sert Konuştu [Erdogan Spoke Harshly about the Gezi Park Call].' 30 May 2014. http://www.cnnturk.com/haber/turkiye/erdogan-gezi-parki-cagrisi-icin-cok-sert-konustu.

CNN Turk. 2014b. 'Erdoğan: Kadın ve Erkeğin Eşit Olması Fıtrata Ters [Erdoğan: Male-Female Equality is Against Nature].' 24 November 2014. http://www.cnnturk.com/haber/turkiye/erdogan-kadin-ve-erkegin-esit-olmasi-fitrata-ters.

Cohen, J. L. 2019. 'What's Wrong With the Normative Theory (and the Actual Practice) of Left Populism.' *Constellations* 26 (3): 391–407.

Confessore, N., and D. Wakabayashi. 2017. 'How Russia Harvested American Rage to Reshape U.S. Politics.' *New York Times*, 9 October 2017. https://www.nytimes.com/2017/10/09/technology/russia-election-facebook-ads-rage.html.

Confessore, Nicholas, and Karen Yourish. 2022. 'A Fringe Conspiracy Theory, Fostered Online, is Refashioned by the G.O.P.' *The New York Times*, 15 May 2022. https://www.nytimes.com/2022/05/15/us/replacement-theory-shooting-tucker-carlson.html.

Cooper R., and B. Ellem. 2008. 'The Neoliberal State, Trade Unions and Collective Bargaining in Australia.' *British Journal of Industrial Relations* 46: 532–54.

Cosentino, Gabriele. 2020. *Social Media and the Post-Truth World Order: The Global Dynamics of Disinformation*. Cham: Palgrave Pivot. https://doi.org/10.1007/978-3-030-43005-4_3.

Croft, A., and O. Coskun. 2014. 'Turkey's Erdogan, On Brussels Visit, Criticized Over Crackdown.' *Reuters*, 21 January 2014. http://www.reuters.com/article/2014/01/21/us-euturkey-idUSBREA0K1J320140121?irpc=932.

Cumhuriyet. 2015. 'Gezi'de faiz lobisi yalan çıktı.' 24 October 2015. http://www.cumhuriyet.com.tr/haber/ekonomi/394359/Gezi_de_faiz_lobisi_yalan_cikti.html.

Cuperus, R. 2018. 'Social Democracy and the Populist Challenge.' In *Why the Left Loses: The Decline of the Centre-Left in Comparative Perspective*, edited by R. Manwaring and P. Kennedy, 185–202. Bristol: Policy Press.

Dahl, R. 1982. *Dilemmas of Pluralist Democracy*. New Haven: Yale University Press.

Daily Sabah. 2016. 'The Rise of Sultan Abdülhamid II's Period in TV Series Filinta: Dawn of the Millennium.' 15 April 2016. https://www.dailysabah.com/arts-culture/2016/04/16/the-rise-of-sultan-abdulhamid-iis-period-in-tv-series-filinta-dawn-of-the-millennium.

Daley, D. M., D. P. Haider-Markel and A. B. Whitford. 2007. 'Checks, Balances, and the Cost of Regulation Evidence from the American States.' *Political Research Quarterly* 60 (4): 696–706.

Davey, Jacob, and Julia Ebner. 2019. *'The Great Replacement': The Violent Consequences of Mainstreamed Extremism*. London: Institute for Strategic Dialogue.

Davis, Eric. 2005. *Memories of State: Politics, History and Collective Identity in Modern Iraq*. Berkeley: University of California Press.

Davis, Joseph E. 2002. 'Narrative and Social Movements: The Power of Stories.' In *Stories of Change: Narrative and Social Movements*, edited by Joseph E. Davis. Albany: State University of New York Press.

De Fina, Anna. 2003. *Identity in Narrative: A Study of Immigrant Discourse*. Amsterdam: John Benjamins.

De Fina, Anna, and A. Georgakopoulou. 2008. 'Analysing Narratives as Practices.' *Qualitative Research* 8 (3): 379–87.

de la Torre, C. 2019. 'Is Left Populism the Radical Democratic Answer?' *Irish Journal of Sociology* 27 (1): 64–71.

De Mesquita, B., J. D. Morrow, R. Siverson and A. Smith. 2001. 'Political Competition and Economic Growth.' *Journal of Democracy* 12: 58–72.

Demuth, Carolin, and Gunter Mey. 2015. 'Qualitative Methodology in Developmental Psychology.' In *International Encyclopedia of the Social & Behavioral Sciences*, edited by James D. Wright, 668–75. Amsterdam: Elsevier.

Der Standard. 2010. 'Die Freiheit, Die Sie Meinen.' 7 September 2010. https://derstandard.at/1282979021446/Wahlkampf-Zitrone-Die-Freiheit-die-sie-meinen.

Deutsche Welle. 2020. 'Viktor Orban Expands Hungary's Anti-LGBTQ+ Measures.' 21 May 2020. https://www.dw.com/en/viktor-orban-expands-hungarys-anti-lgbtq-measures/a-53526969.

Diamond. L. 2008. 'The Democratic Rollback: The Resurgence of the Predatory State.' *Foreign Affairs* 87 (2): 36–48.

Die Presse. 2012. 'Strache: Aufregung über "antisemitischen" Facebook-Eintrag.' 19 August 2012. https://diepresse.com/home/politik/innenpolitik/1280732/ Strache_Aufregung-ueber-antisemitischen-FacebookEintrag.

Diken. 2020. 'Her taşında Ankaralının emeği var: Fotoğraflarla 1'inci Meclis binası.' 23 April 2020. https://www.diken.com.tr/her-tasinda-ankaralinin-emegi-var-fotograflarla-1inci-meclis-binasi/.

Dostal, J. M. 2017. 'The Crisis of German Social Democracy Revisited.' *The Political Quarterly* 88: 230–40.

Dünya. 2013. 'Babacan "operasyon"un faturasını açıkladı.' 31 December 2013. http:// www.dunya.com/babacan-operasyonun-faturasini-acikladi-213724h.htm.

Economist Intelligence. 2015. 'Democracy Index 2015.' http://www.eiu.com/public/ topical_report.aspx?campaignid=DemocracyIndex2015.

Economist Intelligence. 2020. 'Democracy Index 2020.' https://www.eiu.com/n/ campaigns/democracy-index-2020/.

Eder, M. 2016. 'Turkey.' In *The Middle East*, 14th edn, edited by Ellen Lust, 854–94. Los Angeles: CQ Press/SAGE.

Eisenstein, Zillah R. 1994. *The Color of Gender: Reimaging Democracy*. Berkeley: University of California Press.

Ekman, Mattias. 2022. 'The Great Replacement: Strategic Mainstreaming of Far-Right Conspiracy Claims.' *Convergence*, May 2022. https://doi.org/10.1177/ 13548565221091983.

Eley, G. 2002. *Forging Democracy: The History of the Left in Europe*. Oxford: Oxford University Press.

El-Haj, Nadia Abu. 1998. 'Translating Truths: Nationalism, the Practice of Archae-ology, and the Remaking of Past and Present in Contemporary Jerusalem.' *American Ethnologist* 25 (May): 166–88.

El-Haj, Nadia Abu. 2002. *Facts on the Ground: Archaeological Practice and Territorial Self-Fashioning in Israeli Society*. Chicago: University of Chicago Press.

Esen, Berk, and Şebnem Gümüşçü. 2017. 'A Small Yes for Presidentialism: The Turkish Constitutional Referendum of April 2017.' *South European Society and Politics* 22 (3): 303–26.

Esin, Cigdem. 2011. 'Narrative Analysis Approaches.' In *Qualitative Research Methods in Psychology: Combining Core Approaches*, edited by Nollaig Frost. Maidenhead: Open University Press.

Ewick, Patricia, and Susan Silbey. 1995. 'Subversive Stories and Hegemonic Tales: Toward a Sociology of Narrative.' *Law & Society Review* 29 (2).

Ewick, Patricia, and Susan Silbey. 2003. 'Narrating Social Structure: Stories of Resistance to Legal Authority.' *American Journal of Sociology* 108 (6): 1328–72.

Ezzy, Douglas. 1998. 'Theorizing Narrative Identity: Symbolic Interactionism and Hermeneutics.' *The Sociological Quarterly* 39 (2): 239–52.

Facebook. 2012. 'Unser Herz Schlägt ROT-WEISS-ROT!!!' 5 July 2012. https://www.facebook.com/HCStrache/photos/a.226243068590/10150948634068591/?type=1&theater.

Filc, Dani. 2010. *The Political Right in Israel: Different Faces of Jewish Populism*. New York: Routledge.

FPÖ TV. 2017. 'Rot-Schwarz Haben Die Fairness-Krise Geschaffen – Die FPÖ Wird Sie Lösen!' https://www.youtube.com/watch?v=iRyyNj_CBP4.

Fraser, N. 1998. *Social Justice in the Age of Identity Politics: Redistribution, Recognition, Participation*. Discussion Paper. Berlin: Wissenschaftszentrum Berlin für Sozialforschung.

Fraser, N. 1999. 'Social Justice in the Age of Identity Politics: Redistribution, Recognition, and Participation.' In *Culture and Economy after the Cultural Turn*, edited by L. Ray and A. Sayer, 25–52. London: Sage.

Fraser, N. 2000. 'Rethinking Recognition.' *New Left Review* 3 (3): 107–18.

Freedom House. 2013. https://freedomhouse.org/report/freedom-press/2013/turkey.

Freedom House. 2016a. https://freedomhouse.org/report/freedom-press/2016/turkey.

Freedom House. 2016b. https://freedomhouse.org/sites/default/files/FH_FITW_Report_2016.pdf.

Freedom Party of Austria. 2011. 'Parteiprogramm (Englisch) – Freiheitliche Partei Österreichs.' 18 June 2011. https://www.fpoe.at/themen/parteiprogramm/parteiprogramm-englisch/.

Freedom Party of Austria. 2015. 'HC Strache: Wir müssen unser Heimatrecht verteidigen und schützen!' 11 December 2015. https://www.fpoe.at/artikel/hc-strache-wir-muessen-unser-heimatrecht-verteidigen-und-schuetzen-1/.

Freedom Party of Austria. 2016. '333. Jahrestag: FPÖ feierte Ende der Türkenbelagerung.' 13 September 2016. https://www.fpoe.at/artikel/333-jahrestag-fpoe-feierte-ende-der-tuerkenbelagerung/.

Freedom Party of Austria. 2017. 'Das Freiheitliche Wirtschaftsprogramm.' 2017. https://www.fpoe.at/fileadmin/user_upload/2017_freiheitliche_wirtschafts-programm_web.pdf.

Freeman, Mark, and Jens Brockmeier. 2001. 'Narrative Integrity: Autobiographical Identity and the Meaning of the "Good Life".' In *Narrative and Identity: Studies in Autobiography, Self and Culture*, edited by Jens Brockmeier and Donal Carbaugh, 75-99. Amsterdam: John Benjamins Publishing Company.

Frega, R. 2021. 'The fourth stage of social democracy.' *Theory and Society* 50: 489–513.

Freistein, Katja, and Frank Gadinger. 2020. 'Populist Stories of Honest Men and Proud Mothers: A Visual Narrative Analysis.' *Review of International Studies* 46 (2): 217–36.

Gazetevatan. 2018. 'Cumhurbaşkanı Erdoğan: CHP Dün Neydi Ki Bugün Ne Olsun | Siyaset Haberleri.' 7 October 2018. http://www.gazetevatan.com/cumhurbas-kani-erdogan-konusuyor-1207212-siyaset/.

Gec, Jovana. 2019. 'Suspected New Zealand Gunman Fascinated with Ottoman Wars, Named Rifles after Legendary Serbs.' *The Morning Call*, 16 March 2019. https://www.mcall.com/news/breaking/mc-nws-new-zealand-shooter-balkans-20190316-story.html.

Geddes, Barbara. 1999. 'What Do We Know About Democratization After Twenty Years?' *Annual Review of Political Science* 2: 115–44.

Geddes, Barbara. 2007. 'What Causes Democratization?' In *Oxford Handbook of Comparative Politics*, edited by C. Boix and S. Stokes, 317–39. Oxford: Oxford University Press.

Gellman, Barton. 2021. 'Trump's Next Coup Has Already Begun.' *The Atlantic*, 6 December 2021. https://www.theatlantic.com/magazine/archive/2022/01/january-6-insurrection-trump-coup-2024-election/620843/.

Gerçek Gündem. 2018. 'Erdoğan: Ekonomide çok iyi durumdayız.' 5 June 2018. https://www.gercekgundem.com/siyaset/18498/erdogan-ekonomide-cok-iyi-durumdayiz.

Gidron, Noam, and Bart Bonikowski. 2013. *Varieties of Populism: Literature Review and Research Agenda*. Weatherhead Working Paper Series No. 13–0004.

Goetz, Judith. 2021. '*"The Great Replacement"*: Reproduction and Population Policies of the Far Right, Taking the Identitarians as an Example.' *DiGeSt Journal of Diversity and Gender Studies* 8 (1): 59–74.

Goffman, Erving. 1974. *Frame Analysis: An Essay on the Organization of Experience*. New York: Harper & Row.

Göle, Nilufer. 1993. 'Engineers: "Technocratic Democracy".' In *Turkey and the West: Changing Political and Cultural Identities*, edited by Metin Heper, Ayse Oncu and Heinz Kramer. London: I. B. Tauris.

Göle, N. 1997. 'Secularism and Islamism in Turkey: The Making of Elites and Counter-elites.' *Middle East Journal* 51 (1): 46–58.

Groth, Stefan. 2019. 'Political Narratives/Narrations of the Political.' *Narrative Culture* 6 (Spring): 1–18.

Günay-Erkol, Ç. 2013. 'Issues of Ideology and Identity in Turkish Literature during the Cold War.' In *Turkey in the Cultural Cold War*, edited by C. Örnek and Ç. Üngör, 109–30. London: Palgrave.

Gür, Aslı. 2007. 'Stories in Three Dimensions: Narratives of Nation and the Anatolian Civilizations Museum.' In *The Politics of Public Memory in Turkey*, edited by Esra Özyürek. Syracuse: Syracuse University Press.

Gür, Aslı. 2010. 'Political Excavations of the Anatolian Past: Nationalism and Archaeology in Turkey.' In *Controlling the Past, Owning the Future: The Political Uses of Archaeology in the Middle East,* edited by Ran Boytner, Lynn Swartz Dodd and Bradley J. Parker. Tucson: Arizona University Press.

Gürkaynak, R. S., and S. Sayek-Böke. 2013. 'AKP döneminde Türkiye ekonomisi.' *Birikim* 296.

Gürsel, Kadri. 2015. 'Turkey's Perilous Security Package.' 20 February 2015. http://www.al-monitor.com/pulse/originals/2015/02/turkey-security-package-threatens-security.html.

Halil, Ahmet. 1928. 'Ankara'daki Müesseseleri Ziyaret: Etnoğrafya Müzemiz.' *Hayat Mecmuası* 108: 9–14.

Halman, Talat. 2012. 'Literature.' In *The Routledge Handbook of Modern Turkey*, edited by Metin Heper and Sabri Sayari, 76–86. New York: Routledge.

Hammack, Phillip L. 2010. 'The Cultural Psychology of Palestinian Youth: A Narrative Approach.' *Culture & Psychology* 16 (November): 507–37.

Harari, Yuval Noah. 2015. *Sapiens: A Brief History of Humankind*. New York: Harper Perennial.

Harvey, D. 2007. 'Neoliberalism as Creative Destruction.' *Annals of the American Academy of Political and Social Science* 610: 22–44.

Hawkins, Kirk A. 2009. 'Is Chávez Populist?: Measuring Populist Discourse in Comparative Perspective." *Comparative Political Studies* 42 (8): 1040–67. https://doi.org/10.1177/0010414009331721.

Hayward, Clarissa R. 2010. 'Bad Stories: Narrative, Identity, and the State's Materialist Pedagogy.' *Citizenship Studies* 14 (6): 651–66.

Henisz, W. J. 2004. 'Political Institutions and Policy Volatility.' *Economics & Politics* 16 (1): 1–27.

Heper, Metin. 1992. 'The Strong State as a Problem for the Consolidation of Democracy: Turkey and Germany Compared.' *Comparative Political Studies* 25 (2): 169–94.

Her Sey. 2014. 'Ankara Somut Olmayan Kültürel Miras Müzesi.' 6 March 2014. https://www.youtube.com/watch?v=_1EOit3EySE.

Heute. 2017. '1. FPÖ-Wahlplakat gegen rot-schwarzen Speck.' 24 August 2017. https://www.heute.at/politik/news/story/Nationalratswahl--Erstes-FP--Wahl-plakat-gegen-rot-schwarzen--Speck--51051191.

Hobsbawm, E. 1996. 'Identity Politics and the Left.' *New Left Review* 217: 38–47.

Hogg, Jonny, and Hümeyra Pamuk. 2014. 'Fight Against Domestic Violence Stalls in "Patriarchal" Turkey.' *Hürriyet Daily News*, 22 July 2014. http://www.hurriyet-dailynews.com/fight-against-domestic-violence-stalls-in-patriarchal-turkey.aspx?pageID=517&nID=69455&NewsCatID=339.

Hungarian Government. 2014a. 'Prime Minister Viktor Orban's Speech at the 25th Bálványos Summer Free University and Student Camp.' 26 July 2014. http://www.kormany.hu/en/the-prime-minister/the-prime-minister-s-speeches/prime-minister-viktor-orban-s-speech-at-the-25th-balvanyos-summer-free-university-and-student-camp.

Hungarian Government. 2014b. 'Hungary 25 Years after the Opening of the Borders – 25 Years of Democracy and Freedom in Europe.' 6 November 2014. http://www.kormany.hu/en/the-prime-minister/the-prime-minister-s-speeches/hungary-25-years-after-the-opening-of-the-borders-25-years-of-democracy-and-freedom-in-europe.

Hungarian Government. 2015a. 'Viktor Orban's Speech on the Anniversary of the Hungarian Revolution of 1848.' 15 March 2015. http://www.kormany.hu/en/the-prime-minister/the-prime-minister-s-speeches/viktor-orban-s-speech-on-the-anniversary-of-the-hungarian-revolution-of-1848.

Hungarian Government. 2015b. 'Viktor Orban: We Should Not Use Only the Language of Strength.' 5 June 2015. http://www.kormany.hu/en/the-prime-minister/the-prime-minister-s-speeches/viktor-orban-we-should-not-use-only-the-language-of-strength.

Hungarian Government. 2016a. 'Prime Minister Viktor Orban's State of the Nation Address.' 28 February 2016. http://www.kormany.hu/en/the-prime-minister/the-prime-minister-s-speeches/prime-minister-viktor-orban-s-state-of-the-nation-address.

Hungarian Government. 2016b. 'Are You Opposed to Peace?' 13 July 2016. http://www.kormany.hu/en/the-prime-minister/the-prime-minister-s-speeches/are-you-opposed-to-peace.

Hungarian Government. 2016c. Prime Minister Viktor Orban's Speech at the Official Ceremony Marking the 60th Anniversary of the 1956 Revolution.' 23 October 2016. http://www.kormany.hu/en/the-prime-minister/the-prime-min-ister-s-speeches/prime-minister-viktor-orban-s-speech-at-the-official-ceremony-marking-the-60th-anniversary-of-the-1956-revolution.

Hungarian Government. 2017a. 'Viktor Orban's Speech on the Anniversary of the 1848 Revolution.' 15 March 2017. http://www.kormany.hu/en/the-prime-minister/the-prime-minister-s-speeches/viktor-orban-s-speech-on-the-anniversary-of-the-1848-revolution.

Hungarian Government. 2017b. 'Prime Minister Viktor Orban's Speech on the 61st Anniversary of the 1956 Revolution and Freedom Fight.' 23 October 2017. http://www.kormany.hu/en/the-prime-minister/the-prime-minister-s-speeches/prime-minister-viktor-orban-s-speech-on-the-61st-anniversary-of-the-1956-revolution-and-freedom-fight.

Hungarian Government. 2018a. 'Viktor Orban's "State of the Nation" Address.' 18 February 2018. http://www.kormany.hu/en/the-prime-minister/the-prime-minister-s-speeches/viktor-orban-s-state-of-the-nation-address.

Hungarian Government. 2018b. 'Orban Viktor's Ceremonial Speech on the 170th Anniversary of the Hungarian Revolution of 1848.' 15 March 2018. http://www.kormany.hu/en/the-prime-minister/the-prime-minister-s-speeches/orban-viktor-s-ceremonial-speech-on-the-170th-anniversary-of-the-hungarian-revolution-of-1848.

Hungarian Government. 2018c. 'Prime Minister Viktor Orban's Address after Swearing the Prime-Ministerial Oath of Office.' 10 May 2018. http://www.kormany.hu/en/the-prime-minister/the-prime-minister-s-speeches/prime-minister-viktor-orban-s-address-after-swearing-the-prime-ministerial-oath-of-office.

Hungarian Government. 2018d. 'Prime Minister Viktor Orban's Speech at the Final Fidesz Election Campaign Event.' 4 June 2018. http://www.kormany.hu/en/the-prime-minister/the-prime-minister-s-speeches/prime-minister-viktor-orban-s-speech-at-the-final-fidesz-election campaign-event.

Hungarian Government. 2018e. 'Prime Minister Viktor Orban's Speech at the Inauguration of the Monument to the Victims of Soviet Occupation.' 19 June 2018. http://www.kormany.hu/en/the-prime-minister/the-prime-minister-s-speeches/prime-minister-viktor-orban-s-speech-at-the-inauguration-of-the-monument-to-the-victims-of-soviet-occupation.

Hungarian Government. 2018f. 'Prime Minister Viktor Orban's Speech on the 62nd Anniversary of the 1956 Revolution and Freedom Fight.' 23 October 2018. http://www.kormany.hu/en/the-prime-minister/the-prime-minister-s-speeches/prime-minister-viktor-orban-s-speech-on-the-62nd-anniversary-of-the-1956-revolution-and-freedom-fight.

Hürriyet. 2012. 'Dindar Bir Gençlik Yetiştirmek Istiyoruz.' 1 February 2012. http://www.hurriyet.com.tr/gundem/19819295.asp.

Hürriyet. 2013a. 'Turkish PM Erdoğan calls for "immediate end" to Gezi Park protests.' 7 June 2013. http://www.hurriyetdailynews.com/turkish-pm-erdogan-calls-for-immediate-end-to-gezi-park-protests-.aspx?PageID=238&NID=48381&NewsCatID=338.

Hürriyet. 2013b. 'Başbakan: Bu Tayyip Erdoğan değişmez [Erdogan: This Tayyip Erdogan Will not Change].' 12 June 2013. http://www.hurriyet.com.tr/gundem/23479966.asp.

Hürriyet. 2013c. 'Başbakan Erdoğan'dan Gezi değerlendirmesi.' 12 July 2013. http://www.hurriyet.com.tr/gundem/23708621.asp.

Hürriyet. 2013d. 'Faiz lobisi bulunamadı.' 20 December 2013. http://www.hurriyet.com.tr/faiz-lobisi-bulunamadi-25467161.

Hürriyet. 2014. 'Erdoğan'dan 17 Aralık göndermesi.' 22 January 2014. http://www.hurriyet.com.tr/dunya/25620888.asp.

Hürriyet Daily News. 2013a, "Prime Minister Erdoğan blesses Turkish police for 'heroic' action during Gezi unrest," 24 June 2013. http://www.hurriyetdaily-news.com/turkish-prime-minister-erdogan-praises-polices-intervention-in-gezi-protests-as-heroic.aspx?pageID=238&nid=49356.

Hürriyet Daily News. 2013b. 'Banks investigated for transactions over 2 million dollars in Turkey.' 10 July 2013. http://www.hurriyetdailynews.com/banks-under-probe-for-transactions-over-2-million-dollars-in-turkey.aspx?pageID=238&nID=50402&NewsCatID=344.

Identitäre Bewegung Deutschland. 2017. 'Von der Notwendigkeit politischer Aktivist zu sein.' 28 July 2017. https://www.identitaere-bewegung.de/blog/von-der-notwendigkeit-politischer-aktivist-zu-sein/.

Inan, Ayşe Afet. 1999 [1930]. *Türk Tarihinin Ana Hatları* [Guidelines of Turkish History]. Istanbul: Kaynak.

Inan, Ayse Afet. 2000 [1931]. *Medeni Bilgiler ve M.K.Atatürk'ün El Yazıları* [Civics and Ataturk's Handwritings]. Ankara: Atatürk Kültür, Dil ve Tarih Yüksek Kurumu Atatürk Araştırma Merkezi Yayını.

Inan, Ayşe Afet. 1939. 'Atatürk ve Tarih Tezi [Atatürk and the History Thesis].' *Belleten* 3 (10), 245–6.

Kalaycıoğlu, E. 2010. 'Justice and Development Party at the Helm: Resurgence of Islam or Restitution of the Right-of-Center Predominant Party?' *Turkish Studies* 11 (1): 29–44.

Kalaycıoğlu, E. 2013. 'Q&A: Presidential Systems.' *Turkish Review* 3 (1): 62–7.

Kalaycıoğlu, E. 2016. 'Denge ve Denetleme Açısından Yeni Anayasa Değişikliği Teklifi.' *mecliste.org*. http://mecliste.org/bakis-acisi/denge-denetleme-acisindan-yeni-anayasa-degisikligi-teklifi.

Kanal B. 2013. 'Gezi Finansörü "Ayşe Teyze" Çıktı.' 21 November 2013. http://www.kanalb.com.tr/haber.php?HaberNo=52608.

Kandiyoti, Deniz. 2014. 'No Laughing Matter: Women and the New Populism in Turkey.' *OpenDemocracy*. 31 August 2014. http://www.opendemocracy.net/5050/deniz-kandiyoti/no-laughing-matter-women-and-new-populism-in-turkey.

Kansteiner, Wulf. 2002. 'Finding Meaning in Memory: A Methodological Critique of Collective Memory Studies.' *History and Theory* 41 (May): 179–97.

Kapstein, E. B., and N. Converse. 2008. 'Why Democracies Fail.' *Journal of Democracy* 19 (4): 57–68.

Kasaba, Resat. 2008. 'Introduction.' In *The Cambridge History of Turkey, Volume 4: Turkey in the Modern World*, edited by Resat Kasaba. Cambridge: Cambridge University Press.

Kaya, Ayhan, Max-Valentin Robert and Ayşe Tecmen. 2020. 'Populism in Turkey and France: Nativism, Multiculturalism and Euroskepticism.' *Turkish Studies* 21 (3): 361–91.

Kearney, Richard. 2006. *On Stories*. New York: Routledge.

Keefer, P., and S. Knack. 2007. 'Boondoggles, Rent-Seeking, and Political Checks and Balances: Public Investment under Unaccountable Governments.' *The Review of Economics and Statistics* 89 (3): 566–72.

Keyman, E. F. and Z. Öniş. 2010. 'Civil Society: Then and Now.' In *Turkish Politics in a Changing World*, edited by E. F. Keyman and Z. Öniş, 267–87. Istanbul: Istanbul Bilgi University Publications.

Keyman, E. Fuat, and Sebnem Gümüşçü. 2014. 'Civil Society and Democratic Consolidation.' In *Democracy, Identity, and Foreign Policy in Turkey: Hegemony through Transformation*, by E. Fuat Keyman and Sebnem Gumuscu, 143–62. London: Palgrave Macmillan.

Kezer, Zeynep. 2000. 'Familiar Things in Strange Places: Ankara's Ethnography Museum and the Legacy of Islam in Republican Turkey.' *Perspectives in Vernacular Architecture* 8: 101–16.

Kilinç, Kivanç. 2017. '"The Hittite Sun Is Rising Once Again": Contested Narratives of Identity, Place and Memory in Ankara.' *History and Memory* 29 (2): pp. 3–34.

Kioupkiolis, A. 2016. 'Podemos: The Ambiguous Promises of Left-Wing Populism in Contemporary Spain.' *Journal of Political Ideologies* 21 (2): 99–120.

Kitschelt, H. 1994. *The Transformation of European Social Democracy*. New York: Cambridge University Press.

KONDA. 2014. 'Gezi Report: Public Perception of the "Gezi Protests". Who Were the People at Gezi Park?' KONDA, 5 June 2014. See konda.com.tr.

Kültür Bakanligi. 'Ankara – Kurtuluş Savaşı Müzesi (I. TBMM Binası).' https://
www.ktb.gov.tr/TR-96356/ankara---kurtulus-savasi-muzesi-i-tbmm-binasi.html
(accessed 23 May 2022).

Kültür Varliklari ve Müzeler Genel Müdürlüğü. 'Ankara Cumhuriyet Müzesi
Müdürlüğü.' https://Kvmgm.Ktb.Gov.Tr/TR-269401/Ankara-Cumhuriyet-
Muzesi-Mudurlugu.Html (accessed 23 May 2022).

Kuran, Timur. 1991. 'Now Out of Never: The Element of Surprise in the East
European Revolution of 1989.' *World Politics* 44: 7–48.

La Porta, R. Florencio Lopez-De-Sılanes, C. Pop-Eleches and A. Shleifer. 2004.
'Judicial Checks and Balances.' *Journal of Political Economy* 112 (2): 445–70.

Laclau, Ernesto. 1977. *Politics and Ideology in Marxist Theory: Capitalism, Fascism,
Populism*. London: New Left Books.

Laclau, Ernesto. 2005. *On Populist Reason*. New York: Verso.

Levitsky, Steven, and Lucan A. Way. 2010. *Competitive Authoritarianism: Hybrid
Regimes After the Cold War*. New York: Cambridge University Press.

Lipset, Seymour Martin. 1959. 'Some Social Requisites of Democracy: Economic Development and Political Legitimacy.' *American Political Science Review* 53 (1): 69–105.

LSE IDEAS. 2018. 'Understanding the Global Rise of Populism.' *LSE IDEAS* (blog).
12 February 2018. https://medium.com/@lseideas/understanding-the-global-
rise-of-populism-27305a1c5355.

Lueg, Klarissa, Ann S. Bager and Marianne W. Lundholt. 2021. 'Introduction: What
Counter-Narratives are: Dimensions and Levels of a Theory of Middle Range.'
In *Routledge Handbook of Counter-Narratives*, edited by Klarissa Lueg and
Marianne W. Lundholt. London: Routledge.

McAdam, Doug. 1982. *Political Process and the Development of Black Insurgency,
1930–1970*. Chicago: University of Chicago Press.

McClintock, Anne. 1991. '"No Longer in a Future Heaven": Women and Nationalism in South Africa.' *Transition* 51: 104–23.

McClintock, Anne. 1995. *Imperial Leather: Race, Gender and Sexuality in the Colonial
Con-test*. New York: Routledge.

MacIntyre, Alasdair. 2007 [1981]. *After Virtue: A Study in Moral Theory*, 3rd edn.
South Bend: University of Notre Dame Press.

Manwaring, R., and J. Holloway. 2021. 'A New Wave of Social Democracy? Policy
Change across the Social Democratic Party Family, 1970s–2010s.' *Government
and Opposition* 57 (1): 171–91.

Mardin, Şerif. 1973. 'Center-Periphery Relations: A Key to Turkish Politics?' *Daedalus*,
169–90.

Mehta, Akanksha, and Annick T. R. Wibben. 2018. 'Feminist Narrative Approaches to Security.' In *The Routledge Handbook of Gender and Security*, edited by Caron E. Gentry, Laura J. Shepherd and Laura Sjoberg. Abingdon: Routledge.

Mercil, Erdoğan, Taner Tarhan and Zerrin Gunal. 1990. *Lise için Tarih I* [History for High School 1]. Istanbul: Altin Kitaplar Yayınevi.

Metiner, M. 2013. '"Faiz lobisi" ile "kan lobisi" kol kola.' *Yeni Safak*, 24 December 2013. http://yenisafak.com.tr/yazarlar/MehmetMetiner/faiz-lobisi-ile-kan-lobisi-kol-kola/44888.

Miller-Idriss, C. 2020. *Hate in the Homeland. The New Global Far Right.* Princeton: Princeton University Press.

Milliyet. 2010. 'DİSK Genel Başkanı: 2.5 milyon sendikalı sayısı 650 bine düştü.' 21 August 2010. http://www.milliyet.com.tr/disk-genel-baskani-2-5-milyon-sendikali-sayisi-650-bine-dustu/ekonomi/sondakikaarsiv/06.09.2010/1279353/default.htm.

Milliyet. 2012. 'Erdoğan Kuvvetler Ayrılığı Eleştirisi.' 17 December 2012. http://siyaset.milliyet.com.tr/erdogan-kuvvetler-ayriligi-elestirisi/siyaset/siyasetde-tay/17.12.2012/1642954/default.htm (accessed 5 April 2013).

Mishler, Elliot G. 1995. 'Models of Narrative Analysis: A Typology.' *Journal of Narrative and Life History* 5 (2): 87–123.

Mishler, Elliot G. 2006. 'Narrative and Identity: The Double Arrow of Time.' In *Discourse and Identity*, edited by Anna De Fina, Deborah Schiffrin and Michael Bamberg. Cambridge: Cambridge University Press.

Miskimmon, Alister, Ben O'Loughlin and Laura Roselle. 2013. *Strategic Narratives: Communication Power and the New World Order.* New York: Routledge.

Moreno, Eduardo Manzano, and Juan Sisinio Perez Garzon. 2002. 'A Difficult Nation? History and Nationalism in Contemporary Spain.' *History & Memory* 14 (1): 259–84.

Mouffe, C. 2018. *For a Left Populism.* London: Verso.

Mudde, Cas. 2004. 'The Populist Zeitgeist.' *Government and Opposition* 39 (4): 541–63.

Mudde, Cas, and Cristóbal Rovira Kaltwasser. 2015. 'Vox Populi or Vox Masculini? Populism and Gender in Northern Europe and South America.' *Patterns of Prejudice* 49 (1–2): 16–36.

Mudde, Cas, and Cristóbal Rovira Kaltwasser. 2018. 'Studying Populism in Comparative Perspective: Reflections on the Contemporary and Future Research Agenda.' *Comparative Political Studies* 47: 1324–53.

Müller, Jan-Werner. 2016. *What is Populism?* Philadelphia: University of Pennsylvania Press.

Neue Freie Zeitung. 2017. 'Nur wer FPÖ wählt, stoppt Rot-Schwarz!' 24 August 2017. https://nfz.fpoe.at/nur-wer-fpo-wahlt-stoppt-rot-schwarz/59390220.

North, D. 1990. *Institutions, Institutional Change, and Economic Performance.* Cambridge: Cambridge University Press.

Norton, Anne. 2004. *95 Theses on Politics, Culture, and Method.* New Haven: Yale University Press.

NTV. 2013a. 'Erdoğan: Başörtülülere Saldırdılar.' 9 June 2013. https://www.ntv.com. tr/turkiye/erdogan-basortululere-saldirdilar,MY8fETQDTESWrDoEc5_tbQ.

NTV. 2013b. 'Erdoğan: Faizlobisinin neferi oldular.' 22 June 2013. http://www.ntv.com. tr/turkiye/erdogan-faiz-lobisinin-neferi-oldular,hRBnD9YIYkehfPQCWqTF4g.

NTVMSNBC. 2013. 'Babacan: Kayıp 20 milyar dolar.' 22 December 2013. http://www.ntvmsnbc.com/id/25487437/.

Obaidi, Milan, Jonas Kunst, Simon Ozer and Sasha Y. Kimel. 2021. 'The "Great Replacement" Conspiracy: How the Perceived Ousting of Whites Can Evoke Violent Extremism and Islamophobia.' *Group Processes & Intergroup Relations* August 2021. doi: 10.1177/13684302211028293.

Oda TV. 2014. 'Erdoğan: Bu ülkede yıllarca bir doğum kontrolü ihaneti yaptılar.' 22 December 2014. https://odatv4.com/guncel/dogum-kontrolu-ihanettir-2212141200-69030.

O'Donnell, G. 1999. 'Horizontal Accountability in New Democracies.' In *The Self-Restraining State: Power and Accountability in New Democracies,* edited by A. Schedler, L. Diamond and M. F. Plattner. Boulder: Lynne Rienner Publishers.

Oe24. 2013. 'Strache: "Hurra, Es Reimt Sich Wieder".' 28 August 2013. https://www.oe24.at/oesterreich/politik/Strache-Hurra-es-reimt-sich-wieder/114362259.

Oe24. 2018. 'Strache: "Das Kopftuch-Verbot Schützt Mädchen".' 17 November 2018. https://www.oe24.at/oesterreich/politik/Strache-Das-Kopftuch-Verbot-schuetzt-Maedchen/356413914.

Olick, Jeffrey K., and Joyce Robbins. 1998. 'Social Memory Studies: From "Collective Memory" to the Historical Sociology of Mnemonic Practices.' *Annual Review of Sociology* 24 (August): 105–40.

Olson, Mancur. 1993. 'Dictatorship, Democracy, and Development.' *The American Political Science Review* 87 (3): 567–76.

Öniş, Z. 2004. 'Turgut Özal and his Economic Legacy: Turkish Neo-Liberalism in Critical Perspective.' *Middle Eastern Studies* 40 (4): 113–34.

Öniş, Z. 2013. 'Sharing Power: Turkey's Democratization Challenge in the Age of the AKP Hegemony.' *Insight Turkey* 15 (2): 103–22.

Önnerfors. Andreas. 2021. '*Der Grosse Austausch*: conspiratorial frames of terrorist violence in Germany.' In *Europe: Continent of Conspiracies: Conspiracy Theories in and about Europe*, 1st edn, edited by Andreas Onnerfors and Andre Krouwel, pp. 76–96. Abingdon: Routledge.

Oppermann, K., and A. Spencer. 2018. 'Narrating Success and Failure: Congressional Debates on the "Iran Nuclear Deal".' *European Journal of International Relations* 24 (2): 268–92.

Oren, Neta, Rafi Nets-Zehngut and Daniel Bar-Tal. 2015. 'Construction of the Israeli-Jewish Conflict-Supportive Narrative and the Struggle Over Its Dominance.' *Political Psychology* 36 (February): 215–30.

Orhan, G. 2007. 'Institutions and Ideas in the Institutionalization of Turkish Environmental Policy," *Critical Policy Studies* 1 (1): 42–61.

Özbudun, Ergun. 2013. *Party Politics and Social Cleavages in Turkey*. Boulder: Lynne Rienner.

Özbudun, Ergun. 2014. 'AKP at the Crossroads: Erdoğan's Majoritarian Drift.' *South European Society and Politics* 19 (2): 1–13.

Özdoğan, Mehmet. 1998. 'Ideology and Archaeology in Turkey.' In *Archaeology under Fire. Nationalism, Politics and Heritage in the Eastern Mediterranean and Middle East*, edited by L. Meskell, 111–24. London: Routledge.

Özyürek, Esra. 2006. *Nostalgia for the Modern: State Secularism and Everyday Politics in Turkey*. Durham: Duke University Press.

Özyürek, Esra, Gaye Özpınar and Emrah Altındiş, eds. 2019. *Authoritarianism and Resistance in Turkey, Conversations on Democratic and Social Challenges*. Cham: Springer.

Palley, T. I. 2005. 'From Keynesianism to Neoliberalism: Shifting Paradigms in Economics.' In *Neoliberalism: A Critical Reader*, edited by A. Saad-Filho and D. Johnston, 20–9. London: Pluto Press.

Patterson, Molly, and Kristen R. Monroe. 1998. 'Narrative in Political Science.' *Annual Review of Political Science* 1 (June): 315–31.

Payitaht Abdülhamid. [TV series] 2017. http://www.imdb.com/title/tt6536562/.

Pierson, Christopher. 2011. *The Modern State*. London: Routledge.

P-NORC Center for Public Affairs Research. 2022. 'Immigration Attitudes and Conspiratorial Thinkers: A Study Issued on the 10th Anniversary of The Associated Press-NORC Center for Public Affairs Research.' May 2022. apnorc.org/projects/immigration-attitudes-and-conspiratorial-thinkers.

Polanyi, Karl. 1957 [1944]. *The Great Transformation*. Boston: Beacon Press.

Politico. 2021. 'How the Istanbul Convention Became a Symbol of Europe's Cultural Wars.' 12 April 2021, https://www.politico.eu/article/istanbul-convention-europe-violence-against-women/.

Polkinghorne, Donald E. 1995. 'Narrative Configuration in Qualitative Analysis.' *International Journal of Qualitative Studies in Education* 8 (1): 5–23.

Polletta, Francesca. 1998. 'Contending Stories: Narrative in Social Movements.' *Qualitative Sociology* 21 (December): 419–46.

Polletta, Francesca. 2009. *It Was Like a Fever: Storytelling in Protest and Politics.* Chicago: University of Chicago Press.

Polletta, Francesca, and Jessica Callahan. 2017. 'Deep Stories, Nostalgia Narratives, and Fake News: Storytelling in the Trump Era.' *American Journal of Cultural Sociology* 5 (October): 392–408.

Polletta, Francesca, and Pang C. B. Chen. 2012. 'Narrative and Social Movements.' In *The Oxford Handbook of Cultural Sociology*, edited by Jeffrey C. Alexander, Ronald N. Jacobs and Philip Smith. Oxford: Oxford University Press.

Polletta, Francesca, and John Lee. 2006. 'Is Telling Stories Good for Democracy? Rhetoric in Public Deliberation after 9/11.' *American Sociological Review* 71 (5): 699–723.

Polletta, Francesca, Pang Ching Bobby Chen, Beth Gharrity Gardner and Alice Motes. 2011. 'The Sociology of Storytelling.' *Annual Review of Sociology* 37 (August): 109–30.

Posta. 2012. 'Kuvvetler Ayrılığı Önümüze Engel.' 17 December 2012. https://www.posta.com.tr/kuvvetler-ayriligi-onumuze-engel-153008.

Przeworski, Adam, and Fernando Limongi. 1997. 'Modernization: Theories and Facts.' *World Politics* 49 (2): 155–83. http://www.jstor.org/stable/25053996.

Radikal. 2012. 'Kuvvetler ayrılığı engel.' 18 December 2012. http://www.radikal.com.tr/turkiye/kuvvetler_ayriligi_engel-1112491/.

Radikal. 2013. 'Burhan Kuzu: Diktatörlük Gelemesin Diye Başkanlık İstiyoruz.' 3 March 2013. http://www.radikal.com.tr/Radikal.aspx?aType=RadikalDetayV3&ArticleID=1124443&CategoryID=78.

Radikal. 2014. 'Cumhurbaşkanı Erdoğan: Bu Ülkede Yıllarca Doğum Kontrolü Ihaneti Yaptılar.' 22 December 2014. http://www.radikal.com.tr/turkiye/cumhurbaskani_erdogan_bu_ulkede_yillarca_dogum_kontrolu_ihaneti_yaptilar-1256542.

Reed, A., and M. Chowkwanyun. 2012. 'Race, Class, Crisis: The Discourse of Disparity and its Analytical Discontents.' *Socialist Register* 48 (1): 149–75.

Ricoeur, Paul, 1980. 'Narrative Time.' *Critical Inquiry* 7 (1): 169–90.

Riessman, Catherine Kohler. 1993. *Narrative Analysis.* Thousand Oaks: Sage.

Riessman, Catherine K. 2008. *Narrative Methods for the Human Sciences.* Thousand Oaks: Sage.

Roberts, Kenneth M. 1995. 'Neoliberalism and the Transformation of Populism in Latin America: The Peruvian Case.' *World Politics* 48 (1): 82–116.

Roberts, K. M. 2008. 'Is Social Democracy Possible in Latin America?' *Nueva Sociedad* 217: 70–86.

Roediger, Henry L., and James V. Wertsch. 2008. 'Creating a New Discipline of Memory Studies.' *Memory Studies* 1 (January): 9–22.

Rueschemeyer, Dietrich. 2006. 'Why and How Ideas Matter?' In *The Oxford Handbook of Contextual Political Analysis*, edited by Robert E. Goodin and Charles Tilly. Oxford: Oxford University Press.

Sabah. 2013a. 'Gençleri Korumak Devletin Görevi [It is the State's Duty to Protect the Youth].' 7 November 2013. http://www.sabah.com.tr/Gundem/2013/11/07/gencleri-korumak-devletin-gorevi.

Sabah. 2013b. 'Başbakan Erdoğan: İşte operasyonun 9 sebebi.' 25 December 2013. https://www.sabah.com.tr/gundem/2013/12/25/basbakan-erdogan-konusuyor.

Sabah. 2015. 'Erdoğan'dan *New York Times* değerlendirmesi. 2 June 2015. https://www.sabah.com.tr/gundem/2015/06/02/erdogandan-new-york-times-degerlendirmesi.

Sabah. 2016. 'Milletin adamları "Büyük Türkiye" için çalıştılar.' [video] https://www.sabah.com.tr/webtv/turkiye/milletin-adamlari-buyuk-turkiye-icin-calistilar.

Sahlstein Parcell, Erin, and Benjamin M. A. Baker. 2018. 'Narrative Analysis.' In *The SAGE Encyclopedia of Communication Research Methods*, edited by Mike Allen. Thousand Oaks: Sage.

Savage, Ritchie. 2012. 'From McCarthyism to the Tea Party: Interpreting Anti-Leftist Forms of US Populism in Comparative Perspective.' *New Political Science* 34 (January): 564–84.

Schatzberg, Michael G. 1993. 'Power, Legitimacy and "Democratisation" in Africa.' *Africa: Journal of the International African Institute* 63 (October): 445–61.

Schatzberg, Michael G. 2001. *Political Legitimacy in Middle Africa: Father, Family, Food*. Bloomington: Indiana University Press.

Schmidt, Vivien A. 2010. 'Reconciling Ideas and Institutions through Discursive Institutionalism.' In *Ideas and Politics in Social Science Research*, edited by Daniel Béland and Robert H. Cox. New York: Oxford University Press.

Schmitter, P. C., and T. L. Karl. 1991. 'What Democracy Is . . . Is Not.' *Journal of Democracy* 2 (3): 75–88.

Schwartzburg, Rosa. 2019. 'The "White Replacement Theory" Motivates Alt-Right Killers the World Over.' *The Guardian*, 5 August 2019. https://www.theguardian.com/commentisfree/2019/aug/05/great-replacement-theory-alt-right-killers-el-paso.

Sedlaczek, Robert. 2010. 'Wennst dem Mustafa ane aufbrennst – Sedlaczek am Mittwoch.' *Glossen – Wiener Zeitung Online*, 28 September 2010. https://www.wienerzeitung.at/meinungen/glossen/36843_Wennst-dem-Mustafa-.

Shaw, Wendy. 2007. 'Museums and Narratives of Display from the Late Ottoman Empire to the Turkish Republic.' *Muqarnas* 24: 253–79.

Shaw, Wendy. 2011. 'National Museums in the Republic of Turkey: Palimpsests within a Centralized State.' In *Building National Museums in Europe 1750–2010*, edited by Peter Aronsson and Gabriella Elgenius. [Conference Proceedings from EuNaMus, European National Museums: Identity Politics, the Uses of the Past and the European Citizen, Bologna 28–30 April 2011 and EuNaMus Report No 1]. Linköping: Linköping University Electronic Press, http://www.ep.liu.se/ecp_home/index.en.aspx?issue=064.

Shepherd, Laura J. 2015. 'Ideas/Matter: Conceptualising Foreign Policy Practice.' *Critical Studies on Security* 3 (February): 334–7.

Shohat, Ella. 1999. 'The Invention of the Mizrahim.' *Journal of Palestine Studies* 29 (October): 5–20.

Silverman, Craig. 2016. 'How the Bizarre Conspiracy Theory Behind "Pizzagate" was Spread.' *Buzzfeed News*. https://www.buzzfeed.com/craigsilverman/fever-swampelection.

Şimşek, Çiğdem. 2015. 'Halk Bilimi Müzeciliğine Bir Örnek "Ankara Somut Olmayan Kültürel Miras Müzesi".' Masters thesis, Gazi University, Department of Folklore.

Smith, Rogers M. 2003. *Stories of Peoplehood: The Politics and Morals of Political Memberships.* Cambridge: Cambridge University Press.

Smith, Rogers M. 2015. *Political Peoplehood.* Chicago: University of Chicago Press.

Smith, Rogers M. 2020. *That Is Not Who We Are! Populism and Peoplehood.* New Haven: Yale University Press.

Snow, David A., and Robert D. Benford. 1988. 'Ideology, Frame Resonance, and Participant Mobilization.' *International Social Movement Research* 1 (1): 197–217.

Somers, Margaret R. 1994. 'The Narrative Constitution of Identity: A Relational and Network Approach.' *Theory and Society* 23 (October): 605–49.

Somers, Margaret R. 1995. 'What's Political or Cultural about Political Culture and the Public Sphere? Toward an Historical Sociology of Concept Formation.' *Sociological Theory* 13 (July): 113–44.

Squire, Corinne, Mark Davis, Cigdem Esin, Molly Andrews, Barbara Harrison, Lars-Christer Hydén and Margareta Hydén. 2014. *What is Narrative Research?* New York: Bloomsbury Academic.

Star. 2013a. 'Başkanlık Sistemi Türk Ekonomisini Uçuracak. [The Presidential System will make Turkey fly]' 17 March 2013. http://haber.stargazete.com/yazar/baskanlik-sistemi-turk-ekonomisini-ucuracak/yazi-736668.

Star. 2013b. 'Tekrar da olsa yazacagim yazı. [A piece that I will write despite repeating myself]' 4 September 2013. http://haber.stargazete.com/yazar/tekrar-da-olsa-yazacagim/yazi-786150.

Steinmetz, George. 1992. 'Reflections on the Role of Social Narratives in Working-Class Formation: Narrative Theory in the Social Sciences.' *Social Science History* 16 (3): 489–516.

Steinvorth, Daniel. 2012. 'Erdogan the Misogynist Turkish Prime Minister Assaults Women's Rights.' *Der Spiegel*, 19 June 2012. http://www.spiegel.de/international/europe/turkish-prime-minister-erdogan-targets-women-s-rights-a-839568.html.

Stinchcombe, Arthur L. 1968. *Constructing Social Theories*. New York: Harcourt, Brace and World.

Sümer, Faruk, and Turhal Yüksel. 1986. *Tarih Lise 1* [History High School 1]. Istanbul: Ders Kitapları Anonim Şirketi.

Süngü, Y. 2013. '"Faiz lobisi" ve 'Gezi'ci gençler ne iş yapar.' *Yeni Şafak*, 9 June 2013. http://yenisafak.com.tr/yazarlar/YasarSungu/faiz-lobisi-ve-gezici-gencler-ne-is-yapar/38060.

T24. 2013. 'Erdoğan: Onlar milyonlarca tweet atsınlar, bizim tek bir besmelemiz oyunları bozar.' 22 June 2013. http://t24.com.tr/haber/erdogan-onlar-milyon-larca-tweet-atsin-bizim-bir-besmelemiz-yeter,232546.

T24. 2016. 'Erdoğan: Eğitimde Attığımız Her Adım Kilisede Ölen 'Haluk' Tarzı Batılılaşmayı Savunanlarca Engellenmek Istendi.' 26 March 2016. http://t24.com.tr/haber/cumhurbaskani-erdogan-uluslararasi-egitim-zirvesinde-konusuyor,333625.

T24. 2021. 'Bloomberg, Erdoğan'ın bin 56 konuşmasını analiz etti: 2021'de 'yatırım', 'üretim', 'büyüme' ifadeleri rekor seviyede kullanıldı.' 21 December 2021. https://t24.com.tr/haber/bloomberg-erdogan-in-bin-56-konusmasini-analiz-etti-2021-de-yatirim-uretim-buyume-ifadeleri-rekor-seviyede-kullanildi,1002401.

T. C. Kültür Bakanlığı, Ankara İl Kültür ve Turizm Müdürlüğü. 'Ankara Somut Olmayan Kültürel Miras Müzesi.' https://ankara.ktb.gov.tr/TR-152965/muzeler.html (accessed 25 May 2022).

Tansuğ, Sabiha. 1990. 'Ankara Etnoğrafya Müzesi.' *Atatürk Araştırma Merkezi Dergisi* 18: 659–63.

Tanyeri-Erdemir, Tuğba. 2006. 'Archaeology as a Source of National Pride in the Early Years of the Turkish Republic.' *Journal of Field Archaeology* 31 (4): 381–93.

Taraz, Nazli. 2021. 'An Inquiry into the Construction of National Memory in the Republican Period: Assembly Buildings of Turkey.' PhD diss., Izmir Institute of Technology, Department of Architecture.

Taylor, Charles. 1989. *Sources of the Self: The Making of the Modern Identity*. Cambridge, MA: Harvard University Press.

Teisman, Rachel. 2022. 'Putin's Claim of Fighting Against Ukraine "Neo-Nazis" Distorts History, Scholars Say.' *NPR*. 1 March 2022. https://www.npr.org/2022/03/01/1083677765/putin-denazify-ukraine-russia-history.

The Economist. 2013. 'Alcohol in Turkey Not So Good for You.' 1 June 2013. http://www.economist.com/news/europe/21578657-mildly-islamist-government-brings-tough-alcohol-restrictions-not-so-good-you.

The Guardian. 2011. 'The Rise of Vienna's Far Right' [Video] 11 February 2011. https://www.theguardian.com/world/video/2011/feb/11/vienna-far-right-video.

Therborn, G. 2018. 'Twilight of Swedish Social Democracy.' *New Left Review* 113 (September–October): 5–26.

Thomas, Gwynn. 2011a. *Contesting Political Legitimacy in Chile: Familial Ideals, Citizenship and Political Struggle, 1970–1990*. University Park: Pennsylvania State University Press.

Thomas, Gwynn. 2011b. 'The Legacies of Patrimonial Patriarchalism: Contesting Political Legitimacy in Allende's Chile.' *The Annals of the American Academy of Political and Social Science* 636 (June): 69–87.

Tilly, Charles. 1977. 'Getting it Together in Burgundy, 1675–1975.' *Theory and Society* 4 (4): 479–504.

Tilly, Charles. 1985. 'War Making and State Making as Organized Crime.' In *Bringing the State Back In*, edited by Peter B. Evans, Dietrich Rueschemeyer and Theda Skocpol, 169–87. Cambridge: Cambridge University Press.

Tin Medya. 2018. 'Somut Olmayan Kültürel Miras Müzesi'[film] 5 August. https://www.youtube.com/watch?v=PHnMvxTqpsE&t=1s.

Tokdoğan, Nagehan. 2018. *Yeni Osmanlıcılık: Hınç, Nostalji, Narsizm*. İstanbul: İletisim Yayınları.

Traverso E. 2019. *Geçmişi Kullanma Kılavuzu: Tarih, Bellek, Politika*. İstanbul: İletişim Yayınları.

TRT Avaz, 2015. 'Ankara Somut Olmayan Kültürel Miras Müzesi – Yeni Gün.' 28 April. https://www.youtube.com/watch?v=1Cf156Z2aaU.

Türk, B. 2014. *Muktedir: Türk Sağ Geleneği ve Recep Tayyip Erdoğan*. İletişim, İstanbul.

turkiyegazetesi.com.tr. 2013. 'Erdoğan, "Başkalık sistemini tartışmak herhalde günah değil".' 9 June 2013. http://www.turkiyegazetesi.com.tr/gundem/72277.aspx.

Ugur Cinar, Meral. 2015a. *Collective Memory and National Membership: Identity and Citizenship Models in Turkey and Austria*. New York: Palgrave Macmillan.

Ugur Cinar, Meral. 2015b. 'Letter from Ankara.' *The Political Quarterly* 86 (3): 359–63.

Ugur-Cinar, Meral. 2017. 'Embedded Neopatrimonialism: Patriarchy and Democracy in Turkey.' *Social Politics* 24 (July): 324–43.

Ugur-Cinar, Meral, and Berat Uygar Altınok. 2021. 'Collective memory and the populist cause: The Ulucanlar Prison Museum in Turkey.' *Memory Studies* 14 (5): 1106–26.

Ugur-Cinar, Meral, and Gökhan Şensönmez. 2022. 'Making Sense of Senseless Times: Religious Narratives and Identity in the Memoirs of Far-right Militants in Turkey.' *Politics, Religion & Ideology* 23 (3): 327–48.

Ugur-Cinar, M. and R. M. Smith. 2014. 'Nation-Building Narratives: Implications for Immigrants and Minorities.' In *The Nation State and Immigration, Vol. III: The Age of Population Movements*, edited by Anita Shapira, Yedidia Z. Stern, Alexander Yakobson and Liav Orgad, 1–29. Brighton: Sussex Academic Press and Israel Democracy Institute.

Ugur-Cinar, Meral and Rogers M. Smith. 2015. 'Narrative Structures and the Politics of Peoplehood.' In *Political Peoplehood: The Roles of Values, Interests, and Identities*, 66–91. Chicago: University of Chicago Press.

Uğurlu, Nurer, and Esergul Balcı. 1989–1992. *Tarih Lise I-II-III* [History for High School I-II-III]. Istanbul: Serhat, Orgun.

Vekam, 'Taşhan.' https://libdigitalcollections.ku.edu.tr/digital/collection/AEFA/id/174/ (accessed 23 May 2022).

Waldner, D., and E. Lust. 2018. 'Unwelcome Change: Coming to Terms with Democratic Backsliding.' *Annual Review of Political Science* 21 (1): 93–113.

Walker, Shaun. 2019. 'Viktor Orbán Trumpets Hungary's "Procreation, Not Immigration" Policy.' *The Guardian*, 6 September 2018. https://www.theguardian.com/world/2019/sep/06/viktor-orban-trumpets-far-right-procreation-anti-immigration-policy.

Wedeen, Lisa. 2002. 'Conceptualizing Culture: Possibilities for Political Science.' *The American Political Science Review* 96 (December): 713–28.

Wedeen, Lisa. 2013. 'Ideology and Humor in Dark Times: Notes from Syria.' *Critical Inquiry* 39 (Summer): 841–73.

Wegner, N. 2015. 'Fünf Fragen zur Demo gegen den "Großen Austausch" am 6. Juni in Wien.' *Sezession*, 4 June 2015. https://sezession.de/49945/fuenf-fragen-zur-demo-gegen-den-grossen-austausch-am-6-juni-in-wien.

Wertsch, James V. 2000. 'Narratives as Cultural Tools in Sociocultural Analysis: Official History in Soviet and Post-Soviet Russia.' *Ethos* 28: 511–33.

Wertsch, James V. 2004. 'Specific Narratives and Schematic Narrative Templates.' In *Theorizing Historical Consciousness*, edited by Peter Seixas. Toronto: University of Toronto Press.

Wertsch, James V. 2007. 'National Narratives and the Conservative Nature of Collective Memory.' *Neohelicon* 34 (December): 23–33.

Wertsch, James V. 2008. 'Collective Memory and Narrative Templates.' *Social Research* 75 (Spring): 133–56.

Wertsch, James V., and Henry L Roediger. 2008. 'Collective Memory: Conceptual Foundations and Theoretical Approaches.' *Memory* 16 (3): 318–26.

Weyland, Kurt. 1996. 'Neopopulism and Neoliberalism in Latin America: Unexpected Affinities.' *Studies in Comparative International Development* 31 (3): 3–31.

Weyland. Kurt. 2018. 'Populism and Authoritarianism.' In *Routledge Handbook of Global Populism*, edited by Carlos de la Torre, 319–33. London: Routledge.

White, Geoffrey M. 1999. 'Emotional Remembering: The Pragmatics of National Memory.' *Ethos* 27 (4): 505–29.

White, Hayden. 1973. *Metahistory: The Historical Imagination in Nineteenth-Century Europe*. Baltimore: The Johns Hopkins University Press.

White, Hayden. 1978. *Tropics of Discourse: Essays in Cultural Criticism*. Baltimore: The Johns Hopkins University Press.

White, Hayden. 1980. 'The Value of Narrativity in the Representation of Reality.' *Critical Inquiry* 7 (1): 5–27.

White, Hayden. 1987. *The Content of the Form: Narrative Discourse and Historical Representation*. Baltimore: The Johns Hopkins University Press.

Wibben, Annick T. R. 2010. *Feminist Security Studies: A Narrative Approach*. Abingdon: Routledge.

Wiener Zeitung Online. 2018. 'Europa schützen und sichern.' 29 May 2018. https://www.wienerzeitung.at/nachrichten/oesterreich/politik/967686_Europa-schuetzen-und-sichern.html.

Wilson, A. 2019. 'Fear-filled Apocalypses: The Far-Right's Use of Conspiracy Theories.' *Oxford Research Group*. https://www.oxfordresearchgroup.org.uk/blog/fear-filledapocalypses-the-far-rights-use-of-conspiracy-theory.

Wodak, R. 2004. 'Critical discourse analysis.' In *Qualitative Research Practice*, edited by C. Seale, J. F. Gubrium and D. Silverman, 197–213. London: Sage.

World Justice Project. 2015. http://data.worldjusticeproject.org/#/groups/TUR.

Wuthrich, F. M., and M. Ingleby. 2020. 'The Pushback Against Populism: Running on "Radical Love" in Turkey.' *Journal of Democracy* 31 (2): 24–40.

Yeni Şafak. 2014. 'Faiz lobisi hortladi.' 3 January 2014. http://yenisafak.com.tr/ekonomi-haber/faiz-lobisi-hortladi-04.01.2014-601140.

Yeni Şafak. 2016. 'Masallardan ninnilere "kültürel miras" müzede.' 2 March 2016. https://www.yenisafak.com/hayat/masallardan-ninnilere-kulturel-miras-muzede-2427864.

Yıldırım, D. 2009. 'AKP ve Neoliberal Popülizm.' In *AKP Kitabı Bir Dönüşümün Bilançosu*, edited by İlhan Uzgel and Bülent Duru, 66–107. Ankara: Phoenix Yayınevi.

Young, Iris M. 1990. *Justice and the Politics of Difference*. Princeton: Princeton University Press.

Young, Iris M. 2003. 'The Logic of Masculinist Protection: Reflections on the Current Security State.' *Signs Journal of Women in Culture and Society* 29 (Autumn): 1–25.

Yuval-Davis, Nira. 2006. 'Belonging and the politics of belonging.' *Patterns of Prejudice* 40 (3): 197–214.

Zalewski, Piotr. 2012. 'Why is Turkey's Prime Minister at War with a Soap Opera?' *Time*, 26 December 2012. http://world.time.com/2012/12/26/why-is-turkeys-prime-minister-at-war-with-a-soap-opera/.

Zencirci, G. 2015. 'From Property to Civil Society: The Historical Transformation of Vakifs in Modern Turkey (1923–2013).' *International Journal of Middle Eastern Studies* 47: 533–54.

Zerubavel, Eviatar. 2003. *Time Map: Collective Memory and the Social Shape of the Past*. Chicago: University of Chicago Press.

Zerubavel, Yael. 1995. *Recovered Roots: Collective Memory and the Making of Israeli National Tradition*. Chicago: University of Chicago Press.

INDEX

EU representative:
Easy Access System Europe
Mustamäe tee 50, 10621 Tallinn, Estonia
Gpsr.requests@easproject.com

www.ingramcontent.com/pod-product-compliance
Lightning Source LLC
Chambersburg PA
CBHW050650270326
41927CB00012B/2955